politics@media

David D. Perlmutter, Series Editor

Also by Edwin M. Yoder Jr.

The Night of the Old South Ball (1984)

The Unmaking of a Whig (1990)

Joe Alsop's Cold War (1995)

The Historical Present: Uses and Abuses of the Past (1997)

EDWIN M. YODER JR.

Telling Others What to Think

recollections of a pundit

with a foreword by
JONATHAN YARDLEY

Published in cooperation with the
Kevin P. Reilly Center for Media and Public Affairs

 Louisiana State University Press   Baton Rouge

Designer: Barbara Neely Bourgoyne
Typefaces: Sabon, text; Franklin Gothic, display
Typesetter: Coghill Composition Co., Inc.
Printer and binder: Thomson-Shore, Inc.

Library of Congress Cataloging-in-Publication Data

Yoder, Edwin M. (Edwin Milton), 1934–
    Telling others what to think : recollections of a pundit / Edwin M. Yoder ;
    with a foreword by Jonathan Yardley.
        p.   cm.—(Politics@media)
    ISBN 0-8071-3033-8 (alk. paper)
    1. Yoder, Edwin M. (Edwin Milton), 1934–   2. Journalists—United States—
Biography. I. Title. II. Series.
PN4874.Y54A3   2004
070′.92—dc22   2004048583

This book is for Bill and Flo Snider

And for other members of the
Occasional Dining Club of Greensboro,
past and present

[He] was [the] eldest son . . . and the first page or two of this narrative must be consumed in giving a catalogue of the good things which chance and conduct together had heaped upon this young man's head.

—ANTHONY TROLLOPE, *Framley Parsonage*

Your connection with any newspaper would be a disgrace and degradation. I would rather sell gin to poor people and poison them that way.

—SIR WALTER SCOTT to an aspiring newspaperman

Contents

Illustrations follow page 62.

Foreword

If memory serves me correctly—and in this instance I believe it actually does—I met Ed Yoder in Charlotte, North Carolina, in the autumn of 1960. Ed was writing editorials for the afternoon newspaper, the *Charlotte News,* and I was editor of the *Daily Tar Heel,* the student newspaper at the University of North Carolina in Chapel Hill. I had come to Charlotte on the press plane that trailed John F. Kennedy's *Caroline* around the state, and had stayed to visit my fiancée, who was working for the *Charlotte Observer* on what was known, in those pre-Enlightenment days, as the women's section.

Ed was five years older than I and already, at twenty-six, a legendary figure at Chapel Hill. As co-editor of the *Tar Heel* in 1955–56 he had fought numerous battles, the noisiest of which he describes in the chapter entitled "Chapel Hill," and upon graduation had promptly marched off to Oxford as a Rhodes Scholar, the first *Tar Heel* editor to achieve that distinction. Whether I was in awe as I dropped by his office at the *News* I do not recall, but I certainly was impressed, and he did nothing to disabuse me of that. Tall and slender, friendly and correct but somewhat distant, he was the embodiment of the adjective applied to certain southern gentlemen of that day: *courtly.*

Our meeting was brief and inconclusive. Half a decade was to pass before the beginning of what is, as I write, a friendship of forty years. I graduated from U.N.C. the following June and went off to work at the *New York Times,* where I stayed until the summer of 1964, when I was hired by the *Greensboro Daily News* to replace . . . Ed Yoder. Ed had moved from Charlotte to Greensboro not long after our first meeting, but had succumbed to the blandishments of his friend Otis Singletary, chancellor of what was then still called the Woman's College of the University of North Carolina (now U.N.C.—Greensboro), and had agreed to teach in its history department; readers of this memoir will quickly understand that he was eminently qualified to do so.

Ed moved a couple of miles across town to the campus and I took over his little office in the editorial department. I was low man on the totem pole that had H. W. "Slim" Kendall at the top and Bill Snider in the middle; there is much about these two in the pages that follow. Doubtless Ed gave me counsel as I began the job—here memory fails me—but he also did me the kindness of staying out of my way, suppressing whatever urge he may have felt to backseat drive as I ventured into editorializing for the first time since *Tar Heel* days.

Then, a year later, everything changed. The Greensboro papers (the *Record* was published in the afternoon) were purchased by Landmark of Norfolk, which had a good newspaper in its home town (the *Virginian-Pilot*) but over the coming years showed little interest in publishing good ones in Greensboro. In the beginning, though, all was sunshine and Santa Claus. Landmark appointed Snider editor-in-chief and brought Ed back as editor of the editorial page. Suddenly Ed was a daily presence in my life, the person who set the tone for the page (there was only one, op-ed pages not yet having been invented), who read and edited my copy, who was, in a word, my boss.

It never felt that way. Ed had acquired the Oxonian habit of collegiality, and ran his small department accordingly. It was a strange place. By default I rose to the middle position on the totem pole, with various people taking the third one over the decade to follow. Jim Wagner and Kate Blackwell served honorably, though I do not remember precisely when, and special honors went to Jim Ross, about whom more presently. But the atmosphere was controlled by the secretary, a tiny, wrinkled, dyspeptic woman named Dot, whose quick temper and sharp tongue kept everyone on edge, and whose fondness for the bottle turned her into a time bomb at the occasional office social gathering.

The oddest thing about Dot—and believe me, there were many to choose among—came to her by way of her grandfather. He had been a minor factotum in the Lincoln White House, and had been on the scene in those terrible hours after John Wilkes Booth fired his fatal shot. Somehow he had come into possession of the clothing Lincoln had on when he was in Ford's Theater, and somehow this had made its way to Dot. When she told me about it I looked at her in astonishment and protested that it belonged in the Smithsonian Institution. Her beady little eyes narrowed as she made plain that the clothes would go there (or somewhere else) only at her profit, which a few years later indeed happened. I believe the proceeds underwrote her retirement and the many bottles of bourbon necessary to its full enjoyment.

Ed presided over this slightly wacko menagerie with avuncular patience mixed in, at times, with lordly disdain. All that really interested Ed was writing his editorials and occasional signed columns, so he simply closed his ears and eyes to the firestorms that erupted in Dot's vicinity, though I do recall that from time to time a look of mild exasperation passed across his face. The rest of us were less immune to disruption, or perhaps more inclined to play our own roles in this comical soap opera. But Ed's patience with all of this, and all of us, bordered on the infinite. So long as his two subordinates wrote their editorials and Dot licked her stamps, or whatever it was she did, he was happy.

As an editor he was astonishingly tolerant and permissive. Editorialists at big newspapers—the *New York Times* and the *Washington Post* rush to mind—would not know what to make of Ed's system, if "system" is the word for it. The big boys (and, now, big girls) sit on editorial "boards" and hold endless meetings in which topics are so thoroughly hashed out and opinions so compromised that all life is drained from the editorials that ensue. So far as I know Ed never held a staff meeting in more than two decades of editorial writing, most of them as editorial-page editor. We got to the office around eighty-thirty or nine in the morning (Ed was always the first one there) and started reading the newspapers. At around ten Ed would poke his head into our offices and ask what subjects we had in mind that day. Each of us was expected to write at least two editorials—on one nightmarish day, holding the fort alone, I wrote *ten!*—but Ed only wanted to know what we would write about, not what we aimed to say about it.

The result, as Ed notes in his chapter about the Greensboro years, was that the editorial columns were susceptible to occasional internal contradiction, but this made them more interesting rather than less. The page's tradition of literate prose seems to have meant more to its readers than the uniformity of its opinions, and many of those readers apparently agreed that it was, overall, the best editorial page in a state that, at the time, had many good ones.

They read the page closely, as I learned to my considerable discomfort in the fall of 1973. Jim Ross had gone on a tear about "prayer for judgment continued," a practice in the North Carolina Superior Court that permitted judges to let off without punishment persons who had the right friends. He wrote a couple of pungent, funny editorials about it, treating the judges just as they deserved. Unfortunately, at the time I was in court myself. I had managed to get myself charged with leaving the scene of an (exceedingly minor) accident, and was haled before the bar. While my lawyer stood helplessly by, the judge asked if I was in fact the Jonathan Yardley who wrote editorials for the *Daily News*. When I conceded that I was, he then asked if I had written those inflammatory editorials about the Superior Court. How the rest of the exchange played out I have managed to forget, but I clearly remember the closing words: "Prayer for judgment will *not* be continued!" The long editorial arm of the *Daily News* ended up costing me a pretty penny.

A word must be said about Jim Ross. When I joined the paper in 1964 at the age of twenty-four, Jim was in his mid-fifties, covering politics and other subjects as its star reporter. He was a wonderfully gifted writer, and at first opportunity Ed lured him onto the editorial page. Despite the difference in our ages, we became good friends. Jim was a superb storyteller—it ran in the family: his sister is the distinguished poet Eleanor Ross Taylor, and his brother-in-law was Peter Taylor, the great short-story writer and novelist—and loved to stay up late telling tales over frequently refilled glasses of bourbon.

What I did not know, until Jim finally and reluctantly confessed it—he was shy, and reticent about his private life—was that Jim was, or had been, a novelist himself. In 1940 he published a book called *They Don't Dance Much,* which was praised by Raymond Chandler, Ernest Hemingway, and others but allowed to fall into neglect. Jim didn't want to talk about it. In the early 1970s, though, it was rediscovered by editors at Southern Illinois University Press, which reissued it in 1975 as part of the Lost American Fiction series, with an admiring and perceptive afterword by George V. Higgins. That edition has remained in print ever since, and Jim, who died in 1990 at the age of seventy-nine, is honored by students of *noir* fiction as a master of the genre.

By the time that reissue appeared I had left Greensboro and joined the *Miami Herald* as its book editor. I had gotten sick of writing anonymous homilies that had no apparent influence on anything (except in a certain courtroom), and my interest had turned to books, first writing about them and eventually actually writing them myself. Ed and I stayed in occasional touch, always in a friendly way, but I assumed our professional association was over. Then, in June 1975, Ed became editorial-page editor of the *Washington Star,* and soon he and I were trying to arrange a reunion. It didn't come about until three years later, when I went to the *Star* as its book editor and part-time editorial writer. I did well in the first capacity but not in the second—my heart just wasn't in it—though Ed was kind enough to pretend otherwise.

Two and a half years after I got there the *Star* succumbed to its inevitable fate; I especially commend to you Ed's chapter about his years there. I joined the *Washington Post* and Ed started his own syndicated column. We saw each other far too infrequently, but Ed remained—as he had been since late 1965—the reader I had in the back of my mind whenever I wrote anything. He remained that until 1998, when Marie Arana entered my life and gently nudged him aside. To this day, though, he is the most important journalistic presence in my life. Among all journalists whom I have known—and I have known many, including many of the best—he is the wisest, the most erudite, the most humane, and the wittiest. Evidence of all that is on every page of this lovely book.

JONATHAN YARDLEY

Author's Note

Any book is a collaborative effort and many hands, chronicled and un-chronicled, have contributed to this one. I am grateful to Jonathan Yardley for writing the foreword and for valuable structural sugges-tions. I first noticed his exceptional talent when he was a college editor at Chapel Hill. We later worked together for many happy years at the *Greensboro Daily News* and at the *Washington Star.* I have watched his development over the years as a critic and writer on books and on the quirks of American culture second to none. I also owe a word of thanks to William Dickinson, my editor at the Post Writers Group, who as Manship visiting professor at the Louisiana State University invited me to the succulent dinner tables of Baton Rouge as a visiting journalism fellow, and also put me in touch with David Perlmutter and others con-nected with the LSU Press, distinguished regional publishers. Perlmut-ter's counsel and that of Lee Campbell Sioles, managing editor, im-proved this memoir in countless ways. My fellow Tar Heel, Prof. Tim Tyson of the University of Wisconsin, read the chapter entitled "A Ra-cial Education" and encouraged me to believe that I had written truly and honestly of the great subject of which he is an accomplished master.

The dedicatees of this work, William Davis and Florence Lide Snider of Greensboro, have been virtual family, as well as wise and encouraging mentors, for almost half a century. Their hearth and dinner table have provided gathering places for happy reunions with old friends of the Oc-casional Dining Club. The ODC began with farewell parties when Jane and I were leaving Greensboro—reluctantly—in the summer of 1975 and has continued in robust liveliness ever since. My wife, Jane, and my children, Anne Daphne and Edwin Warwick (Teddy), have stimulated and nurtured me over the years, as has my brother, James Colin Yoder, and as have my delightful new grandsons, Spencer and Evan Yoder and Dylan Blankenship. It is my hope that the three newcomers will eventu-ally find in these pages a guide to their heritage at a time when Ameri-cans are often casual about their roots and traditions.

A few acknowledgments: "Star Wars" appeared in a slightly different form in the *Virginia Quarterly Review* (69:4, Autumn 1993), whose editor, the late Staige Blackford, published my work for more than three decades. Parts of the sketch of Willie Morris appeared in *The American Oxonian* (86:4, Fall 1999). Parts of the chapter entitled "Meg Greenfield and the Perils of Punditry" appeared, in a different form, as a review in the *Washington Times* of the late Ms. Greenfield's memoir *Washington.* For these assignments I thank David Alexander, then editor of the *Oxonian,* and the late Colin Walters, book editor of the *Times.* I have borrowed a few lines for the chapter entitled "Fossil's Farewell" from my essay in the *Sewanee Review* (Spring 2004) and thank its distinguished editor, George Core, for permission to do so. I also wish to acknowledge the help of my former Washington and Lee colleague John Jacob, archivist of the Lewis Powell Collection, who graciously granted permission to quote from my extensive correspondence with the late Justice Powell.

A Preface: That David Copperfield Business

"The first thing you'll probably want to know is where I was born, and what my lousy childhood was like, and how my parents were occupied and all before they had me, and all that David Copperfield kind of crap." The voice is that of J. D. Salinger's Holden Caulfield, of *The Catcher in the Rye*, taking a sassy bow before adding, belligerently, that he doesn't want to go into any of it.

Some stuffy words were written on the fiftieth anniversary of the novel's appearance in 2002, about Holden as the spoiled prototype of youthful rebelliousness. More to the present point, his resistance to "all that David Copperfield kind of crap" foreshadowed an era when ancestral memories would fade and our children would often fail to recall, or even bother to learn, the last names of their friends, let alone how their parents were occupied. I came of a different vintage and from a South whose storytelling tradition was still intact. So the urge to reminisce comes naturally to me and thrusts me into territories Holden avoided, not least how my parents were occupied and all before they had me.

Obviously, there are as many styles of reminiscence as there are writers to write them. Some these days, so I hear, are as precious as Holden Caulfield's. Readers whose judgment I trust speak of a proliferation of memoirs of introspection and neurotic confession, hothouse blooms unseasoned by the experience of larger worlds and longer years, perhaps indeed the belated progeny of *Catcher in the Rye*. The reminiscences that follow are emphatically not of that self-conscious or self-pitying school. I was blessed with a sunny childhood—"a surfeit of honey," my wife Jane says—and I am far too jaded for the confessional mode. Among the models and precedents for what follows are such dry-eyed, amused, and ironic works as *The Education of Henry Adams*, Henry James's *Notes of a Son and Brother*, T. S. Matthews's *Name and Address*, and John A. Rice's *I Came Out of the Eighteenth Century*.

The autobiographical writings that have stirred or amused me deal with two universals common to such works—memory and permanence and their elusive connection. William Faulkner, the greatest writer of fiction ever bred on these shores, claimed—with what candor is uncertain, since he could be as crafty as the rural Mississippi horse-traders he portrayed so affectionately—that he wished to be "as a private individual, abolished and voided from history, leaving it markless." He left no personal memoir that we know of, but abolition was not his fate and he is the subject of many a fat biography. The vital point, however, is that he was of that enviable tribe whose works constitute so imposing a monument as to require no "private" elaboration. Such works as *Absalom, Absalom!* and *The Sound and the Fury* alone, to say nothing of half a dozen other brilliant novels, suffice as surety against oblivion.

For us lesser beings, it is not easy to gaze with airy serenity into the great void of Time. Human vanity craves lasting mark. Finding the right mode for it is always a challenging question. A great soldier or explorer need only recite his adventures and, unless he is a dull dog, the story will convey its drama. For the rest of us, and especially if our labors smell of the lamp and the library, the strategy must be more subtle. The writer of the ensuing reminiscences, though he can boast many adventures of a quieter sort, has no tales of shot and shell or quests for the source of the Nile to relate. He must fall back on different modes in which memory pursues permanence, perhaps with a cue from Marcel Proust. In a famous passage in *Le temps rétrouvé,* the last volume of his great "search for lost time," Proust's narrator Marcel revisits an old social scene after years of sickness and seclusion. He is in a blue mood; he feels death near and has all but abandoned his youthful literary ambitions. But, dodging an approaching carriage, he stumbles over some uneven paving stones in the courtyard of a great Parisian hotel and the sensation recalls, unbidden, the stones and pleasures of Venice. He grasps the intensity of involuntary memory and realizes its centrality. Its yield may be homely, but it usually is more vivid and reliable than that reconstruction of the past that we attempt by conscious effort.

Memory, allowed to speak for itself, will often locate what is significant in the coordinates of a life, and bring one as close as ordinary talent allows to permanence. Unforced memory has a special tale to tell. The content may be deceptively trivial in appearance, modest and private, like the taste of the famous cookie dipped in lime tea, but it glows with an authenticity that conscious effort can't contrive. Memory may certainly be aided by documents, as are some of the recollections that follow; but it is memory that gives life to documents, not documents to memory.

While much of this book is personal, more of it is professional and tells of an education in its broadest sense. I have been a journalist off and on now for more than half a century, if you count my early work in my sixteenth year as a summer fill-in sports editor, reporter, and advertising salesman for the *Mebane Journal*. I have tried to make these reminiscences exemplary of a formative phase or influence. For instance, the opening sketch of my brainy, dutiful, and authoritative father is a study in character and in the Stoic virtues that shape it. "A Racial Education," with my generous, life-loving, and affectionate mother in the central role, tells of a transition that those of us who grew up in the old southern world have experienced, or should have. The sketch of Justice Lewis F. Powell Jr. is representative of the role of mentors, among whom he was one of the best. "Willie" is the story of a life-friendship, individualistic in flavor because he was the most original of men; but also, I hope, universal in its echoes. A regrettable trace of acerbity may have crept into the account of some few of my professional associates and experiences in Washington. But better sober truth than that "social simper" Henry James speaks of that masks sharp emotions that the eyes, peering through peep-holes, give away. It is saddening to realize how many of the actors of my small drama are gone, some snatched away far too early, for in memory and affection they remain vitally present. I would like to think—small vanity—that through craft I have in some modest way helped to gather them into Yeats's "artifice of eternity."

Telling Others What to Think

CUE

Fathers and Sons *"Which of us has looked into his father's heart?" asks Thomas Wolfe in the prose-poem that opens his novel* Look Homeward, Angel. *The question may be unanswerable, but in any case we are condemned by the human condition to judge the hearts of others, even in the most intimate kinships, by what they do and say. As I have indicated in this sketch, my father, a small-town school superintendent, was one of the most honest and demanding men I have known, and also one of the most intelligent and persevering. A powerful brain and character were compelled by a physical calamity in midlife to struggle with a damaged body unequal to their will and capacity. Yet how he, the least self-pitying of men, would have loathed the privileges of victimhood now so widely claimed by those who struggle with handicaps.*

In the introduction to the Appendix, below, I say that it is useful for a political commentator to be "opinionated"—and that I came by the trait naturally, meaning by both genes and example. My father, grandfather, and great-grandfather on the paternal side seem to have been all too kin in that respect. But, as I hope this portrait of my father will show, in his case I mean "opinionated" in the better sense of that disagreeable word. The common iniquities and outrages of public life occasionally put him in a lather of indignation, for he was an unbending Yellow Dog Democrat and never tired of denouncing the misdeeds of Republican administrations. (He made exceptions of Theodore Roosevelt and Herbert Hoover, whom he regarded as able and honest men.) In all fairness, however, I can't recall a single opinion of his about anything of importance that was uninformed or half-cocked. The distinction is essential, though it is little observed today, especially in electronic journalism. God knows what he would have thought or said about the vast volumes of misinformation flying about on the Internet, which he died too early to know of.

I am a decade older now than he was when he first began to seem old to me. The sense that he was suddenly aging first struck me one day, not long after I returned from Oxford, when we attended a neighborhood friend's wedding together. He was then fifty-eight. As we walked up the sidewalk toward the church, he leaned heavily on my arm. I believe the weakness he felt had something to do with the "heart attack" his doctors had diagnosed a few months earlier, when I was still abroad, though he declined to believe them and had strictly forbidden my mother to notify me of it, knowing that I was facing my final examinations in a few weeks. I was familiar with those moods when he seemed tired and ailing or out of sorts, though he displayed few of the neurotic tics of the hypochondriac or valetudinarian.

In fact, however, more or less constant pain had been his companion since the physical disaster that bisected his life at age forty.

I recall the beginning vividly. It was a bright autumn morning in 1940 and the leaves were turning outside our house in the small North Carolina town whose schools he had, by then, supervised for five years. While the maid puttered about making beds and dusting, my mother was running the vacuum cleaner in the living room. I might or might not have been practicing at the piano. She turned the machine off and gazed out the front windows. To my surprise, I saw that she was fighting back tears.

"Edwin, we have to be brave," she called, noticing my alarm, but without further elaboration that I can now recall. Of course I know the whole story now; but just when I learned the details is uncertain; I was then only six.

Some months earlier, my father had begun to suffer episodic but nagging pain, stiffness, and tingling in his neck and left leg. He was a strong, muscular, and sturdy man, a college football player in his day, compact without being fat, and immensely energetic. The experience of persistent pain was new to him, and I suppose he procrastinated in a very human way in the face of its scary signals, denying to himself that it might mean that something was seriously wrong with his serviceable body. He consulted the local doctors, whose judgment he had no great faith in— whom, in fact, he tended to deride. But doctors were doctors. They represented for him—he had very much wanted to be one—an authority not to be idly questioned. They peered and probed but could find nothing amiss. The pain and dullness were put down to "neuralgia," which, they assured him, would vanish as mysteriously as they had come on when the season changed and winter dryness prevailed. Still, the cycles of pain gradually intensified and it could no longer be safely denied that something was wrong. Finally, he went to Duke Hospital, the best medical center in the state, to a neurologist and surgeon named Barnes Woodhall, who for obvious reasons was to become a sort of family hero.

Woodhall, who would later serve as dean of the Duke Medical School, gasped when he examined the X-rays of my father's spine. "My

God, man," he exclaimed—his exact words were too grim to be forgotten—"My God, man, a slipped disc is severing your spine at the top of your back. Another month and you'd have been too late, in fact a dead man."

But even this eleventh-hour discovery brought only slight encouragement, as I later learned. What, if detected earlier, might have been relieved by traction or minor repair called for dangerous and intrusive surgery. The whole area, Woodhall explained, was medical terra incognita. At least half of the (few) patients who had undergone the unperfected procedure had died. Happily, Woodhall was himself among the earlier pioneers of delicate spinal surgery, but he candidly put my father's chances of survival at no better than fifty-fifty, and it must have been those dismal odds that haunted my mother when I saw her in tears that sunny autumn morning, trying to distract herself with household routine. Even her great buoyancy of spirit was threatened.

He had the surgery, of course, but I remember little about the sequel, except for the daily drive from our town to Duke Hospital, twenty-three miles, to visit as he recuperated. I was not allowed to see him in the hospital for more than one or two brief glimpses; and that was no doubt part of the shielding of small children from painful sights and situations that was a fixed feature of my parents' approach to child-rearing. I do remember the day he came home by ambulance. He limped about the house in his bathrobe with a heavy plaster cast on his neck—itself a novelty since he was rarely without a necktie during the daylight hours when he was on duty. The cast, however, soon grew so oppressive in the spring heat that he got Woodhall's permission to have it cut away by one of the local doctors. Ever after, one could see the livid railroad-track scar from his collar to his hairline that the crude sutures of that time left behind.

This close and physically devastating brush with death, leaving him seriously impaired, was almost certainly the signal physical event in his life, and it deeply affected my life in elusive, but decisive, ways. The wreckage of his body and his nerves shortened his patience; he was often on edge, and his energy needed more careful husbanding than would have been usual for a vigorous man in his early forties. And there was the chronic pain—he told me more than once that he could not remember a single day since the "accident" when he had not felt it somewhere, usually in his left leg or neck. In later years, he found relief from the pain in the arid climate of the Southwest, where we traveled extensively by car with my parents' close friends the Doyle Earlys; and in the waters of Hot Springs, Arkansas, where he and his great friend Tom Carter would repair once a year to soak themselves and play cutthroat bridge with Jewish widows. But even in his reduced state, my father was a man of titanic self-control and willpower.

No doubt the pain was no easier to bear in that he had no idea what stroke of bad luck had caused the spinal insult. One theory, depending on mood and season, was that it had been caused by a freak golfing accident. He had been playing one day without spikes on the nine-hole course near our house and as he stepped off an elevated tee he lost his footing and sat hard on his rump. He came to connect this jolt with the problem because it was not long afterward that the pain and tingling set in. But there was another, less plausible, theory that the trauma dated all the way back to his boyhood on the family farm in Catawba County, when he fell from the roof of a toolshed and was knocked unconscious. All this was shrouded in rueful speculation; he simply didn't know. But for this and other reasons—and here we reach the subtle and mysterious effects of a father's condition on the son—he became ultra-cautious about my physical well being. He knew that I must inevitably go through the boyish gun craze common in the South in those days, and he was too wise to prohibit my adolescent access to rifles and shotguns. It would have been pointless anyway, as he knew, since my next-door friends, the two Wilkinson boys, were inveterate hunters. But guns were a matter of compounded dread for him because his younger brother Hubert had mortally wounded himself climbing over a fence with a loaded shotgun, and it had been he who had driven the dying boy to the hospital, begging him pathetically to hold on. His injury further intensified his determination that I would not, could not, play high school football, much as I longed to. (A good thing too, I see now, given my lanky build.) He claimed, with permissible exaggeration, that playing in the crude football equipment of the World War I era (when he had captained the team at Lenoir-Rhyne College) he had "broken every bone that could be broken." (He *had* broken his nose and collarbone.) What mattered far more for me, and for us as a family, was the limp that resulted from the paralysis in his left leg that limited his mobility and the constant alimentary problems stemming from the intestinal paralysis and impaired peristalsis: a daily preoccupation, ministered to with ritual bedtime doses of mineral oil. I am sure now that I have been a compulsive exerciser—even to the point of marathon running—as a sort of compensation for what he missed in the second half of life.

As I look back now on our life together, it is clear—clearer of course than it could have been when I was a boy—that certain conventional expectations of the father-son relationship were disappointed. He occasionally took me hunting, and then only, I imagine, as a sort of duty; but he and his companion Tom Carter weren't serious hunters. They were poor wing shots, carried no hunting dog along and were, I'm sure, uninterested in shooting anything. Our range on these expeditions was, moreover, limited by the paralysis in his left leg. In fact, he and Carter devoted more energy on the hunt to their long-running, if civil, dialogue over politics, Carter's only major flaw being that he was a Republican and believed that the New Deal was "socialistic," a view that my father, a far better informed historian than his friend, rightly regarded as absurd and irrelevant.

My father's occasional irritability over minor matters was so constant a factor in our relationship that I formed the habit of evasion and, when he was in a bad mood, made every effort to stay out of his way. The awkwardness was reinforced by an impersonal factor: he was the superintendent of the schools I had to attend, there being no acceptable alternative. When pre-adolescent silliness pushed me over the line—and in my early teens I am sure that I was one of the silliest boys who ever walked the earth—and I was expelled from class, scenes of mutual embarrassment became inescapable. Some teacher (as I recall, especially, the devoted Miss Reba Vernon, my sixth grade teacher) would send me to stand in the hall. I lurked there, praying that this would be a lucky day and that I would not hear in the hallway that unmistakable step that signaled his approach on his rounds of inspection. Then it would happen. He would round the corner of the corridor and pause as if amazed. "What are you doing here, sonny?" he would ask, peering at me sternly through his rimless glasses. I could feel my face blaze and there was no acceptable answer. One awful day, it must have been when I was in the sixth or seventh grade, Milton Breeze, my constant companion in harmless silliness, and I were "sent to the office." Being sent to his office was a dreaded fate, putting one in danger of the mythic "electric paddle" that every school administrator was rumored to keep locked away in some inner cabinet—not that anyone, even the worst cutups and delinquents, ever had experienced its legendary sting. Our offense had occurred on the playground just after lunch and we found him at his desk, opening mail. We stood waiting. Finally he looked up, ignoring me. "Milton, what are you doing here?" he asked. "We threw rocks on the playground." More silence; more letters being slit by his letter-opener. "Are you going to do it again?" "No, Mr. Yoder." "Then go back to class." Looking back, I can see that these were probably far less memorable or humiliating episodes for him than for me, and he rarely mentioned them at home. But I can still hear the dreadful echoes of his rocking footsteps in the hallway, a tempo dictated by his gimpy left leg, and the tearing sound of the envelopes being slit with his letter-opener as Milton and I stood before him, awaiting his verdict.

As these fragmentary memories suggest, his influence on the development of my character and outlook was decisive, in fact overwhelming. Like all growing boys, I had what I assumed to be a secret life (not that it was particularly scandalous) and assumed that parents knew far less than they actually did about what I was up to. Perhaps it is only when one has children of one's own that one grasps the unspoken and inexplicit side of a relationship otherwise marked by so much admonition: what parents *don't* say, when it seems that they say so much.

Beyond measure my most humiliating experience in my relationship with him stemmed from a case of petty embezzlement. The wartime years and late Forties were not yet marked by the carefree affluence of our age. My allowance was small and hard earned, and I was always short of money. I cared for the chickens we kept for years at the bottom of the back lawn, between the edge of the woods and the small stream that ran through it. On cold winter mornings before school, the drinking trough had to be defrosted—a nasty job, since mash and droppings tended to become mixed in the water. But I soldiered through for the privilege of selling two dozen eggs, at twenty-five cents a dozen, every Saturday morning to the mother of my movie-going pal Janice Rae Veal, who lived just up the hill. Most of the proceeds went to Saturday and Wednesday afternoon movie matinees, plus popcorn, then ten cents a box. I can't recall now what shortfall tempted me one day to dip with light fingers into the box of loose change and bills that he routinely brought back from the Friday-evening basketball game and placed carefully on a hallway shelf above the telephone. I believe I had thoughts of replacing the money later, but that may be self-flattering afterthought. I was passing by and before I could catch myself I stealthily raked three or four fifty-cent pieces out of the box and jammed them in my pocket. Of course, in his meticulous way, he had already counted the money and given someone who had been selling concessions at the game a receipt, and when he found a dollar or two missing I was the obvious suspect. His detective work was gentle but direct.

"Sonny, did you by chance borrow two dollars from the cigar box?" he asked.

I burst into tears and confessed all—concealment has never been among my talents, even in devious moments. What others have flatteringly called my "honest face" is no more than a stark inability to lie or dissemble about anything of importance. I had none of the actor's talents. I gave the money back to him, absorbed the lesson, and nothing was ever said about the matter again. I suspect that the pity of the incident and my own sorrow stirred his warm heart, which he so deeply concealed; for when he was not stern he was often on the verge of tears. But I felt degraded and dishonored in his eyes. I see now that he knew enough about small boys to know that honesty and truthfulness are usually acquired, rather than native, gifts.

Fortunately, most of the early and memorable lessons he taught me are less painful, and some are amusing. Once when I was about twelve, I wrote an English or history theme for school on what I would do to improve the world if I were president. I was immensely pleased with it and with myself and asked him if I could read it aloud—I think now that this demonstration had something to do with my habitual scholastic indolence, which distressed him. I always scored well beyond my grade or years on standard tests, but in that I was merely lucky because application to humdrum schoolwork was not my habit. Yet I coveted his approval. He listened patiently as I outlined my plan, which seemed to me terribly original, a sort of vision over the isthmus, like the one famously described in the poem, something no one else had thought of before. My basic idea was the communitarian possession and management of just about everything—the premise being that if public schools and roads were such a good idea, there should obviously be no limit to the benefits of sharing more widely. I noticed that he was smiling—in stunned admiration, I assumed—as I outlined my utopian vision. He asked me if I had heard of "socialism," a word not then in my vocabulary. I'm not sure that I had, and in any case had no notion of what it meant and perhaps had not considered it at all. He patiently explained, though with a smile of amusement that he couldn't quite suppress, that communitarian plans like mine, while reflecting a creditable idealism and generosity, had in fact been tried—in Russia, for example—and had invariably ended badly because no one had ever learned how to control the endemic selfishness of mankind, man's inhumanity to man, one of his pet phrases. I believe he mentioned other experimental utopias, Brook Farm perhaps, which he surely knew of; but that also had failed for different reasons. He had learned Latin, an expected skill for anyone earning a college degree, especially if he planned to go on to medical school, so perhaps he knew the tag *Quis custodiet ipsos custodes?*—the essence of his patient response—but would have thought it pedantic to quote it to a boy of twelve. Besides, he didn't regard his pronunciation of foreign words as reliable. He had studied German but not French and his stabs at a term like *laissez-faire* could be a bit comic.

Just how he acquired it as a relatively junior member of a large family of brothers and sisters, several of both sexes older than he, I have no idea; but my father possessed an unblushing habit of command—one so assertive at times that I was often embarrassed by the peremptoriness with which he exercised it. It was certainly among those characteristics that had an inoculative effect on me, so that I find it hard to order, even ask, anyone to do anything at all. Unlike my mother, who was consummately tactful, he was never ceremonious when he wanted something done, and he had a way of assuming that his directives were right (as they usually were) and should be followed without question or quibble. He seemed to assume that those who were commanded found it entirely natural that he would command them, as if it were a feature of the eternal order of things. I suppose his resistance to unction explained his uncommon effectiveness. He was often called "the best school man in North Carolina." Who first said so I don't know, but it was certainly right. Everyone who worked under or for him acknowledged that he was a natural leader and administrator, a talent not so widely distributed, especially among academic folk, as is widely supposed. His schools—and they were his—were models of order, respect, and discipline—and, far from incidentally, of learning as well.

His unselfconscious assumption of authority could at times be amusing, if allowances were made. When Jane and I were first married, we often played a rubber or two of bridge in the evenings when we visited. The unvarying lineup was my father and Jane against my mother and me. When my father held the dummy hand, he never hesitated to circle around the table and tell Jane, card by card, how to play the bid. It was not so much rudeness as what Dr. Johnson called "stark insensibility." He often complained that he had little patience for social bridge, preferring a simpler game called "setback" for casual purposes. His explanation was that he had learned to play bridge in the army, during his brief time at an officers' candidate school in the year of the Armistice. And while he did not say so openly (any more than he admitted that he enjoyed betting on the horses in Arkansas), he let me suspect that the stakes in these early bridge games were too high for silly errors, and that was why casual or "social" bridge was repugnant. He took almost everything in life seriously, including games, his view being that if it was worth one's time it was worth doing well. To that end, he had even devised his own point-counting system and scorned the book-learned alternatives, such as Goren, as imprecise.

It was, as I say, odd that he had been the next most junior among five brothers. It was against the code of family solidarity to which all Yoders of that ilk adhered to say anything really negative about a sibling. The negatives emerged between the lines. His older brother Craig, for many years a fine entomologist and a popular teacher of biology at Lenoir-Rhyne, the family Lutheran College, was not—at least in youth—among his favorite people. My father felt that he had been bullied by him. Uncle Craig as I remember him looked the part. He was everyone's image of the formidable Prussian junker: taller than others (most of the brothers were short), with a small, bristly blond moustache and a swept-back brush of hair of the same color. At the large gatherings on the porch of my grandfather's huge and forbidding stone house in Hickory, Uncle Craig smoked fragrant cigarettes and tended to talk through his nose when he spoke at all, which was seldom. My father's defining memory of their early relationship was summed up in a story I heard repeatedly all through boyhood. (If a story made a point, my father never feared to repeat it for fear that it might have grown stale.)

The two of them, he and Craig, and another younger brother, were sent out to pick cotton by my imperious grandfather, a stern taskmaster. My father's two brothers, he recalled with undiminished indignation many decades later, seized every opportunity to slack off and goldbrick, while he himself picked industriously. In relating this exemplary tale, in which he emerged as virtuous, my father would work himself into a lather. I dutifully absorbed the tale at face value, insofar as it mattered to me. One day, however, having heard the story more than once herself, Jane observed that the story could be reframed to reveal unsuspected complexities. Wasn't the real question, the paradox, she asked, why *he* felt compelled to pick the cotton as ordered rather than join his brothers in boyish evasion, the latter being far more natural? When she ventured to ask him as much one night, in her disarming way, he had no answer at all; he was struck dumb by the question. Filial duty was filial duty, and that was that. So deeply was he imbued with it, in fact, that he told me more than once that the biblical parable of the Prodigal Son had always seemed to him to get the emphasis backward, since he identified with the elder son who had loyally stayed at home and obeyed his father. The secret of the matter may lie in the personality of my grandfather, to me in his old age a benign presence with curly white hair and a beautiful Roman nose. The fact that by then he was almost stone deaf also subdued him in company. But earlier photographs tell quite another story and reinforce my father's deeply internalized reverence for his authority. There must have been something menacingly willful in his manner that my father, as a child and young man, had been as reluctant to challenge as I was to challenge his. My father had absorbed my grandfather's almost religious work ethic and had little but scorn for those who lacked it. He definitely entertained the fear that I would grow up good for nothing, without *learning* to work. The word itself—work—had an ominous ring on his lips, and for all his brainy intellectuality it sometimes seemed to have an exclusively physical meaning. The countless hours I spent crouched over my drawing or painting upstairs, for instance, didn't seem to count as work—not even when I experienced for the first time the joy of appearing in print. It visited me early. When I was ten or eleven, *Child Life* magazine published my drawing of Columbus's *Santa Maria,* emblazoned with the heroic caption "Sail On." When I found the drawing there on the contributors' page, I ran pell-mell to the edge of the garden to show it to him. He nodded approvingly but took it in stride. I knew somehow that he really would prefer that I be mowing or raking leaves.

And there is more to say about his devotion to *work*. Every so often he terrorized my mother (and me) by saying that just about any day he might sell our house in town and buy a farm in the country, so that we, my younger brother and I, could really be taught to work. Fortunately, his closest approach to this fantasy—though how could we be sure it was only that?—was to cultivate a large vegetable garden in the vacant field that ran down the long hill from my mother's rose beds beneath the power lines that bordered our property. It perhaps began as one of those ubiquitous "victory gardens" that everyone cultivated in the World War II years, then took on a larger life of its own. Before age and infirmity began to overtake him, he would put on an old pair of khaki shorts on blazing summer afternoons and push a hand-held plow between the rows of corn, beans and squash, his tongue resolutely tucked in the corner of his mouth as it always was when he applied himself to a close physical task, his pale skin gleaming and turning pink in the sunlight. But this was sporadic, and for the most part the garden was tended by the help, men and boys, black and white, whom he hired in the summers.

No doubt a psychological profile, if one had been imaginable in his case and in those days, would have disclosed substantial "ambivalence" in the celebration of the harsh physical regimen to which his taskmaster father had subjected him. He idealized it in retrospect, but I see now, as was probably evident even then to any detached eye, that the three oldest Yoder boys, my father and his older brothers Fred and Craig, were intensely cerebral beings like their grandfather, Col. George Yoder. This ancestor of ours had been so natural a scholar that at the age of seventeen (this would have been about 1840, before the common-school movement took hold in North Carolina) he had absorbed all the local schoolmaster had to teach. And having done so, he inherited at that tender age the schoolmaster's mantle at what was known thereafter, for the better part of a century, as "the Yoder school." This rude but effective rural institution held a cherished place in family tale and legend; for it was my father's fond memory that since before Civil War days, each generation, down to my own—George, Colin, Edwin—had taught his son and presented him with a high school diploma. Accordingly, at my high school commencement in the spring of 1952, I was startled when my name was called and my father snatched my diploma from the hands of the school-board chairman who had been presenting them to others and handed it to me himself. As he explained later, he was keeping a family tradition intact: a tradition of sober learning. My father had few idols, but aside from Franklin D. Roosevelt and Frank Porter Graham, the president of the University of North Carolina, the closest approximation was his oldest brother, Fred R. Yoder. Uncle Fred, having acquired his master's degree at Chapel Hill, had left his schoolteaching job to fight as an infantry officer on the western front in 1917–18, in a unit that had seen much hard fighting and suffered 50 percent casualties. After the Armistice, he attended the London School of Economics, where he began a long friendship with the controversial British socialist Harold Laski. After taking his doctorate in sociology under Thorstein Veblen at Wisconsin, he began a long academic career as a professor and dean at Washington State University. After his retirement there, he ran for Congress as a Democrat (unsuccessfully), then took over as dean of academic affairs at a small Kentucky college. Well into his eighties, this tireless scholar, a man of catholic interests, was burrowing in the manuscript collections at Chapel Hill, preparing to write a biography of his father's political mentor and model, the Fusionist senator Marion Butler. When he visited in North Carolina, as he often did, to teach in summer-school sessions at Duke or Chapel Hill, he and my father would make a pilgrimage to visit Dr. Joseph G. deR. Hamilton, the notable architect of the great Southern Historical Collection, who had taught them both in graduate courses in history. On these warm, cricket-chorusing summer nights, I would sit patiently on the bank overlooking the porch of Dr. Hamilton's little bungalow, wondering what on earth the interminable chatter could be about. I wish now that I had been more interested and a better listener. Meanwhile, however, the farm-buying fantasy, the proposed return to the soil, gradually receded and was spoken of no more.

There is a familiar, if informal, category of self-identified sufferers who speak of themselves as "PKs," preachers' kids, and believe themselves to exhibit common scars. I can identify with the special brand they bear, as sons or daughters of the stricter Protestant sects whose clergy (and their children as well!) are expected to exhibit a preternatural piety.

It often turns out the other way, of course, like the cobbler's shoes. No equivalent category known as principals' sons has been defined. But similar strictures applied. I was supposed to set an example of model behavior in the classroom, although as I have confessed I missed that mark by a mile. Meanwhile, the rougher boys under my father's tutelage—those who smoked forbidden cigarettes in the bushes behind the gym, or slipped off during school hours to Clark's grocery store across the street, or who bombarded our house with fireworks on Hallowe'en night— those he labeled "the elements" (as in "undesirable elements") or "rag-tag and bobtail"—had ingenious ways of mocking him. They imitated his voice, and some even went so far as to joke about his limp and whether he had a cork leg and perhaps a penis of the same material. The shameless among them did not conceal this mockery from me; in fact, they taunted me with it. My father in those years was a stocky man of medium height whose most striking physical characteristic (other than the searching, benevolent, and slightly astigmatic brown eyes behind the rimless spectacles—and of course the limp) was a dome-like bald head, a classic egghead. To the more imaginative detractors, however, this dome suggested a cue-ball; so my father was referred to by them as cue-ball, or "cue" for short. I was "little cue." I hated and was embarrassed by both terms, though they seem no more than mildly insulting now. There were occasions, infuriating to him, when I was taunted by the school bullies if they thought they could get away with it—they knew I was not a tattle-tale. "There goes little cue!" one of them would shout, making as if to stop my bicycle. One of those days became famous in family annals as the "day I ran over Mr. Grant's car." Some of the usual rowdies were gathered at the bottom of the long hill on Fifth Street, waiting to hitchhike to the golf course. When I came coasting down the hill on my bike, headed home, they began shouting for me to stop. As I pedaled hard to get past them, looking back over my shoulder, I collided with Mr. Grant's old tan Ford auto, parked on the street, its jagged fender cutting a gash in my thigh. The incident enraged my father, yet he couldn't help laughing at the conceit that I had *run over* a car and never stopped teasing me about it. The direst threat was that the rowdies would make off with my pants—a small-town American version, I guess, of the English schoolboy ritual of "debagging" that I was to hear threatened on frolicsome evenings with the "Lizzie" (Elizabethan Society, named in honor of the royal founder of my college), a drinking club

I belonged to in Oxford, though never enacted outside the novels of Evelyn Waugh.

As a boy, I was mildly terrorized by the experience of being a principal's son; but it came with the territory and I doubt that I suffered permanent psychic damage. Far worse were the accidental unfairnesses of my father's resolve to avoid, at all costs, the barest hint of favoritism to me. But this resolve had its limits, for as I have said he hated cruelty or the humiliation of any student, whoever the perpetrator or victim might be. One night at a high school basketball game when I was playing second-string center, some of the bench players were wearing practice uniforms, I have forgotten why—perhaps some had simply worn out and the new ones had not arrived. The coach beckoned to me from his perch down the bench. I naturally assumed that he intended to put me into the game and eagerly stripped off my warmup suit. "Ed," he said, however, in the dry tone that was usual with him, "swap shirts with Jesse." So in plain view, I removed my jersey with the numeral on it and put on the numberless black practice jersey; and my classmate Jesse Raines—who was, certainly, a better player than I—went into the game. Several hundred eyes had witnessed the change of costume and the slight pushed me close to tears of anger and embarrassment. The evening passed, but no such scene was ever lost on my father. He said nothing, but by the next season that coach had been retired from the basketball scene. The oddity, given his acute sense of justice, was that it had almost nothing to do with the fact that I happened to be his son as well as the humiliated party.

I have mentioned my father's keen, polymathic mind. When he died, suddenly, in July 1985, I wrote as follows in the obituary column:

> Careful, observant scrutiny of a world he could no longer even barely affect, let alone control, suggested his unquenchable curiosity. Early in the morning of his funeral, a few days later, I watched a long freight train crawl through the small North Carolina town whose schools he had administered for forty years. I thought: He was the only man I knew who could have told you what those odd-shaped cars were built to carry, whether they still did and, if so, where the cargoes were mined and made. For good measure he could have named the founders of the rail lines—rascals in his book, most probably—and told by what imposture against the public interest they had prospered. His information was vast and

seemed especially so to a boy. . . . A few summers ago, he sat patiently listening as a babbling mob of newsless children and grandchildren on vacation idly guessed where the United States had recently shot down two Libyan planes. The Gulf of . . . of . . . . ? Persian Gulf? "Sidra," he finally said. Others guessed; he knew. . . .Education was so central to his family's vision of the world that to be without it, or to treat it lightly, was unimaginable. And by the way, to know was to know exactly. Once he ran through a geometrical demonstration with me as I sat, only half comprehending, by his reading chair. "See, sonny?" he asked. "I think I do," I responded. "In geometry," he said, "proofs are not a matter of opinion. They are either right or wrong." He felt that way about many things—not only math and science but history, behavior and politics. Especially behavior. He conceded little to the twilight.

Had his intellect enjoyed a polish as high as its potential, it would, I think, have shown virtually unlimited promise. I came slowly to an accurate estimate of its power—certainly not before I had cleared that stage of juvenility at which we become abashed (often as college sophomores) by the astonishing ignorance and intellectual limits of parents. This incisiveness (literally, the *bite*) of my father's mind was to be seen in any errand requiring cognitive grasp, especially of a historical, mathematical, or scientific kind. The only signal limiting factor was that his was sense without sensibility; the literary, the poetic, the imaginative realm, was not his forte.

The first time I recall noticing the dimensions of his learning came one Sunday morning when he unexpectedly appeared to teach the lesson in the young persons' Bible class. The usual teacher was a neighbor, a prominent citizen, whose take on biblical texts was moralistic, sometimes maudlin as well, though it was not always easy to detect the transition. He suffered from an apparently hereditary tear-duct disorder, and appeared to weep as he was moved by his keynote: his own exemplary virtue. On the day when my father substituted for him, businesslike as always when discharging an academic task, the lesson of the day was the story from *Genesis* of Jacob's sharp practice against his brother Esau and his shameful deception of his father, the blind and aged Isaac—a story replete with potential for moralizing. But my father, reared in the Lutheran tradition of serious biblical scholarship, framed it historically rather than moralistically and gave us a spellbinding account of the context of Hebraic custom in which the tale played out: the birthright expectations of first-born sons, and the institution of primogeniture, of which I am not sure I had ever heard. He added, for perspective, that primogeniture was an important feature, still, of English common law and had prevailed in a number of the American colonies until Thomas Jefferson led the movement to abolish it in Virginia. He went on to say that Jacob, having tricked his father, would in turn be tricked by his prospective father-in-law, Laban, who substituted his homelier elder daughter for the younger and more beautiful Rachel. I am sure this appealed to his unwavering sense of fair play. But I wonder, even now, how many Sunday School teachers anywhere could have matched this bravura performance. For years I had watched him settle down for an hour or so on Saturday evenings, after rapping the dottle of spent Prince Albert tobacco from his after-dinner pipe, to prepare his lesson for the next day's men's Bible class. But until I had the experience first hand, it had not been clear to me what a natural he was, with the master teacher's capacity for cutting through stale conventionalities to the heart of the matter.

My father continued to teach the men's Bible class for something like a quarter century, doubtless seeing it as a duty; but it could hardly be said that piety or fervor (as distinguished from natural reverence) ran deep in either the Yoders or the Logues. My father remained faithful to the Lutheran church in which he and many generations of ancestors had been christened, and to its characteristic traditions of sober learning and theological reserve. Religious practice in the Mebane of my parents' era was that of many small southern towns, though narrower in range. There were neither Lutheran nor Episcopal churches; it was Presbyterian country. Otherwise, as someone once said, there are more Baptists than people in North Carolina, and they abounded also. My parents attended, and my mother eventually joined, the Presbyterian church. It was there that my father for years taught the class I've mentioned. He also liked singing the fine old hymns (off-key), but otherwise kept his religious views to himself—in part, I suspect, to avoid disconcerting my mother, whose faith was traditional, though not assertively so. He never volunteered, and in the spirit of reticence that prevailed in our household when it came to the "forbidden things," I never asked what he believed. Given his otherwise abundant flow of opinions, the silence was probably significant. Nor did his preferences extend to indoctrination of any sort. His keenest interest was in the ethical and social consequences of religion, and not in mystery or metaphysics.

It was very much in character that on Reformation Sunday, 1960, when John F. Kennedy's Roman Catholic faith was under attack from such prominent bigots as the Rev. Norman Vincent Peale, and for squalid and prejudicial political reasons, my father made a point not only of attending church but of sitting toward the front, prepared to stare down the mousy parson should he dare to preach about the dangers of popery. Whether because of his eagle-eyed stare or otherwise, the subject was avoided. The sight of him sitting there with his arms skeptically folded would not have loosened anyone's tongue.

As the foregoing stories would indicate, his cast of mind, trained as he was in history and biology, was analytical and skeptical and never credulous or superstitious. I can't help wondering now what he believed about what W. J. Cash calls "the questions that have no answers." Religion was of obvious importance to him, but when he spoke of it the usual topic was parables and other New Testament dicta that made ethical points. I have already said that while he regarded the parable of the Prodigal Son as a beautiful story, he identified with the sober son who stayed at home and, as southern people said in my youth, "amounted to something" while his prodigal brother was dissipating abroad. This was in character; as was his hatred of bigotry and bullying, religious or political. His resolute refusal to join the Presbyterian church stemmed, I suspect, from his sense that Calvinists were much too obsessed with doctrine, sometimes at the expense of charity. That determination, even after many years of attending and teaching Bible studies for adults, was certainly strengthened, and indeed sealed for good, by an episode of the early 1950s. When I was a freshman at Chapel Hill in 1952, the pastor of the university Presbyterian church there, Charles Jones, a notable preacher and ethicist with strong views on social issues, fell afoul of the governing Orange presbytery. The elders of that body were alarmed by reports of Jones's unorthodox views and practices (he rarely celebrated Holy Communion, for instance). On this pretext, Jones was subjected to a sort of heresy trial and deposed. The immediate result was to foster a schism in the church, and the more liberal half of the congregation formed the Chapel Hill community church and immediately hired Jones as its pastor. My father suspected, however, that Jones's real offense was that he was a liberal who saw no virtue in racial segregation—this of course was a couple of years before the Supreme Court's decisive repudiation of the "separate but equal" doctrine—and said so and, furthermore, entertained interracial groups at his parsonage. The Jones *auto da fé* followed close on the heels of a depressing U.S. Senate race in the summer of 1949 in which Dr. Frank Porter Graham, the former president of the university and an idol of my father's (as of all liberal North Carolinians), was defeated in a nasty racist campaign instigated by Jesse Helms. The Jones case seemed to my father part and parcel of the smear campaign against Dr. Graham, and Jones's deposition did not endear the Presbyterian church to him. Almost from the day—I don't think this is mere imagination—I noticed a subtle but progressive drift away from it. But perhaps it was only that I was growing up and he was willing to confide his doubts to me.

The outcroppings of racial and religious bigotry in our previously tranquil North Carolina were clearly an aspect of the troubled and fearful spirit of those years, the years of McCarthyism. I am still thankful that, unlike so many of my college friends, I did not have to fear dreadful arguments over segregation or Joe McCarthy during home visits. My mother was the most tolerant and unassertive of persons, especially with her sons. My father despised "thought control," as he called it, and shared Harry Truman's view that the self-serving red-baiting then so popular in Washington was a "red herring" designed to distract the public from more substantive issues, such as the state of American medical care. He identified the wizened and blinkered elders of the Orange Presbytery who had cast out Charles Jones as a heretic with the inquisitors of Washington. Their works alarmed and exasperated him; and since this was a crucial period in my own political development I readily absorbed his views and feel the imprint to this day—not that I regret that stamp in the least.

Occasionally, his skepticism in religious matters would peek briefly, almost antically, above the surface, like a burrowing animal at the door of its den. One summer evening when my Aunt Rubye was visiting from Augusta, and Jane and I and the children had driven over from Greensboro for dinner, she held forth about an eccentric acquaintance who still sat for long hours by her late husband's grave in the conviction that he would one day arise and rejoin her. "History is against it, Rubye," my father commented dryly. *History is against it*—those spare words intimated far more about his outlook than they said.

He had planned to study medicine and with that goal in mind took his undergraduate degree in biology. It is a field that seems to run in the family genes. His older brother Craig (the one who looked like a junker) was an entomologist of local note known to generations of Lenoir-Rhyne students as "Bugs." But while my grandfather contrived to build a big house near the college during the cotton boom, and send ten children through it, there were no funds for medical school, and college loans had not yet been thought of. Thus my father soon found himself a school principal at Mint Hill, in Mecklenburg County, and that was to be his professional destiny. But his medical interest persisted, even after he gave up all hope of medical school and began taking summer courses at Chapel Hill with the thought of earning a doctorate in history.

He was not exactly a hypochondriac but seemed to me to consult doctors quite a lot, for himself and for me; and the doctors who treated him were often impressed by his up-to-date knowledge of the advances in their art. It often exceeded their own. He probably knew the story of Alexander Fleming and penicillin long before most of the pill-rollers who attended his medical needs. And since for the first six years of my life I was a sickly boy, suffering from a cornucopia of childhood illnesses—mumps, measles, whooping cough, chicken pox, plus innumerable colds, earaches, and fevers—he got to practice his amateur medicine on me. I can still see him standing by my sickbed and shaking down one of those old thermometers of the 1930s and 1940s, which had to be gripped silently under the tongue for seven minutes or more before they registered. (I can still see myself inhaling air in an attempt to manipulate the reading and escape from quarantine.)

What adds a special poignancy to this thwarted medical ambition is a might-have-been of uncertain meaning. During one of his stays at Duke Hospital—perhaps it was while he was convalescing from disc surgery—his grasp of medical lore so impressed one of the attending doctors that this man made him a stunning proposition. He would pay for my father's medical schooling if my father would only agree to go into practice with him.

I heard this story more than once in his later life, when he was embarked on that process known as "life review." There must have been truth in it. He attached a high, indeed prohibitive, value to truth-telling and it is inconceivable to me that he would have fabricated such a tale. But I did not often press for details or try to pin him down to times and places when he was reminiscing and the subject was one of those representative stories that are perhaps of greater personal significance than notable for historical exactitude. I wonder now whether my father magnified a kindly and conditional gesture—not much more, maybe, than a flattering remark—into a proposition more definite and considered than it was. But he attached great meaning to it, as a glimpsed and savory resurgence of an earlier dream that impecuniousness had dashed. Medicine's loss was education's gain; and perhaps there was ironic compensation in his marriage into my mother's Georgia family, the Logue-Laseters, where for several generations physicians have abounded. My father was not embittered. But he thought, probably correctly, that most doctors were basically incompetent and occasionally vented his conviction that medical schools practiced an outrageous favoritism, that their admissions were rigged so that sons or grandsons of doctors, even when dumb as posts, got a leg up.

Whatever his other gifts and disappointments, one success was striking: He was a wizard with money and the wizardry was all the more remarkable considering how modest his pay and resources were. He occasionally observed that a public-school administrator in his position, with three schools and more than a score of teachers and coaches under his supervision, was paid almost as well as a full professor at Chapel Hill—a comparison that suggests his preference for the latter. Even so, however, the pay was modest by any professional standard. His case proved that it is what you contrive to save that matters. He certainly was no miser; he was far from stingy and could be extraordinarily generous. He allowed me to write checks on his bank account as a student in Chapel Hill. When I won my scholarship to study at Oxford, his monthly subsidies arrived as predictably as the turn of the calendar page, and financed opportunities for continental travel and other amenities that the Rhodes stipend didn't cover.

How did he manage this Midas touch (without Midas's fateful handicap)? Soon after we moved from Greensboro to Mebane in 1935, in the pit of the Depression years, he contracted for a house—a standard-model frame house of typical configuration and absolutely no architectural distinction—living room, dining room, kitchen, bath, entrance hall, and two bedrooms downstairs; two bedrooms, a roomy hallway, and another bath upstairs—the latter usually occupied in the early years by one of my mother's live-in Georgia maids.

The house was convenient enough for a family of four but hardly spacious, and in later years he often spoke of enlarging it or even of swapping houses with an elderly neighbor, Ed White, whose imposing hilltop colonial on spacious grounds two doors up from ours was one of the town's showplaces. His good financial planning had made either of these steps possible. But like his fantasies about farming, they finally came to nothing. The crucial fact is that he had disposable income in the mid-thirties, when the economy was down and prices deflated, so that with the onset of prosperity and inflation in the early World War II years, the twenty-five hundred dollars he had borrowed became easy to repay and the mortgage could be retired by 1942. After that, the substantial portion of income that most people spend for housing—30 to 40 percent by standard estimates—were free for saving and investment. He felt that he had learned a useful lesson when he had unloaded some depreciated oil stocks during the 1929 crash, in companies that ultimately recovered spectacularly, whose post-Depression expansion alone would have made him financially comfortable. He never repeated the error, followed the stock market closely, and did well.

His investing acumen produced at least one significant coup. Whenever a national company announced plans to move to North Carolina or open a plant or subsidiary there, his practice was to buy shares of the company's stock. He routinely did so when P. Lorillard announced in the early 1950s that it would build a Greensboro plant. By happy chance, the purchase fell a year or so before the *Reader's Digest* named Kent filter-tip cigarettes (a Lorillard product) the "safest" cigarettes, igniting a boom in Kent sales. His Lorillard stock commenced to double and split, double and split, and the windfall was considerable. (As I write, half a century later, cigarette companies have been demonized as the new evil empire, now that the Soviet Union has collapsed—mainly the work of television networks deprived by congressional edict of cigarette advertising.)

When he retired, he had accumulated a sizable estate. And when he died in July 1985, he left my mother comfortable while also leaving generous bequests to my brother and me. His foresight had vital personal consequences for me. The *Washington Star* failed in 1981 and I launched a syndicated column. The income from the column yielded only a base, however, and for special expenses I benefited from the handsome interest generated by my modest inherited capital—thanks to the high real interest rates occasioned by the Reagan administration's huge deficits and heavy borrowing. Thanks to my father's stewardship, I could operate independently. Incidentally, I denounced the Reagan-Bush fiscal policies that produced those personally useful interest rates several score times, biting at the hand that fed me while it famished and stunted national investment. I claim no special virtue; but at least I could hardly be accused of using my column for financially self-serving purposes.

I mention all this because my father's economic management was in many ways strangely incongruous with his usual interests and attitudes, political and educational. No child ever grew up in a household so blessedly free of money anxiety or talk: it went along with the companion reticence about so many topics of obsessive American concern—not only money but sickness, family scandal and misfortune, death, sex, etc.—that was my parents' policy and manner. I was kept away from all funerals as a child; and while neither of my parents was in the least prudish about sex, I can't recall any plain or direct discussion of that universally fascinating topic—ever. My excellent tenth-grade biology teacher, Iris Abernathy, explained human reproduction and its essential physical equipment with cheerful aplomb and candor, almost certainly because my father instructed her to do so. These mysterious matters— mysterious in that buttoned-up age, at least, for sheltered boys in their early teens—were spoken of as natural aspects of the biological order. Today, the same lessons, inevitably mixed with contraception and abortion, would be labeled "sex education" and denounced by ostrich-like cranks as indoctrination and the usurpation of parental authority. In those more deferential days, before rank-and-file Americans began to fancy themselves experts on education, a school administrator could make intelligent curricular decisions that no one ventured to challenge. In my father's case, it would have been fruitless to contest them and he would have paid no attention at all. It wasn't democratic; it was merely sensible.

It was only when he grew infirm and capricious in his mid-eighties, and bedridden, that he occasionally brandished his money as a weapon—an obvious symptom, for so generous a man, of his rage at physical incapacity. And of life's unfairness he had suffered doubly. He whose luck had turned bad at the physical summit of life became its victim again in age, and in much the same freakish way. My parents were visiting my favorite aunt in Augusta, as they frequently did. Walking down the dark central corridor of her house, he slipped on one of the many small throw rugs that lined it and fell hard—again—on his rump. An ambulance was summoned and he was driven, no doubt protesting, to the small private hospital of my uncle's medical-school classmate, Dr. Gray, the Logue family physician for well over half a century. The early X-rays showed no damage to bones and it was assumed that when the bruises healed all would be well. My brother flew to Augusta to drive them home.

But the pain persisted and increased, as if in a demonic reprise of the earlier catastrophe. When he finally consulted orthopedic specialists at the university hospital in Chapel Hill, the new X-rays showed countless hairline fractures of the pelvis—probably missed at Dr. Gray's clinic because, the doctors explained, it is often only when healing begins that these faint and spidery fractures become detectable. For a man now in his early eighties and none too steady on his legs, the injury was a sentence to bleak deterioration. He soon relied on a walker to get about the house. After several attempts at physical therapy, he became all but immobile and had to move to a nursing home, which he bitterly hated. It was a harsh struggle, for his mind and will were intact and stoic resignation had never been his style. The outrage now occasionally surfaced. In bad moods he threatened to change his will and take off for Florida with a female nurse who, unlike his own family, would not forsake him and would care for him properly—a proposition not to be debated on its merits, for as he understood in calmer moments, it had none.

As the years passed, our reticent relationship deepened into mutual respect, seasoned by broad agreement on most public issues. There was often a note of hectoring indoctrination in his views; but I valued his wisdom, and politics became for us a bonding agent. It is sometimes said that in our search for the missing father—that Telemachus's quest immortalized by our state bard Thomas Wolfe—we seek some compensatory element that is missing in the original. I was to develop many close bonds with teachers and mentors—Jim Caldwell and Fred Weaver at Chapel Hill, Bill Williams in Oxford, Ed Hudgins and Bill Snider in Greensboro, Lewis Powell in Washington.

But if the compensatory theory had been correct, it would surely be clearer to me just what missing ingredient of the incomplete father these mentors supplied. In fact, it is easier at a glance to see them as echoing and amplifying features of my relationship with my father, as if that were the basic motif and these variations upon it.

When he died suddenly that day in July 1985 I could say goodbye with a good conscience, content that I had been a son worthy of such a father. But there was one mystifying qualification. It had come up one summer some years earlier when Jane and I came for a week to keep him company while my mother paid her usual visit to Georgia. One night he suddenly asked: "Why did you say you don't love me?"

I was stunned, all the more because this was so far from his usual tact and because I could not imagine, let alone recall, saying so wounding a thing.

"I have no idea what you're talking about," I said. "Of course I love you."

This seemed to reassure him, though he went on to elaborate. "You once said you respected me but didn't love me. I've never been able to forget."

He was in full possession of his faculties, so dementia or forgetfulness or hallucination could be ruled out.

"I'm positive I never said it and couldn't say it even if I thought it—and I don't," I said. "Maybe you dreamed it." I was aware, of course, that dreams sometimes are a subliminal reflection of unspoken words.

"I'm sure I didn't dream it," he said, "but I take your word for it."

To this day, I can't imagine what this complaint was all about. But having in my mature years observed a greater variety of father-son relationships, I know that they all differ; and I can see that ours, often so close and confidential, was also almost entirely comradely, as if we were fellow members of some cozy club, bonded by fraternal feelings or similar political inclinations. Certainly I had a lifelong opportunity to see how undemonstrative all the Yoders were, himself included. It was their inbred and indelible hallmark. Always cordial and courteous, if unceremonious, they maintained a wary distance from emotional display—as if the open demonstration even of the closest familial affection were somehow in bad taste. The wild scenes of demonstrative affection, whether of happy greeting or tearful farewells, that marked my mother's warm-blooded Georgia family were entirely avoided by the Yoders. They did not shout, they did not weep, they neither embraced nor kissed; and the deepest sorrows and joys, even when near the surface, were sternly controlled. I fancy, moreover, that my father and his brothers and sisters suffered, if that is the right term, from a double dose of this temperament, insofar as it might be genetic in origin. My paternal grandfather and grandmother were second cousins, both surnamed Yoder, and both models of self-containment. It may be, then, that my father in this curious episode was groping to articulate a hereditary lack he sensed in our relationship: that it was missing some quite ordinary, yet vital, affective spark which had never quite been compensated for in our fraternal agreement and cordiality—and "respect."

In the sketch I wrote when he died (quoted in part above, and in full in the Appendix), I said that some weeks of reflection had turned up no unusual variations on the old theme of fathers and sons; and at a longer remove that remains so. I see him now with more objectivity, according to that advice tendered to the hero of my friend Peter Taylor's brilliant novel *A Summons to Memphis,* whose worries about his powerful father virtually obsess him: We should make the imaginative leap to cut away the last intimidating veils of filial dependency and see fathers as persons in their own right, with their own lives and histories: "She [the hero's girlfriend Holly] was teaching herself to admire and respect her old patriarch of a father as she had not done since before her adolescence. Moreover, she began teaching me at this point to seek a still clearer understanding of my own father. *She wished me to try to see him in a light that would not require either forgetting or forgiving. She frequently urged me to talk to him. . . . and to try to give her a whole picture of what his life had actually been and to try to imagine how it must always have seemed to him*" (my emphasis).

I gather, not only from Peter's short stories and novel but from many casual conversations, that his father had presented the same challenging presence in his life as mine had in my own, and in some ways a presence as problematical also. As I have tried to follow Holly's good advice in this longer portrait, I am, at the end, impressed by my father's massive strength of character and his exhibition of those qualities—justice, fortitude, prudence, and temperance—that in traditional wisdom constitute the cardinal virtues. Certainly he was just, though in later years his judgment of others could at times be severe. There was prudence in his stewardship of the never too abundant earthly treasure he was granted, and always temperance and consideration in his behavior; he was never impulsive. And perhaps most admirable of all, there was the self-command—the classic fortitude—with which he faced physical catastrophes that would have defeated lesser men.

A RACIAL EDUCATION

Mothers and Sons *I sometimes say, only half in jest, that I am for better or worse the product of a "mixed marriage"—mixed, in the sense that the qualities of my parents were very different, if complementary. When I encountered that pervasive thematic musing in the tales of Thomas Mann about the northern, austere, businesslike father and the southern, artistic mother, it was familiar territory. As I have indicated, the Yoders were (almost) all seriousness and scholarly sobriety, with little sense of play (no homo ludens they), austere, analytical, masking even deep emotion. My mother and her remarkable family, the Logues, were fun-loving, arty, overflowing with sensibility and poetry, living in a world "too fine to be violated by ideas." For them, the social revolutions of their time came and went, as if powerful underwater currents, felt of course, adjusted to without bitterness, but registering little visible disturbance on the surface of their happy world.*

In the following chapter, I deal primarily with what is still the great American issue, "the American dilemma" as Gunnar Myrdal called it. Several revolutions and substantial improvement later, it strikes me that we are still as a nation in some denial, still reluctant to confront the race issue honestly and historically. I am sometimes asked how it was that unreflecting racial prejudice pervaded the society I grew up in—as indeed it did much of the nation—and I have no simple answer. Certainly it was not confined to the hoodlums and nightriders who cheered demagogues like Bilbo, Wallace, and Barnett, among many others, and sometimes stooped to atrocity. It was in the churches and the country clubs no less than in the back alleys. I can only maintain, as I do in this chapter, that a form of prejudice that was long accepted by my mother, the gentlest and kindest of people, could and did find a place in the best of hearts. And still sometimes does, no doubt.

One day in her later years, my mother greeted me during a visit with a teasing question: "Edwin, do I seem to be getting darker?" She laughed as she asked.

"Darker? Not that I can see. Why?"

"Well, because Magdalen and I eat our lunch together now at the dining room table. It seemed silly for us to be talking to each other through the doorway. So one day I said to her, 'Magdalen, for goodness' sake, just bring your plate and sit in here.'"

Magdalen was her black maid, "colored" as she always said. And if you knew my mother as I did you knew that light-years of evolving social custom had been bridged in that simple gesture, growing as it did out of the loneliness of two elderly southern ladies. By the time of which I speak, my mother was approaching her ninetieth year and had been living alone for some time.

She had grown up in central Georgia when race was an overriding obsession, agitated by the horrors of lynch law (some two thousand persons, most of them black, had been murdered in the South by mobs in the decade before her birth in 1900) and yet shrouded in the insulating denials that allowed white people of decent instincts to live with themselves and with the atrocities their newspapers reported. And when it came to mob action, Georgia, as the later Leo Frank case would show, was among the more violent places.

Her heritage, then, was a deep ambivalence about the race barrier, a blend of affection for particular persons with a deeply inbred conviction that there was a fixed "place" or station for black people generally. She had once mentioned casually to me that her father, my grandfather, had been a friend of Sen. Thomas Watson's and that Watson had often stayed with them when he traveled in that part of Georgia, south and east of Augusta. Readers of Vann Woodward's brilliant biography of Watson, *Agrarian Rebel,* will recall that Watson was then among the South's preeminent race demagogues. As a young man, a writer and editor, he had been a literate and, for his time, liberal and enlightened apostle of progress. In his later years, those once flexible views had coagulated into a hideous compound of racism and anti-Semitism.

Perhaps it was my chilling knowledge of the character of the later Watson that silenced the questions I might have asked: "Why Watson? Did they agree?" But her father had died in 1928, six years before I was born; and the truth was that while my father had once said that the old man's thinking accorded with our own, I knew nothing about his political views. I also could imagine that those far-off visits to the Logue household could well have been anodyne affairs. So ingenious were the disguises and evasions that had been woven about the great fact of race that I could envision a courtly Watson abiding under my grandfather's roof, or dining at his table, served in serenity by patient black people without so much as a hinted reference to his bleak demagoguery. But I mustn't exaggerate; civilized life often demands the concealment of raw and awkward truths.

In any event, when she came one day to the realization that her affection for Magdalen—and her loneliness, for she was the most gregarious of persons—had vanquished all the inbred taboos (one did not dine with servants), she had moved light-years. Hence her typically joky way of taking the edge off this late-life pilgrimage: "Do I look darker?"

My mother was not, I hasten to add, in any sense a "racist"—at least as I would define the term. She had been imbued with the racial culture of her time and place, early twentieth-century Georgia; but it had been moderated by many decades in the easier climate of North Carolina and I can't recall a single instance in my childhood or after when she or my father intimated, or countenanced, the slightest disrespect for black people. True, they were amused when one of their black employees who'd been looking after the house in their absence left a note reading: "i have warsh the dish, I have fed Charm (Chum, my fox-terrier) and now I have went home to study my French." But she would have called it "common," her word for underbreeding, to say or suggest anything compromising to another's dignity, black or white. In fact, gentility, for want of a better term, was an integral part of the infinitely refined and subtle way in which the matter of race was dealt with when I was a boy. It was not that the elephant in the room was ignored; the elephant was treated as deferentially as if it were displaced royalty. In the world of my childhood, in central North Carolina and Georgia, black people were a constant and intimate presence and often stood for me in the role of surrogate parents.

For reasons that I failed to clarify during her lifetime, my mother in my own earliest years preferred imported maids from her native Georgia as my caretakers. They would typically arrive in late summer and stay with us through the school year. My mother was a schoolteacher who had married a school principal when they worked together in the small North Carolina mountain resort of Hendersonville. It was never clear to me just why she had left Georgia as a young woman of twenty or so; certainly not because she disliked it. But she was the youngest of three sisters of celebrated beauty, and as my daughter (who was very close to her) once put it: "If your two sisters were noted beauties, maybe you would have wanted to get away, too." But having transplanted herself, first to upper South Carolina and then to North Carolina, she never ceased to mean Georgia when she said "home." Perhaps she thought of her Georgia maids as consoling reminders of the life she had left behind.

Of these ladies, my own favorite was a monumentally plump, cheerful, kind, and very dark woman of indeterminate years, Susy. Who had recruited her to work three hundred miles to the north, and what loved ones she had left behind her in those Depression years, it was beyond a child's curiosity to wonder; and anyway, prying or awkward questions would have been gently discouraged. In most such matters, reticence was my parents' fixed policy, whatever the subject—and especially in any matter impinging even vaguely upon race, the darkest and most mysterious subject of all.

In Susy's case, and that of a successor named Daisy, my vivid memories center on departure, or even in Daisy's case of abject flight. During her second tour with us, Susy decided just after Thanksgiving that she must return to Georgia. I am sure she gave plausible reasons, but it may have been a case of homesickness. But since both my parents were busy with school work, her departure would remove my caretaker from the scene. So I traveled southward with Susy, a skinny little white boy of four or five in the company of a huge black woman. In those days, the Southern Railway special from New York to New Orleans passed through Greensboro at about 3 A.M., and I can vividly remember our departure, though the other details of the journey are foggy. But until my grandmother and aunt appeared at trainside to take over, I was in Susy's care and custody; she was my security, and quite enough of it.

As for Daisy, my memory is sketchier, perhaps for good reason. Daisy was as slight as Susy was ample. I liked her well enough, if not as well as Susy; but perhaps she came to like me less well after I barged one day into her upstairs bathroom as she was administering what I took to be an enema. It was probably a douche, but at that age I knew nothing of such things, so this could hardly qualify as a primal scene. Daisy, too, had come to us from warmer climes and I wonder in the light of the outcome whether she had ever seen a snowflake.

The routine in our household was simple. My parents would stay in bed in their room, as I did, awaiting the reassuring sound of Daisy descending the stairs and entering the kitchen to prepare breakfast, with the usual echo of skillets rattling, the clatter of china and glasses and silverware being laid out, attended by the agreeable smell of bacon frying. On the memorable day in question—it must have been a weekend day, a Saturday or Sunday, for otherwise Daisy's disappearance would have been discovered somewhat earlier—the usual sounds of breakfast-making failed to materialize. None of us was a late sleeper; and at about 8 o'clock on this chilly winter's morning (there had been a huge snowfall the day before), my father got up to adjust the thermostat. When he found the kitchen empty he went to the staircase and called gently up into the gloom: "Daisy? Daisy?"

No answer. A tentative tap at her bedroom door also went unanswered. Daisy was not to be found, nor was there any sign that her quarters had been occupied as recently as the previous evening by a living person—no shoes or dresses or personal items. Alarmed for her safety, my father quickly dressed and drove the circuitous mile or so to the "niggertown" house of her best friends. There, he encountered two very embarrassed black people, man and wife, and soon drew from them the admission that they had met Daisy (with her suitcase) near our house at about 4 o'clock that morning and driven her down to the station to flag the early-morning local train to Greensboro. From there, they said, she had undoubtedly caught a train to Georgia.

"She skeered of de snow," it was explained. Daisy, it further developed, had lowered her suitcase from an upstairs window with knotted bed sheets and vanished into the snowy night, no doubt persuaded that the Lord Jesus had condemned this bleak and forlorn outpost of the near-North to a new ice age. Both my parents had the gift of finding humor in even the most inconvenient situation, and dismay gave way to amusement. "Daisy has *vamoosed*," my father announced, and his choice of this colorful and unfamiliar verb formed, afterwards, a Proustian trigger for bardic retelling of the saga of Daisy. "Daddy, tell about when Daisy vamoosed," I would beg. And he would comply, with more patience for narrative suspense than came naturally to him. Daisy's abrupt and surreptitious departure was undoubtedly the stroke that brought an end to my mother's succession of maids from "down home."

I am aware, as I write this memoir six decades and many worlds removed from the world of my boyhood, that the tales of Susy and Daisy may strike some as offensive. But I am merely describing the reality as I knew it and I can only contend that "attitudinizing" (as Dr. Johnson would have called it) about these vanished customs is a poor guide to their color and nuance; for they were more subtle and complex than it is now fashionable to admit.

I had a lesson in this kind of well-intentioned denial when, in 1970, I wrote a brief newspaper reminiscence of the most influential black woman in my early life. The occasion was a so-called "riot" in Augusta in the summer of 1970, and the subject of my sketch was Mozelle Jordan ("Jerden," as Georgians pronounce it). She had gone to work for my grandmother as a girl, before my mother was born, and had moved with the family to Augusta when my grandfather died and the Stapleton house was closed. The wire stories about the Augusta incident told how a number of disorderly black youths had been shot by the police, some in the back; and in the banal jargon of "long, hot summer" journalism it was said that they lived in the black ghetto.

> One thing Augusta did not have [*I wrote, recalling the days of my boyhood visits there*] was a "ghetto," unless one might have meant the white ghettos of the new suburbs on the Hill, or perhaps Fort Gordon, with its endless rows of barracks. The relationships of white to black were neither managed nor perceived in such stark or abrasive terms. . . . No doubt there were unwritten rules about where one could live. But they were never mentioned, and of no concern to a ten-year-old boy. At any rate, they drew no lines; black houses checkerboarded the town in that Southern pattern of proximity without propinquity. For us—for my aunt and for my grandmother as long as she lived—one supreme and unalterable presence ruled the household. This was Mozie: ageless, tyrannical, irascible, mirthful, a gold tooth glinting in her mouth. Unfailingly at 7 A.M. her footsteps would ring, as they had for decades and still do now, the paved driveway. My first consciousness of the rules of segregation came one morning as I heard Mozie's footsteps outside the window and wondered why she never entered the front door in the first instance. To ask that question, and others, as adolescence came on and with it the vague and ineffectual guilt so familiar to Southern white boys, was to be firmly and kindly hushed. . . . She ruled everyone, deferring only to my grandmother, treating most grown men (except my father) with contempt and the women who had been her charges since infancy with a peremptory, mocking despotism. She thought nothing of commanding the removal of an unsuitable dress, new or not, as "trashy"; and usually this command would be obeyed. It was a mortifying day when this grande dame discovered me surreptitiously puffing a Kool cigarette behind the garage, subduing my terror with great hoots of laughter. Yet for her, magnificent in her loyalty and friendship, we who loved

her in so many ways wove a web of picayune custom that in ways invisible to us (and perhaps even to her) circumscribed her womanhood and humanity.

As I review this portrait almost thirty years later, it still seems true to life, notwithstanding that brief burst of piety at the end about the "web of picayune custom," true enough but gratuitous. Yet when this piece appeared in the *Greensboro Daily News,* my friend Hall Patrick, an Episcopal priest who taught history at North Carolina A & T (Jesse Jackson's alma mater), admonished me that younger blacks, including the students he was teaching, did not like the tone of such pieces. I have forgotten Hall's explanation, though no doubt some of his students found even scrupulously honest recollections subtly patronizing, and painful reminders of the servitude that marked segregationist paternalism of even the most benign stripe. And as a recovering segregationist (in practice, for I accepted its considerable benefits, if never in theory) I could not second-guess their reactions, then or now; for I could only see the story from the top down and for me it was a benevolent and very human story.

At about the time when she invited Magdalen to join her at the dining room table, my mother attempted to write a reminiscence of Mozelle and asked me to read her draft. She was a graceful writer who in her college years in Milledgeville had edited the school's literary magazine and written poetry (and memorized even more, so that decades later she could correct my memory of Shakespeare soliloquies), but her profile failed. It was regrettably saccharine, missing the darker shadings and chromatic tones. Of course, I did not say so; I knew that she retained from that far-off Georgia girlhood the fixed view that black people were constitutionally simple and childlike creatures who needed patronage and protection; and that matrix of perception naturally obstructed a sense of individuation. I suspect, too, that it was beyond her range of vision to imagine how the experiences of the paternalist relationship that charmed her had taught women like Mozelle to gratify white expectations and thus avoid conflict. But my view was not without condescension, for Mozelle too may have been as guileless as I thought my mother was. Certainly she was at least equally scornful of egalitarian alternatives—"uppityness," as they both would have called it. Mozelle kept cherished photographs of us all, especially "her children" (me, my brother, and a few other cousins she had known and cared for) on her television set. When I last visited her in the small garage apartment behind the old house on Telfair Street, she showed them proudly to me: tokens of ungrudging affection. And I am sure she didn't remove them when white folks left.

There were others of this company in my early life, some of them vivid presences but of smaller emotional resonance today because they came to work for us when I was no longer a child and had begun to work my way, warily, to a critical distance from the paternalist system that enmeshed us all in a bland, pleasant, and evasive civility. There was, for instance, Gussie Baynes, proud and tiny—she couldn't have weighed more than eighty pounds—whose false teeth jiggled and rattled when she spoke, usually with a cheek full of snuff. And she spoke a great deal; she was easily the most verbal of all. This spare woman was a master cook, so good at traditional country cooking that in the long, hot summer days when southern households took their main meals at midday, Gussie spent the whole morning cooking and the early afternoon, before her departure, washing up. This was later, for she had first come to us as a caretaker for my younger brother Jim. Her authority had been compromised when he fastened her in the large playpen that had been constructed in the driveway median to contain him, his tricycle and sandpile. Gussie was found there, still incarcerated, when my father returned some hours later. It pleased her to tell me, repeatedly, that she had not so much as spent the interest on her late husband's money. In fact, she and her two sisters lived in unusual comfort in a spacious frame house, well painted and furnished. She brooked no condescension, certainly not from bratty boys. Once when she was pursuing my mobile brother through the neighborhood, she thought, mistakenly, that she had overheard my older playmates and me making slighting remarks.

"If you say things like that," she said, "I will have every right to call you a little cracker." Whatever she had overheard had nothing to do with her, but the incident was alarming. Nothing would have guaranteed speedier punishment than a racist remark. The mere use of the absolutely forbidden word "nigger" would have brought parental wrath down on anyone who uttered it; and like all properly brought up southern whites, I had this mannerly restraint drilled into me. What few or none of us grasped then was that the rigid *politesse* that accompanied the otherwise demeaning fetishes of segregation (the most obvious of which were the "white only" and "colored" signs that marked public accommodations) was an integral part of its armor. Not that it was, as might be assumed, two-faced or hypocritical, nor that those indoctrinated in the intricate code of good manners did not believe also in their independent value. There are those who did not know the world I grew up in who think of segregation as crude and brutal, but it was neither, at least by design, and was marked throughout by a nearly Oriental refinement.

But my memories of Gussie, who alarmed me that day by accusing me of racial insult, remind me that she was easily the most verbal of all our caretakers. When in the late 1960s "soul food" and "black English" became cult subjects, I could boast to skeptical friends that I had eaten the one much of my life and was fluent—bilingual—in the other. Lacking a dramatic flair, I rarely ventured to speak black English except in imitation of Prissy's immortal lines in *Gone with the Wind*: "Lawdy, Miss Scarlett, I don't know nothin' 'bout birthin' babies." But because she could see that I was a bookish and verbal child, it amused Gussie to tease me with polysyllabic phrases and questions. "How's your corporosity segatuating?" was her favorite. I never heard the words used anywhere else, by anyone. Then one day four years ago, I was rereading Joyce's *Ulysses* for a spring seminar I was to teach at Washington and Lee, and suddenly the very words jumped out of the page. There it was, in the Oxen of the Sun episode: "Your corporosity sagaciating, OK?" The spelling varies, but that is a minor matter. I thought with wonder of Gussie and the verbal links that bind English-speakers across the earth: an Irish genius with a tiny black woman in North Carolina.

What am I trying to do here? Simply to tease from these assorted and fragmentary shards of memory, and early experience, some clues to the formation of one man's view of the great American issue—attitudes, really, to be distinguished from convictions, since these are as much matters of temperament as of mind. Many of my contemporaries, growing up in the paternalist world, never stood apart from it or attempted to grasp the ways in which it was historically conditioned. I was more fortunate than most southerners in that, because in our household I could observe first-hand the effects of two quite distinct traditions. There was my mother's outlook, already described at length, which could not be abstracted from personal experience and custom, the paternalist tradition in its essence, at once benevolent and accepting. And yet my mother voiced no objection to the civil rights revolution that commenced as I was maturing politically in the late 1940s. The embrace of the cause by John Kennedy and Lyndon Johnson did not in the least diminish her loyalty to the Democratic Party; and when I became a newspaper editorialist she was well aware of my "liberal" views because she could and did read them every morning—and again, never voiced the slightest objection. *Amor omnia vincit*, perhaps. On the other hand, my father's views on race—not that they were assertive, for he was a public servant and had to be reasonably diplomatic—belonged to the liberal tradition, stronger in North Carolina than elsewhere in the South, and stronger still in its unique citadel, Chapel Hill. He believed to his core in justice as a principle; and no one of his sentience and intelligence could miss the patent injustice of Jim Crow; it was obvious to all with eyes to see. He took satisfaction in describing to me how my grandfather had been active in Fusionist politics at the turn of the century, an occasional embarrassment to him as a boy when he was accused of being "a dirty little Populist." Being a dedicated Fusionist meant collaborating with the Black Republicans and their Negro voting base, and opposing the high-minded (and high-handed) chicanery that aimed to strip black voters of their ballot: literacy tests and such. It was by such measures that the self-styled "redeemers," conservative Democrats, wrested political control back into white hands in North Carolina and other southern states at the turn of the century, creating the one-party South. They argued, and some actually believed, that it was far better for everyone, including blacks, to "remove the Negro as a political issue" by the bizarre expedient of nullifying his voting power. Few saw through this huge fraud, but my father and grandfather were among them. For one thing, they could see that the literacy test for voting would disqualify illiterate whites as well as blacks.

Thus the familiar examples and attitudes I grew up with—affectionate and respectful if patronizing and marked by an almost paralyzing reticence—gave me a base for further self-education. As I grew up and the racial climate changed, at first slowly and then with earthquake intensity, I found myself pulled in two ways: one by conviction, the other by temperament. My colleagues and mentors in student journalism at Chapel Hill—Barry Farber, Rolfe Neill, Charles Kuralt, Chuck

Hauser, among others—had no patience with Jim Crow. Their dedication was contagious. Then, there were studies. The freshman course known as Contemporary Civilization included a number of readings in anthropology, a perspective new to me. I remember digesting them with great interest in the reserve reading room at the library and recognizing, with no noticeable mental struggle, that the perspective they offered was right and appealing: "race" was a myth, an artifice of the human imagination and in obvious ways a debilitating one. But even if there were such a thing as race, objectively measurable, it could not overcome the claims of justice nor justify the tissue of restrictions and discriminations that constituted the Jim Crow system of law. And anthropology was reinforced by history. Studying the pivotal court cases, I learned how the "white primary" system had employed a legal fiction—that political parties in a state pretending to be democratic functioned as private clubs—to sustain white supremacy. I suffered no indigestion, probably because all of this was congruent with my father's own outlook, and certainly with the gentle solicitude that I had observed in my mother. But whatever the political or journalistic implications of this new learning might be, I was no sophomoric or impatient critic of the domestic order. I was content to await its gradual leavening by law. One and all, we racial liberals of that time were not unhappy with the label "gradualist" and took the view that it would be best for economic improvement to precede and prepare the way for legal equality. These climacteric strategies tend to be forgotten or denied today, though not by all. In 1994, when I taught a seminar called "The Journalism of the Civil Rights Movement" on the fortieth anniversary of the Supreme Court decision in *Brown v. Board of Education,* my friends Hodding Carter and Pat Derian came to Lexington as guest lecturers.

"I guess you were elated when the Brown decision came along," one of my students suggested to Hodding. To his credit, he kept the record straight and denied premature enthusiasm.

"I wish I could say so," Hodding said, "but I remember how John Stennis [the son of the longtime senator from Mississippi] and I met on the Princeton campus that day and lamented that it had come too early, without proper economic preparation." Hodding is right as well as honest, for this was the enlightened view in those days, for Yoders of North Carolina as well as Carters and Stennises of Mississippi. What we failed to grasp then was that the convulsive issue for black people was not economic status but simple dignity: the unquestioned right to be dealt with as fully human.

Of course no one comes to a mature view of race by cognitive inquiry alone—or if he does, it is likely to be brittle and to lack emotional resonance. The Jim Crow system was replete with irrationalities, however, and merely to list them is to astonish those who grew up, as my children did, in a radically different South. Black servants in the South of my boyhood worked in intimate closeness with their employers, cooking, feeding and dressing children, waiting table and washing dishes, handling laundry and bedclothes. Yet for all this—whatever its origins in some grotesque notion of hygiene or separateness—black servants often had separate drinking glasses and cups and sometimes separate plates, bowls, and eating utensils. They were forbidden by custom to sit down anywhere other than the kitchen, at least when white people were present, and then usually in some appointed place. When arriving for work in the morning (as I noted in my reminiscence of Mozelle), they always entered by the back door. As the day's routine passed, sweeping a front terrace or retrieving small children from the yard to be fed, or dealing with vendors or postmen or callers, they were free to come and go by any door, though not to depart at the end of the day by other than the back door! In commercial establishments, similar lines were drawn, a fact essential to understanding why the direct-action phase of the civil rights movement erupted at the counters of five-and-dime stores in Greensboro and elsewhere in 1960. Every sentient American knows, or should know, the basic story of the sit-ins and the earlier Montgomery bus boycott, and most are probably vaguely aware of Rosa Parks's memorable challenge to seating custom on public transport. What custom decreed, moreover, literal-mindedness often drove into the ground. My wife Jane, who grew up near Knoxville, Tennessee, remembers being threatened by a bus driver that he would stop and call the police when she shared a front seat (the only empty one in the bus) with a black woman. She chose to stand for the long ride to her ballet lesson. How many thousands of such petty indignities there were it would be impossible even to estimate. What is less familiar, unless you grew up with them, is the network of subtle commercial taboos that were cousins to segregation on public transport. A black person could buy an ice-cream cone or a soft drink at the drugstores in my small town, but that meant approaching, as unobtrusively as possible, a designated zone at the end of the soda fountain, and standing patiently there while white people sat. Remarkably, few if any of these taboos and customs seemed strange, prima facie, to me or to children of my generation; they were, again, simply part of a social landscape that seemed to have existed forever. It was not until these petty rules came under challenge in the early 1960s that their absurdity became glaring, even to whites. They were tellingly satirized by Harry Golden in his *Carolina Israelite* newspaper, published in Charlotte until his death in late 1981. Since a black person carrying or otherwise supervising a white child could pass anywhere, for any purpose, Golden proposed a "white baby plan": a black person entering some place of commercial accommodation would be issued a white baby-doll to carry; and before that talisman, segregation would bow. And inasmuch as black people could be served in most stores so long as they remained standing, Golden added his satirical "vertical integration" plan: the wholesale removal of seats and stools from drug stores, dime stores and the like. Golden needed no plan for movie theaters, for their balconies were customarily open to black patrons in the small-town South, where there was apt to be only one theater, or two at most. Blacks, however, were served by separate entrances and bought their movie tickets on the opposite side of the box office, usually after a patient wait. A maid shepherding a white child could, on the other hand, sit anywhere in the theater. I was taken by my black nurse of the time—Susy, perhaps—to see *The Wizard of Oz,* but she had no sooner settled her ample bottom into a comfortable seat near the front—a luxury for her no doubt—than I began to scream with terror when the Wicked Witch appeared on Dorothy's roof and I had to be taken home.

Just what notions originally inspired these demeaning fetishes are perhaps lost in the mists of time today, but there was a widely held view that blacks were less well scrubbed than whites, or likelier to harbor contagious diseases. But even on that insulting premise, a moment's reflection would have suggested a manifest inconsistency, given the thousand daily situations in which whites and blacks with perfect unselfconsciousness commingled at close quarters. Whatever else it was, southern segregation in my boyhood was not "American apartheid," as ignorant people took to calling it, melodramatically, at one point; it was more like inextricable "togetherness" than apartness. I am sure that children bolder or more inquisitive than I questioned their parents at length about these anomalies; but what answers might have satisfied a child's piercing logic I can't imagine. *It's that way because it's always been that way,* I suppose. But even that was not true. Custom aside, the actual fabric of segregation law was woven late in the game, as Vann Woodward's classic account *The Strange Career of Jim Crow* established. Mercifully, by the time my own children (born in 1959 and 1963) were old enough to grow curious, the civil rights movement was running full tilt and many of the extreme absurdities of Jim Crow were falling and no longer needed explanation. I was spared the need to account for them.

How could I have explained, for instance, why most small trades were closed to blacks, unless they operated establishments serving an exclusively black clientele? Here again, however, there were interesting exceptions. One was Tom's Barber Shop on Clay Street in Mebane, across from the medical clinic, where most of the white gentry (including my father and me) had their hair cut. Tom Holt had two associates, one of whom, Freddy, had once worked for us and had served as my caretaker on beach visits. It was he who pulled me, dripping and sputtering, from a gray sea one day when the sandy bank we were walking along suddenly gave way. Tom's Barber Shop of course predated unisex hair parlors—which, had such places even been imaginable in that world, would have been dismissed as a French perversion or affectation, to be expected in Paris but nowhere else. So there was no awkwardness about women, an important point as I shall explain below. Tom Holt was a skilled barber and a thoughtful man. But he considered that the racial code of that day, and the prosperity of his trade, demanded an obsequiousness approaching parody (and perhaps *was* parody, in his mind), with elaborate bowing and scraping and "yessiring," even of underaged boys like me.

There were the traditional professions and trades—teaching, preaching, and undertaking—but only to serve fellow black people. As the superintendent of schools my father was nominally in charge of the black elementary school (black students attended a consolidated county high school nine miles away). When Mr. Petway, the black principal, came to our house, the business was conducted on the back steps overlooking the driveway, with my father standing above and Mr. Petway beneath. I am sure no insult was meant; *de haut en bas* was my father's manner with most persons, whatever their station or race. I doubt that it occurred to him to pretend that he and Mr. Petway were equals, but I am sure that if the two of them had consulted in our living room word of it would have spread, as if of revolutionary activity.

When I said, above, that Tom Holt's barber shop bypassed the awkwardness of ladies' presence, I brushed lightly on what I now believe to have been, all along, the unacknowledged heart of the whole matter. The irrationalities and indignities of racial segregation as I knew it could be accounted for—the pieces of the puzzle would fall as if by magic into place—if you took as your theory one great unmentionable. Implicit in almost every detail of this exquisite tissue of rules and rituals, deferences, fetishes, and taboos was Sex, and on its harsher side the goal, sometimes crudely stated by ill-bred defenders of the system, was the protection of the chastity of white women. Such a barefaced suggestion would have utterly puzzled me as a boy; and equally it would have shocked many genteel defenders of the old order. But what solid purpose could the intricate web of law and custom have had, other than to avert the supposedly catastrophic danger of intermarriage (and, if possible, the lesser evil of surreptitious interracial sex) and thus to maintain what was frequently described as the "purity" or "integrity" of the white race? Once grasped, this was as clearly the ultimate source of its oddly distancing courtesies as it was of its coarser horrors like lynching. My old friend Willie Morris, in his antic takeoffs on the Mississippi demagogues of his youth, had them bellowing to their bumpkin audiences: "And if these-here inte-grationists from Yankeeland get their way, the result will be a *khaki race*." Well might these brummagem orators have imagined so; for any glance at the varieties of pigmentation that already existed, after some three centuries of proximity between the two races in the South, offered tell-tale evidence that the aggressive solicitude for racial purity was a one-way street. It was accompanied by a secret laxity regarding the "racial integrity" of Africans. Dear Mozelle, whom I described earlier, was of a light coppery color, pale enough to suggest mixed ancestry; and there were occasional ribald whispers among some of my Georgia cousins that she might be kin to us.

This underlying tension not only accounted for the elaborate panoply of laws and customs. It also inspired, and usually explained, the thousands of atrocities committed over decades, the darker side of the story. Even after lynch law gradually faded, no longer defended as a mode of social control by respectable southern politicians, the brutal murder even of children remained a danger. Young Emmett Till was accused of whistling at a white woman and ended up in chains on a river bottom.

There are muted discussions of this dispiriting theme in many places now, historical and fictional. But for a long time the only notable white writer of fiction who looked the demon in the eye was William Faulkner. Beginning as early as the late 1920s, his treatment of the subtle themes of sexuality and miscegenation and the tangled social and family tensions they gave rise to, was definitive. Closely read, Faulkner's fiction—in novels like *Absalom, Absalom!, Light in August,* and *Go Down, Moses*—offers schooling in depth on this forbidden subject, infinitely subtle and never didactic. The pursuit, persecution, and murder of Joe Christmas; Thomas Sutpen's callousness to the claims of his own mulatto children; surmises of ruthless sexual exploitation of slave women in the McCaslin family—these tales remain the best sources for those who would venture across this heavily veiled threshold.

But I can hardly claim that any of this was for me other than after-the-fact history. By the time I began, as a man, to explore the darker historical and fictive aspects of race, the lingering boy in me had long benefited from the care and love of strong and affectionate women like Susy, Gussie, and Mozelle; and their examples were firmly inscribed on the heart. With every reason to be soured by unspeakable grievances, they redeemed injustice with generosity, sacrifice, and love.

CHAPEL HILL

"The Southern Part of Heaven" *That was, I recall, the title of a book about Chapel Hill that appeared at about the time I went there, or shortly before. It expresses what most of us feel about that blissful place, now well launched into its third century. Many of both the North Carolina and Georgia branches of my family have studied there, including my father and mother. I never thought of going elsewhere. Nor did my daughter Anne, a quarter-century later. My wife Jane, a classmate who came there from Tennessee, still speaks of her days there as an English major as the happiest time of her life. I suppose there have been a few who found themselves misfits in Chapel Hill. But I've never met, or even heard of, one. It remains, though infringed by urbanization and an overflow of automobiles, a place of surpassing beauty. For me, as the following sketch suggests, it was above all a place of humanistic learning, imparted by splendid teachers, whose traditions of student self-government and lux libertas—light and freedom—also molded habits of citizenship and reflection.*

Speaking of light and freedom, this account would be incomplete without an account of my time at the Daily Tar Heel, *the student newspaper, where I not only learned the rudiments of journalism but was lucky to have as an associate Charles Kuralt, the most original of twentieth-century journalists, excelling in both print and television. And there were others, almost as distinguished if not so imaginative. The* Tar Heel *was heir to a long tradition of independence from administrative supervision. I was told by my mentor Phillips Russell (Class of 1904) that when the president of the university asked to preview* Tar Heel *editorials he was politely told that he was welcome but would have to visit the* Tar Heel *offices to do so. President Venable declined, and so have his successors to this day. Wisely.*

If Princeton had its Scott Fitzgerald and Sewanee its William Alexander Percy, Chapel Hill had its Thomas Wolfe (class of 1921) and he was more than enough. It was Wolfe who conferred literary immortality on the thinly veiled "Pulpit Hill" of *Look Homeward, Angel.* As he wrote, viewing it through the eye of his awkward young hero, Eugene Grant, it was "a charming, an unforgettable place . . . buried in a pastoral wilderness, on a long, tabling butte, which rose steeply above the country. . . . The central campus sloped back and up over a broad area

43

of rich turf, groved with magnificent ancient trees. . . . There was still a good flavor of the wilderness about the place—one felt its remoteness, its isolated charm. It seemed to Eugene like a provincial outpost of Great Rome: the wilderness crept up like a beast."

Chapel Hill has inspired other writers for two centuries. For like all old and beloved places it is easy to write about, deceptively easy, perhaps, inasmuch as a stock of prefabricated images is there to be tapped if imagination or memory falters. When I went there as a freshman in the fall of 1952, Chapel Hill was as familiar to me as any place I knew. And it was undoubtedly closer in climate and appearance to the Chapel Hill of Wolfe's day than to the noisy, auto-crowded segment of the Research Triangle conurbation it has become.

Wolfe himself went on to grumble that the university and its encompassing village had declined since his day, had forfeited the sweetness and beauty conferred by poverty and remoteness and a "century-long struggle in the forest." Even so, Wolfe, who died in 1938, could hardly have foreseen what the high-tech research boom, not to mention the furtive aggression of Durham county real-estate developers and a student body now swollen to more than twenty thousand, would do to its "isolated charm." Charm remains; but it is hardly "isolated."

When I arrived as a freshman, however, Chapel Hill was still the "village" old-timers imagined. The postwar tide of returning veterans had receded. The enrollment, at just over five thousand, was as small as it would be in the post–World War II era; and undergraduate life retained an intimacy that has now been lost, probably forever. The beautiful old campus, clustered on McCorkle and Polk Places about the original eighteenth-century triangle of creamy-colored brick with, yes, the requisite Virginia creeper and ivy clinging to it. On bright autumn and spring days the rear steps of South Building were the perch, infinitely sophisticated to a freshman eye, of urbane-seeming young men in their worn and faded khaki pants, dirty white buck shoes and button-down blue or white Oxford shirts with carefully frayed collars. Beautiful young women, junior transfers from elite women's colleges far and wide, danced attendance. Keeping my intimidated distance, I nonetheless sensed I was in the right place and would someday be at ease in that charmed company.

Of course, I had never given a thought to going elsewhere. My father, a devoted alumnus (M.A. '29), had often checked boyish mischief by threatening—idly, I'm sure—to send me to Duke: a fate too terrible to be imagined. Duke was not then the "national" university it was to become under Chapel Hillians Terry Sanford and Joel Fleishman in the 1970s, but, to us, a strait-laced and parochial Methodist school with a mid-Atlantic clientele incapable of pronouncing the name of its rustic, tobacco-rich benefactors correctly—"Dook," many called it. Its prim neo-Gothic architecture was scorned in age-burnished Chapel Hill as a "poor imitation of Princeton," and it was said that Duke freshmen—still wearing beanies!—were required to sand the stair steps to make them look old. These differences, some no doubt imaginary, have now given way to a ferocious and single-minded basketball rivalry, with great gain in vitriol and little or none in color or depth of imagination. No one, so far as I know, has had the wit of one bygone prankster who on the eve of a Duke-Carolina football game added a wooden sign to the Latin motto emblazoned over the gates of Duke, *religion et eruditio:* "et tobacco," the sign said.

As I have noted elsewhere, my father's affection for Chapel Hill, which he had communicated to me, was rooted in his political outlook and his admiration for Frank Porter Graham, its diminutive former president, and for faculty members like Howard Odum, a Georgia-born sociologist who with Rupert Vance and others had pioneered the dispassionate examination of southern life and values (even as to race).

In the 1920s when he had been a graduate student there, and still in my day, its openness to challenging ideas and notions remained a virtual novelty in the South—and to more than a few, a novelty feared and hated in a region still haunted by defeat and resentment and what W. J. Cash called "the savage ideal" of ideological conformity. It was the university's valiant resistance to that constricting ideal, and the quest for scholarly excellence by a national and international standard that had begun in the 1920s under Harry Woodburn Chase, that my father and his brothers valued. He did not relish the rumors of sexual license and hard drinking that came, perhaps, as the price of political and social boldness. But that price was not prohibitive.

The Chapel Hill that I entered in that far-off fall of 1952 is easy to conjure back to mind. It was, after all, the same leafy and familiar Chapel Hill to which my father had often taken me on perfect autumn Saturdays to watch the football exploits of Charlie "Choo-Choo" Justice in the matchless natural setting of Kenan Stadium. Little did I imagine, that early September day when my parents discharged me with suitcase and steamer trunk at the doors of Ruffin Hall, that my boyish romance with UNC football would evolve into a head-on collision. Which is only to say that the young man of eighteen who entered the university that autumn is, these fifty years later, a stranger even to me. He had abilities as a scholar and knew it; for he had heard his usually modest father quietly boasting to friends about his son's sharpness of mind. But he was raw, untested, and unshaped; and while not exactly provincial, he was unversed in larger worlds that would eventually open before him: the classic situation, no doubt, of many before him. He had spent a quiet summer at the golf course, reading and tending the pro-shop, fraternizing with the caddies and sharpening a golf game soon to rust. He brought with him the benefit of excellent teaching—by his father in economics, by Merle Riggs in French and Latin, and by Eleanor Harris in English. But he faced a quantum jump in academic challenge and competition. The luckiest stroke was that he ended up in J. R. "Speck" Caldwell's section of Western Civilization. Caldwell, a kindly and attentive teacher, was the first to intimate that he might be bet-ter—at history—than merely good. While others would repeat the com-pliment, boosting his already adequate self-regard, he would look back with a grateful eye on Caldwell's particular influence:

In his deliberate and methodical way, J. R. Caldwell brought the past to life: at the least he made sense of it. As the last echo of the bell died, he would stub out his pre-class Raleigh 903 cigarette, prop a foot upon the handiest desk, and begin: "When the bell sounded, gentlemen, we were examining into . . ." Examining into! That was the trademark phrase of his teaching; it seemed novel and attractive to those of us for whom, at this stage, history remained an unmemorable muddle of dates, names, person-ages, treaties, and other matters vaguely known and certainly of no practi-cal consequence. History something to be "examined into"—not a static or fixed pattern, not a lie agreed upon, but something for scrutiny? Here was something new.

I shall not urge the claim here that J. R. Caldwell was the most spectac-ular lecturer of his time; he was merely the most effective. If the subject was Napoleon—"a man on horseback," as he invariably called him—J. R. Caldwell gave you five reasons why Napoleon came to power; and when the proper time came, he gave you five reasons (all equally plausible) why he fell. . . . J. R. Caldwell, lecturing without a glance at the notes before him from a memory of startling retentiveness and accuracy, said all the important things twice. It was enough. His notes parsed; they were beautifully studiable; they were, more than that, interesting. Like all historical accounts, J. R. Caldwell's account of modern history was of course an artifice, as a good parquet floor is an artifice. You knew that the design was imposed by human craft upon an odd assortment of rough-hewn lumber. But there was no looseness about it, no ill-fitting joints. It would bear weight. . . . I would in due course encounter other and different kinds of history teaching but none had the memorable force of J. B. Caldwell's "Contemporary Civilization in the West." What he did, as I look back on it, was to move his students from the naïve view that history was "facts" to the more intriguing and reliable view that it was at least a process in which believable people had been involved, whose motives were sometimes mysterious but in their humanness worth "examining into."

In the same freshman year, there was also J. B. McLeod, a courtly and nattily dressed instructor with a sharp aquiline nose, a neatly trimmed and rather sinister moustache and wavy white hair who had joined the political science faculty after a career at the bar in eastern North Carolina. "Black Jack" McLeod was said to live up to his nickname. By the time the spring quarter began, some of the rough edges of the novice had been smoothed away; but the freshman, despite his A average and Phi Eta Sigma key, was disconcerted to find himself in McLeod's section of Political Science 41. As McLeod called the roll, that first day in Caldwell Hall, he paused when he called out the freshman's name. "Mr. Yoder," he said, "please see me after class." I went forward when the bell rang. He remained seated at the small instructor's table, looking me up and down.

"I see that you are a freshman."

"Yes, sir."

"I have asked the registrar not to put freshmen in this class. Do you know what happened to the last freshman who took this course?"

"No, sir."

McLeod drew his forefinger, knife-like, across his Adam's apple and smiled.

"That's what happened to him."

I said that if it were all the same to him I would take my chances. He nodded grimly, as if to say "you asked for it," and I left the room chilled by his warning.

It was soon apparent that I had every reason to be chilled. As I leafed through the thick mimeographed syllabus, I began to see why McLeod's course might be considered inappropriate for freshmen. McLeod's aim was to see that no one survived Political Science 41 without a thorough-going command of every essential of the American polity, including every significant Supreme Court holding since *Marbury v. Madison*. These were to be read and briefed. We were to master the Constitution verbatim and prepare to gloss its most recondite clauses. We were to di-gest large stretches of Tocqueville and the Federalist Papers. As if in mere afterthought, we were to master the terms of political art, many of them esoteric and unfamiliar, listed in Smith and Zurcher's *New Dictionary of American Politics*. For dessert we were to read and annotate a thick anthology of classic political journalism and scholarly pieces, featuring Walter Lippmann, Richard Rovere, Maury Maverick, and many others. (When I compare this menu with the quantitative vogue that has now reduced the classical study of politics to a bogus pseudo-science, aping econometrics, I weep.)

McLeod made no concession to the possibility that one might be tak-ing other courses, as I was. Nor did he strike me, in spite of the mischie-vous good humor that twinkled in his mild blue eyes, as an instructor to whom one offered flimsy excuses for work not done. The class met in the early afternoon, with the windows open to the warm and blossom-ing spring landscape. It was a drowsy time of day and one young man from deepest Alabama, a fraternity brother of my roommate, who was often to be seen even in daylight hours at the Goody Shop, the local beer hall, had a tendency to nod off. One day, McLeod stole catlike to his side, continuing to discuss some aspect of the First Amendment, loomed above him as he snoozed, and leaning down with cupped hands shouted: *"Poker again, Mr. Moreton?"* Moreton awoke with a start, never to sleep again—in class, anyway.

Meanwhile, I had all but chained myself to a seat in the library read-ing room, exploring the subtleties of Marshall and Madison and other-wise slogging my way slowly through the thick syllabus. Even on some fine spring weekends, when every fiber of my gregarious and indolent being cried out for dates and drinking companions, I beavered away. But apart from the fact that most of the material interested me intensely, I doubtless recall it so vividly because it was my first experience with weekend study—or indeed any study of that intensity. I had grown up in the spirit of the famous story told of W. Kerr Scott, North Carolina's dairyman governor. He had been asked why the lush green fields and pastures of eastern North Carolina had never fostered a dairy industry like Wisconsin's. "Simple," he is reported to have said. "They ain't yet bred a cow that don't have to be milked on weekends." But the sacrifice of my temperamental disinclination to work on weekends paid off, and much that McLeod taught me has stuck to this very hour. When the final exam had been given and graded McLeod again summoned me to his presence.

"You do recall my warning about freshmen?"

"Yes sir," I said. I didn't add, "How could I forget?"

"You obviously took it to heart. You worked hard and learned a great deal; indeed, you wrote the best exam in the class—better by far than even the graduate students. I have given you an A-plus."

"Thank you, sir," I said. "You are kind."

McLeod chuckled. "You are the first student here who has ever accused me of kindness."

There were to be other memorable teachers—Harry Russell, Clifford Lyons, Lyman Cotten, and Peter Phialas in English; Jim King and Jim Godfrey in history; Maynard Adams and Bill Poteat in philosophy; Lee Wiley and Alfred Engstrom in French; Albert Suskin and Bert Ullmann in Latin; and others. Of these, I especially admired and learned from Cotten and Poteat. The former, an elegant and well-born bachelor who lived with his mother and a parakeet on Hooper Lane, was the nephew of the eminent Archibald Henderson, a former professor of mathematics and the authorized biographer of George Bernard Shaw. (Their fine profiles, as Jane noted one night when we were attending a performance of *Pygmalion* and they were present, side by side, were identical.) Cotten was an urbane and challenging teacher; and while I earned A's in his Chaucer, Milton, and Shakespeare course and in Modern Poetry, he discerned my budding arrogance and didn't mind cutting me down to size in his friendly way. One day when we were discussing John Crowe Ransom's difficult poem, "Prelude to an Evening," he asked for a gloss and could hardly ignore my eager hand. He called on me and I confidently embarked on what I regarded as an ingenious interpretation.

"Very interesting, Mr. Yoder," he said, "but as it happens one hundred percent wrong." The class laughed appreciatively, for at that age I was undoubtedly, in the idiom of the time, *too much*. On the other hand, Bill Poteat, who came from an old Wake Forest family of great academic distinction and was perhaps the most charismatic of the younger faculty members (though the term was not in currency then) was usually too deeply absorbed in his own stimulating excogitations to tease his students. But he was as stimulating as Cotten and perhaps a shade deeper. I can still see him standing before our small class in "the philosophy of literature," brooding upon the contrast between the bleakly determinist Greeks of Aeschylus's *Oresteia* and the more hopeful, if equally tragic, vision of the post-Christian dramatists, gripping his high forehead and asking "Now why did I say that?" It was not a rhetorical question; he meant it. Every moment of every class became an interrogation not only of the reading and the students but of himself. But by the time I reached these mentors, I had been in the trenches with Black Jack and survived, and most academic tasks seemed almost downhill. One was occasionally tempted to coast—not that I wanted to; for I was reaching that stage when one begins to realize, with dismay, that every lesson learned merely opens a tantalizing window on one's fathomless ignorance.

But all was not study and grind; far from it.

My generation, with a few exceptions, went to college without the precocious experience of sex and drink that now prevails; and this was true even at allegedly licentious Chapel Hill. Sex in those days answered to the witty observation of the British playwright John Osborne, prophet of England's "angry young men," who had recently written that America "is as preoccupied with sex as a medieval monastery"; and for much the same reason, he might have added. The university admitted women only as junior transfers, and then only in such limited numbers that the prevailing male-female ratio was about seven to one. For the first two years, we all imported dates for the big dance weekends, or sought them elsewhere. Two of my Georgia cousins, Dede Candler of Atlanta, and JoAnne Logue, whose father, my favorite uncle, was a navy surgeon and hospital administrator, were in the freshman class at Sweet Briar and my friends and I kept the road to Lynchburg warm.

As for sexual experience, it varied from virginity in a suspect majority of cases to a quite astonishing precocity in others. Whether of deficit or surfeit, however, sex and the quest for it were of constant and consuming interest. The most colorful, and one of the most brilliant, of our classmates had been to sea on merchant ships (or so he claimed) and told arresting stories of his visits to the whorehouses in friendly ports. One sex-starved dorm mate tried out the only known bordello in the Chapel Hill area, a Durham establishment known as Katie Mae's. He returned with an infestation of pubic lice (popularly, "crabs") that required countless showers and many stinging applications of disinfectant to subdue. If I recall, Eugene Gant, in *Look Homeward, Angel,* comes down with the same affliction—a case of *plus ça change,* perhaps. The double standard distinguished, in those pre-Pill, prefeminist days, between "nice" girls and naughty ones; and there was constant plotting and planning (and occasional, unreliable, boasting) in the quest for naughty girls who in the crude phrase of the time, "put out." They were few in Chapel Hill, so far as I knew. When it became known in Ruffin Hall that one boorish and not very well-liked boy had experienced a ruptured condom in one of his conquests, the ineffable Charles Sharpless ranged up and down the corridor, bellowing: "That will be thirteen dollars fifty cents a week, Mr. P———, thirteen dollars fifty cents a week!": the price, presumably, of child support.

This was also the era of those curious nocturnal swarmings known as panty raids—another symptom of pent-up sexual energy, as strange in its way as the goldfish-swallowing cult and other bizarre antics of the 1920s which, incidentally, were looked back on as a time of delightful licentiousness worthy of imitation if one only had the nerve. We read Scott Fitzgerald's *This Side of Paradise* and aspired to relive its extravagances. Meanwhile, the cry for lingerie tended to break out spontaneously on humid spring evenings. All that was needed was the catalyst of loud outcries beneath the open windows, when everyone was distracted by the gorgeous Chapel Hill spring. Within minutes hundreds of young men would be spilling from the doorways and converging on one of the women's residential quadrangles, baying for undergarments. When a pair of panties, or sometimes a brassiere, would come floating down from an upper window, a throaty cheer would go up. These swarmings were good-natured in tone, and if the doors had suddenly been thrown open with an invitation to rape at large, I doubt that anyone in the crowd would have known how to react; the bluff would have been called.

What were they, anyway, these panty raids? A resurgence, perhaps, of the fetishism associated with the medieval cults of courtly love and the apprentice knight-swains and squires of the feudal age, who rode off to sieges with the lacy little things of their mistresses next to their skin, no doubt facilitating auto-erotic fantasies? Displaced rape? They seemed too lighthearted to qualify for Freudian analysis. Whatever they symbolized, if they rose above mere spring fever, these vernal exercises enraged our gentle, pipe-smoking, Latin-reading, harmonica-playing chancellor, Robert Burton House. On one of these occasions, it was reported, the chancellor had so forgotten himself as to bellow at the swarming mob, "You bastards, get back to your dormitories." Even without prompting, they always did; few of these rituals lasted more than half an hour or so.

"Binge" drinking, as it is now widely known, was not so called in those days. We affected a *savoir-faire* that did not, however, exclude quite a lot of kneewalking, staggering, dizziness, and emergency sickness in handy garbage cans. I heard of one young man who, returning from an evening at the rathskeller, grew alarmed because one of his legs had suddenly grown shorter than the other. He was near hysteria when one of his companions observed that he could cure himself immediately by not walking along with one foot in the gutter. No one had then conceived the unwise under-twenty-one prohibition recently promoted, in national law, by the well-intentioned but well-named MADD—Mothers Against Drunk Driving—which promotes one sort of risky behavior while seeking to avoid another. There were isolated disasters of drunk driving, but no one imagined they could be prevented by giving under-aged students incentive to add concealment and hypocrisy to dangerous behavior by partying at isolated locations, reachable only by car.

It was our aspiration to hold our drink like gentlemen, but given the quantities this didn't always work; and the mixture of suppressed sexuality and alcohol led at times to scenes of gross postadolescent bad taste. One night during a Germans dance weekend mixer at the SAE house, my roommate Bob Angstadt witnessed a typical act of what passed in those tame times for grotesque indelicacy. A drunken pledge came lurching and tottering down the staircase, paused on the landing just above the assembled throng, unzipped his pants, exposed his penis, and cried out: "Meet Willie, the one-eyed trouser worm!" I assume that no house mother was on hand, and I have no idea what happened next. Such a scene must seem less than shocking now. But we were at all times and places expected to adhere to the "the Carolina Code," which obliged us to behave as gentlemen. Unlike violations of the Honor Code, the violation of that lesser code was not necessarily a shipping offense. But at times the rowdy elements sailed so close to the edge as to court expulsion. In my senior year, one of the many drinking clubs whose colorful ads were a prominent and lucrative feature of the yearbook (appropriately called the Ugly Club) staged a cabin party with one of the sororities, decorating the place with blown-up condoms and other obscene decor. The ringleaders were expelled when it became clear that the point of the pary was to offer insult to girls thought to be homelier than others.

Every UNC residence hall prominently posted a regulation: "The consumption of alcoholic beverages on these premises is contrary to trustee policy." It was an ingenious equivocation, since a thing "contrary to trustee policy" was not literally forbidden. Whoever had framed the regulation averted—deliberately, I assume—a gigantic hypocrisy. There is no effective way to police the frolics of college students safely distant from parental supervision and school regimentation, though the dean of students did make a stab at it after one unusually riotous weekend when a grand piano belonging to one of the fraternities was smashed up and burned in one of the residence courts. Henceforth, so the kind and imposing dean Fred Weaver decreed, there would be no drinking in fraternity houses. Charlie Kuralt, then editor of the student paper, later to be a much-loved and highly original CBS correspondent, made elegant and gentle fun of the regulation. It happened that Pierre Mendes-France, the French premier, had launched a milk-drinking campaign to wean French workmen from their murderous consumption of bad red wine. "Pierre, meet Fred," said Kuralt's three-word editorial. Weaver's decree soon fell into desuetude, or perhaps it was rescinded when he and the Interfraternity Council reached a compromise; for Weaver was no prig or Puritan and understood that the best way to cultivate adult behavior in students is to treat them as adults. In larger and longer perspective, the wild intemperance which is now almost expected of American college students as a rite of passage may be seen as a perverse corollary of our Puritanical hypocrisy about alcohol. But to imply a tone of savagery and excess would leave a misimpression of what Chapel Hill life was like in those days. We were, in fact, remarkably decorous; and sometimes even funny.

I recall, for instance, how amusing and chic it seemed to me one Saturday afternoon as my friends and I were making our way to Kenan Stadium for a football game. It was a balmy October day and the good-humored crowd flowing by the Bell Tower was moving slowly. From somewhere in the rear came a cry: "Make way for the lady with the baby! Make way, please, for the lady with the baby!"

The crowd politely parted, but there was no lady with a baby. Instead, there was a procession of four fraternity boys, bearing a hospital stretcher. On the stretcher stood a big block of ice, and recessed within the block of ice was the "baby"—an imposing jug of whiskey.

It was a happy time. There was excitement in the classroom; and I was making a host of new friends. But a parallel attraction for me was the student paper, the *Daily Tar Heel,* whose most famous editor had been Thomas Wolfe. The *Tar Heel* had sponsored a contest during freshman camp, offering to print the best account of that gathering. I entered and "won" though whether there were competing entries I have no idea. A position on the paper was guaranteed me and as instructed, I presented myself at its door upstairs at the south end of Graham Memorial. At the time of the *Tar Heel*'s seventieth anniversary, I recounted what I found there:

> Its editors, remarks the incumbent, "often assume the role of campus god—for lack of any other vaguely responsible element to fill the vacuum." That is essentially true. But the grinding task of issuing a four-page daily with one foot in the classroom permits little basking in this godliness. Indeed, it was only when stripped of his thunderbolts and released onto the tennis courts late in 1956 that this god learned from a charming coed: "I always wanted to stop you as you dashed about the campus—but you seemed so remote, so busy, so important, that I was afraid to try."
>
> What power! What infallibility! . . . How was I to become a part of it? My first attempt at *Tar Heel* punditry—a column about dogs in the Albert Payson Terhune vein—fell flat. Rolfe Neill [the editor] rejected it. "I don't like it," he said, "it's so damned good." (Profanity was *de rigueur.*) One accepted the rejection as a sort of journalistic Purple Heart, considering its source, and lived to write an equally intolerable inquiring-reporter column called "pulling the grass roots," and also bad pieces on Thomas Wolfe . . . an unfortunate prose-style model. . . . Plainly, the *Daily Tar Heel* specializes in effrontery. "No one," boasts the current editor, "is safe from its barbs, from chancellors to student legislators, from coaches to magazine editors." True; and salutary, I believe. But the mystery is why Chapel Hill, unlike more timid universities that muzzle their embarrassing student

press, benevolently tolerates its cheek. I thought I had an insight when Chancellor Robert House confronted me in the lobby of the Carolina Inn just as my year on Mount Olympus was to end. He noted my impending graduation. "Well, Yoder," he asked, "do you think the university can survive without you?" Here, the good old man had probed to the deepest, the unthinkable truth. The *Tar Heel* in its most frenzied tantrums could do no permanent damage. The editorial heavens could shake and thunder, but the campus endured.

Hyperbole allowed for, that piece captures the gamin flavor of the *Tar Heel*. What it omits, and it may explain Chancellor House's tart question at the time of my graduation, is the most colorful of my *Daily Tar Heel* adventures. But I must begin that story at the very beginning.

Louis Kraar, a talented and serious fellow from Atlanta, and I had been Charlie Kuralt's associate editors and it was assumed that we would be rivals to succeed him in the campus-wide spring election. One evening Louis and I had finished our chores at the DTH offices and walked out together into the mild winter twilight of Franklin Street.

"Well, Ed," Louis said, in his friendly way, "when are you going to start eating in Lenoir Hall?"

Lenoir Hall, "ptomaine tavern," was the central dining commons, where most students ate most of the time, unless they belonged to the more affluent Greek letter clubs, which had their own cooks. Lenoir Hall was in theory at least the hangout of *hoi polloi:*, the common folk, and accordingly thought of as a natural venue for politicking. That was the gist and bearing of Louis's question.

"I don't know," I said. "What about you?" Louis laughed and the subject passed for the moment. The truth was that I was beginning to plan my campaign. I had asked my friend Graham Shanks, whose uncle had been president of the university, to manage it. Across the hall in Ruffin, one of my guitar-playing, folk-singing dorm mates had composed a campaign song to the tune of "Happy Days Are Here Again." Louis and I seemed to be set for a friendly but tough campaign, which I had every confidence of winning.

But there was a catch. The *Tar Heel* under a succession of excellent editors—Barry Farber, Rolfe Neill, Charles Kuralt—was unpopular among the more conservative students. Its editorials, especially after the *Brown* decision in May 1954, had offended segregationists, who remained a substantial minority. Its longstanding scorn for what we called "big time athletics," commercialized and subsidized teams, recruited by so-called athletic scholarships, had won few friends in the fraternity courts. Its criticisms of student government pranks had alienated many of those the *Tar Heel* scorned as "student politicians."

What, we began to wonder, if Louis and I split the fragile pro–*Tar Heel* vote and some challenger from outside the intended laying-on of apostolic hands put together a coalition of the disgruntled? And should that happen, what if the *Tar Heel* were to become a mouthpiece for racial segregation or commercialized athletics? Those questions loomed large for us then, when youthful idealism is in spate and one tends to take oneself very seriously. What we regarded as the *Tar Heel's* tradition of enlightened, indeed quasi-professional, journalism might be at risk. Just when those nagging questions prompted Louis and me to begin discussing a joint editorship I can't recall; but I believe it rather quickly followed that conversation about dining for political expediency in Lenoir Hall. The more we talked about a collaboration, the more sense it seemed to make. Louis and I were both exceptions to the tradition that *Daily Tar Heel* editors never studied, in fact all but deserted the classrooms, courting academic dismissal. (Some had actually flunked out.) Louis was planning to marry his fiancée Ebba Freund the following summer and that would bring domestic responsibilities. By splitting the editorial duties, we would reserve time for study and, in his case, for a new marriage. Meanwhile, the coalition would deflect competitors seeking to gain control of the paper and, as we imagined, bend it to unworthy causes. At all events, the idea worked. We ran as a team, won the election that spring, and duly took over from Kuralt. When school ended, Louis and I took up a glittering offer from Time Incorporated in New York to participate in its "summer college editors" program. We sublet an apartment in London Terrace, learned a lot about magazine production and editing, ate and drank too much, and sweated our way through a blistering city summer. My friend Lois Owen and her parents offered generous weekend getaways to Westchester County. In fact, it was at the July Fourth dance at the Westchester Country Club that I experienced a sort of epiphany. The orchestra struck up "Diamonds Are a Girl's Best Friend." "Look!" Lois whispered, as we danced. I turned and there was none other than Bob Hope, one of my movieland heroes, swaying at our elbow. I felt very grownup and sophisticated. I little suspected what a spectacular adventure in student journalism lay just ahead.

I can date the opening shot with precision. One day in the late fall of 1955, as the football season was ending, I came down the long stairway of Graham Memorial from our offices and saw the UNC football coach, George Barclay, pacing up and down the lobby below. He wore a hangdog look. I retraced my steps and told our sports editor what I had seen, and he promptly went downstairs to investigate. The upshot was a sensational scoop for the next day's *Tar Heel*. Barclay had been summarily fired, on grounds that he had not won enough football games. It was the usual thing. The idea that a winning season was the paramount purpose of allegedly amateur athletics was one of the misplaced values we had long objected to. As a matter of routine we ran the usual scolding editorial on the cult of athletic commercialism. That broadside was received with the usual indifference and scorn on our sports-loving campus. The spark that lit the powder keg was only struck a few weeks later, just after the Christmas break, when it was announced that Barclay's successor would be James "Sunny Jim" Tatum, head coach at the University of Maryland. Maryland under Tatum had been in hot water with the NCAA for recruiting violations and other irregularities. Its athletics program was among those—not a few, then or now—over which the sports boosters and athletic director exercised far more authority than the president of the university. It was obvious, despite all the soothing talk, that Tatum could import the same distortions to Chapel Hill. Tatum himself, a UNC alumnus, was a big, bluff, amiable man whose views were no secret. If he hadn't said that "winning is everything," he thought it. That famed Vince Lombardi credo may be acceptable in professional football, a frankly commercial enterprise; but college sports—we frequently said and believed (and I believe still)—were supposed to celebrate the amateur spirit. Tatum's hiring had a sneaky look about it, moreover, and was universally viewed as the prelude to the restoration of UNC as a national football power, as in the recent Carl Snavely/Choo-Choo Justice era. His hiring was announced as a fait accompli during the holiday break and stood at the top of our editorial agenda when classes resumed. Given the *Tar Heel*'s recent editorial line, only one reaction was possible: It was to drop the rhetorical equivalent of The Bomb. I wrote one of my more infamous (and sophomoric?) outbursts of editorial rhetoric. The thought was sound enough, in principle, and there were some good lines. But understatement was not the keynote and I cringe still at the recollection of the deep-purple prose—it spoke of "crazily flapping wings"—of what metaphorical fowl, precisely, I don't now recall—and "the parasitic monster of open professionalism." The syntax was imprecise, and some readers thought we were calling Tatum, not commercialism, a "parasitic monster."

The reaction was immediate and overwhelming. Jonathan Daniels, editor of the *Raleigh News and Observer,* an editor with a streak of mischief, reprinted the screed, vastly broadening its circulation, as did many other newspapers around North Carolina. Those who missed the piece soon heard of it. *Time* magazine, for which Louis and I had worked the previous summer, published a patronizing squib in its press section, loftily pronouncing that student journalists in Chapel Hill were wiser about college sports than the administration and the UNC trustees. This, for some reason, splashed more gasoline on the fire. It is an axiom of provincial controversy that outside kibitzing is unwelcome. Even some of those who agreed in principle thought we had gone too far and overstated the case. Many were shocked by the violence of the language and the harsh references to Chancellor House, who certainly lacked the power or will to veto the choice of Tatum even if he had wished to do so.

Today, of course, I would write less floridly; but a more measured and temperate editorial would probably have been discounted and ignored as more of the usual *Tar Heel* line. The nuclear device had worked. This blast had gotten the mule's attention. Incidentally, the *Tar Heel*'s riper editorial rhetoric was often—falsely—attributed to James C. Wallace. Jimmy, a brilliant polymath, a fine pianist, and a campus gadfly, was teaching a section of the Western Civilization course and managing Graham Memorial. The tea hour often found him hanging out upstairs in the *Tar Heel*'s editorial office, passing the time of day, always entertainingly, or offering editorial copy as needed. Jimmy's flamboyant touch was sometimes detected even in its absence, and he was rumored to have ghosted the Tatum editorial. In fact, he had nothing to do with it. But I considered the rumor flattering, for Jimmy was a fine rhetorician. In any event, the campus was now in a lather and the *Tar Heel*'s inveterate critics saw a chance to pounce.

An obscure provision of the student constitution provided for the recall of any elected student officer, including *Tar Heel* editors. A petition was circulating and gaining signatures by the minute. Just who had dusted off this disused provision of the constitution I never learned; tracks were doubtless covered. By one account, the idea originated in a shower at Cobb dormitory—not among the red-hot sports fans but among the "student politicos," as Louis liked to call them. The chief architect was said to be the friendly-seeming attorney general of the student government, David Reid, a pudgy fellow from the mountains. A spirited campaign ensued, of which I recall few details except for the glaring publicity, including my first experience of television interviews. I remember going one night to my friend Hamilton Horton, a former student-body president then in law school, to try to head off a maverick candidacy he was said to be promoting. I believe the errand was successful. I recall speaking to friendly coeds at the Pi Beta Phi house, but that's about all. Spring was around the corner, I had an exciting new girlfriend, and though the thought was too unworthy to admit even to myself, I half hoped—secretly—that we would be thrown out. It was a selfish impulse; for while the result would be a mild martyrdom and greater freedom to study, party, and play tennis, the precedent would be terrible. The opposition candidate wore the tell-tale livery of our old adversaries among the student politicians. Lewis Brumfield, a bright, gangling boy from Yadkinville, with a comic country twang in his voice, was running against us. I had known him since our freshman year, when we both had the good fortune to sit at the feet of Jack Weston in English II. I knew that he was a good writer. Jack had him read his main paper of the term aloud to the class—an implicit acknowledgment of its superiority. Lewis was destined for a colorful career as a New York night-club pianist and (so he claimed at our twenty-fifth class reunion) as the author of pseudonymous "porny-graphic" novels. The skies wouldn't have fallen if Lewis had won the recall election. He would have been an entertaining interim editor. But whatever the merits of the athletic issue, it would have been unfortunate to entrust the *Tar Heel* to a faction of the Student Party, Lewis's backers. All but the most obtuse defenders of "big time" football could see that the real issue was not sports professionalism but the editorial freedom of the newspaper. For a very long time, the university administration and trustees had wisely declined to limit that freedom. My great mentor in writing, Phillips Russell, of the class of 1904 and the journalism department (he had left the English department on grounds that no one there thought that "any significant writer had lived since Tennyson") had founded the *Tar Heel*'s tradition of editorial freedom, as I noted earlier. Although it was originally founded as a cheerleading sheet by the athletic association, a long line of editors had enjoyed brassy independence. It would be ironic if censorship emerged in the guise of a populist recall election. We needn't have worried. When the issue came to a vote—with Tatum himself graciously endorsing our right to criticize the university sports programs—we prevailed by a margin of more than two to one, winning the "coed" vote overwhelmingly, proving, not for the first time, the superior wisdom of women. The issue quickly died and a glorious spring of dogwoods and redbud succeeded the winter of our discontent. We passed the editorial baton to Fred Powledge, our managing editor, who would prolong and, unfortunately, so personalize the campaign against Tatum that Tatum threatened a libel action. But by then I was three thousand miles away, enjoying my first term in Oxford.

Oxford? I hadn't expected to be going there, and that sudden twist in my fortunes had a curious beginning. One day in late November Fred Weaver, the dean of students, phoned and asked me to come by his office in South Building. The invitation was not unusual. We had become good friends and he and his lovely wife Frances frequently entertained students at their home, the curious old Horace Williams house on Franklin Street. We shared an interest in writing and craftsmanship, and he had pressed on me, among other items of interest, Ezra Pound's essays and Rilke's little book on his great friend Rodin, the sculptor. When I climbed the steps to his office that day, he and Corydon Spruill, the dean of the college, were waiting.

"Ed," Weaver said, "Dean Spruill and I have been looking through the Rhodes scholarship applications and wondered why you haven't applied."

"I hadn't really thought about it," I said truthfully. I was among the many who thought, mistakenly, that the coveted Rhodes scholarship was more or less reserved for varsity athletes and while I was a better than average tennis and golf player and stayed reasonably fit, I certainly was not a varsity athlete. Beyond that, I was well along with plans to study the history of ideas under Crane Brinton at Harvard. He had already written that he would be glad to have me as a graduate student and felt sure that fellowship money would be available. (I sometimes wonder where that path might have led.)

"Why don't you think about it?" Fred Weaver said. "But don't think too long. The deadline is Monday."

I thought about it and decided that there was nothing to lose. I filled out the application form, phoned or visited a number of my professors to ask them for support, and, sitting at my typewriter in the empty *Tar Heel* office on a Sunday afternoon, I composed my essay, something about the value of humanistic education for a journalist. I put it all in an envelope and drove the ten miles to Durham, where I slipped my application under the front door of the state secretary, Dean Davison of the Duke Medical School. I thought no more about it until a postcard arrived in mid-December, inviting me to the state interviews in Greensboro. My classmate Dick Baker, whose uncle had been a Rhodes Scholar, became my companion in both stages of the selection process, in Greensboro and two days later in Atlanta, where both of us were chosen. I was astonished. Favorite cousins of mine, with whom we were lodging, treated us to a celebratory evening at the old Piedmont Driving Club, and we were still flying high early the next morning when we set out for Chapel Hill and soon ran out of gas on a lonely Georgia highway. When I reached my room in Ruffin late that afternoon, my roommates had piled high stacks of books and placed my reading chair on top of them, emblematic, I suppose, of exaltation. But I hardly felt exalted; I felt numb, and it was weeks before the magnitude of this fortunate turn of luck, instigated by Fred Weaver, began to sink in. Meanwhile, it was time to take leave of Chapel Hill.

That last spring, Jane and I sat side by side in Romantic Poetry, whispering and passing notes back and forth, and doing less than justice to the instructor, the kindly but prosaic Dr. Hartsell. For the first time in four years, I cut class several times to play tennis, paying cursory attention to Keats, Byron, Shelley, and Wordsworth and finishing my time at Chapel Hill, and my degree in English, in a blaze of spring fever, after-hours frivolity, and indolence.

The four-year college experience seems to draw itself out, longer and richer than later stages of life—powerful testimony to the deep truth of Bergson's distinction between perceived and measured time, the key inspiration of Proust's great *roman fleuve, The Search for Lost Time.* But that is a matter that youth—this youth, anyway—thinks very little about. Passing time, however thought of, has not yet begun to be a consideration. That is at least one of the reasons why, as someone has wittily said, youth is wasted on the young.

Years later, after our twenty-fifth reunion, in 1981, I wrote, "Most of us would send sons or daughters to this enduringly lovely and beguiling place. Indeed, many of us already do. But that is not surprising, either, since many of us were sons and daughters—and grandsons and granddaughters—of alumni. The teachers we remember best were all in the old humanistic studies: an archeologist whose overflowing Egyptology lectures were good for the grade average; three historians; a professor of Bible studies; three of English." I had known these favorite teachers and I entirely shared the view rendered by our anniversary survey. We were lucky people and coveted the same luck for our children, as our fathers and mothers had before us.

Freshman photo, Chapel Hill, 1952.

"Campus god." The author as *Daily Tar Heel* editor, Chapel Hill, 1955. The fellow in the straw boater on the bulletin board is Socialist presidential candidate Norman Thomas at one of his Princeton reunions.

American Rhodes Scholars en route to England aboard the *Flandre* in October 1956. The author is standing, second from right. Willie Morris is fourth from left in the front row.

My mother in her flapper garb in the 1920s.

My father and his family at his retirement reception in 1965. *From left:* My brother, Jim Yoder (holding my daughter, Anne); Eleanor Hunter Yoder; my mother, Myrtice Mary Logue Yoder; author (holding my son, Teddy); my father; and my wife, Jane Warwick Yoder. *Photo by William Lynch.*

Three former *DTH* editors—*(from left)* Jimmy Wallace, Charles Kuralt, and the author—at the seventy-fifth birthday celebration of the *Daily Tar Heel,* Chapel Hill, 1965.

Farewell luncheon at the *Washington Star,* August 1981, with President Reagan as guest of honor. *From left:* The author, Jerry O'Leary, the president, Murray Gart, Edwin Meese.

The big four at the Washington Star, 1978, just after its purchase by Time, Inc. *Seated:* Murray Gart, editor, and Sid Epstein, managing editor. *Standing:* George Hoyt, publisher, and the author, editorial page editor.

With best wishes
to Ed Yoder

Jimmy Carter 5-80

Luncheon with President Carter on the terrace outside the Oval Office, May 1980. *From left:* Meg Greenfield, Carl Rowan, the president, the author. A mystifying session, just after the failure of the Iran rescue attempt. The three journalists quietly agreed to treat it as a social visit and not to write about it. *White House photo.*

The author next to one of his heroes, historian C. Vann Woodward, University Day, Chapel Hill, 1981. UNC Chancellor Christopher Fordham is to Woodward's left, and UNC President William C. Friday at the far right. Between them are two other Distinguished Alumnus Award recipients. *Courtesy UNC News Bureau.*

The author in conversation with William L. Shirer at the National Portrait Gallery, Washington, c. 1983.

The author explains a delicate point. Situation, date, and photographer unknown.

Jane and I at a reception for the new Archbishop of Canterbury, George Carey, in Washington in 1992.

Speakers at the presentation of the National Press Club's Fourth Estate Award to Charles Kuralt in 1996. *From left:* Bill Moyers, Kuralt, Press Club president Gilbert Klein, the author, Calvin Trillin, and Andy Rooney. *Photo by Marshall H. Cohen.*

" 'What about a chauffeured helicopter?' I asked." The author in a professorial moment, Washington and Lee University, 1992. *Photograph by Patrick Hinely.*

CLERK OF OXENFORD

Far from the Great PX *Recently, addressing the new 2000 class of American Rhodes Scholars, I spoke lightheartedly of "the perils of Oxford." I noted that "my crowd came of age when the Atlantic was not today's busy electronic and supersonic superhighway but the cultural moat it had been since not long after Columbus" and mentioned a few of the signs of creeping modernity that have appeared in the old university city since my time. They can be deceptive. I invited the novice scholars to seek the deeper currents and influences that have distinguished Oxford, in its uniqueness and force, for nearly a thousand years. They are not always easy to detect but they remain.*

I was trying, I suppose, to put in a good word for "alienation" in the better sense. "Who can England know who only England knows?" Browning asked. The same question applies to Americans. Can we really know ourselves if we know no other peoples? There was an anxious time, early in the cold war of the 1940s and 1950s, the time of my youth, when "un-American" became a dreaded charge, often menacingly hurled at those who were merely different. There was even a House Un-American Activities Committee, now, happily, long deceased. As a nation of immigrants, the U.S. has always been vulnerable at times of stress to the herd instinct, to the urge to try to be, or appear to be, more "American" than one's neighbors, whatever that might mean. Tocqueville in the 1830s was not the first to observe a zeal for conformity on these shores. David Riesman found the same instinct in the 1950s. It is an instinct to be resisted; and there is no better cure for it than immersion for a time in another culture. Our world is no more Americo-centric than the universe is geocentric, or even heliocentric. A favorite prayer of mine speaks of "people brought hither out of many kindreds and tongues." Variety is an American national asset, good seasoning for the mix. But when it breeds a rabid nationalism it becomes a blinding liability. To understand our national character you really need to get away from it for a while. Patriotism, yes; nationalism, no. The distinction is important.

We arrived here about 9:30 by ship train. The darkness prevented any view of the dreaming spires by night, but in the glare of the street lights we could see the colleges with their blackened fronts, their Gothic window frames and their jade-green interior quads. In truth, everyone was depressed rather than exhilarated. I was; and I haven't found anyone else whose first night in these tomb-dark and echoing halls fired him up. But

the next day was a different matter. The weather has been beautiful. . . .
We were having tea, today, with friends in Magdalen College, when an En-
glishman came in looking for a French-English dictionary. You can guess
our chagrin when he described this present weather as a heat wave. It is,
as I say, pleasant and beautiful; but it is damp and the chill of the shade
runs right up your sleeves. (Letter to Jane, October 11, 1956)

I have stumbled into some of my greatest adventures. But for randomness, getting to Oxford was like being struck by lightning, freakish
enough to confound any notion that destiny is orderly. According to his
biographer, his wife Julia, the great historian Sir Lewis Namier considered that "life's most teasing game" is "that of chance sequences irrupt-
ing into men's carefully laid plans." Winning the Rhodes Scholarship,
prompted as it was by Fred Weaver's thoughtful summoning of me that
November afternoon (see the previous chapter) was certainly an instance of that "teasing game" par excellence.

Everyone, successful or not, seems to recall his Rhodes interview;
and in my time I've heard some wild tales, usually told by candidates
who did not succeed. I recall both of mine nearly verbatim. In Greensboro, Ed Hudgins, who was to become a dear friend, asked most of the
questions; and most of them were about the *Daily Tar Heel*'s crusade
against commercialized college sports, with an edge implying that I
might not be tolerant of contrary views. Perhaps someone had mentioned (Rhodes referees are encouraged to give negative as well as positive points) that my editorials tended to be a bit preachy.

In Atlanta a few days later, the tenor of the interview was academic.
Professor Gooch of the University of Virginia, a distinguished political
scientist, took his cue from an article I had written for the *Carolina
Quarterly* about Russell Kirk and questioned me about the history of
conservative thought.

"What was Edmund Burke's party?"

"He was a Whig, of course."

"Why 'of course'? Wouldn't it be more natural for him to be a Tory?
Why is he regarded as one of the fathers of European conservatism?"

"I believe that he took an organic and traditionalist view of social
and political institutions and deplored their being uprooted by rationalists," I ventured, wondering how soon the waters would close over my
head. "His writing about the French Revolution is steeped in that view."

Professor Gooch beamed. "Exactly," he exclaimed.

"Ed," asked Dean Spruill, the North Carolina representative on the regional committee, "what sport would you play if you went to Oxford?"

"Golf," I said without hesitation. It was the only game at which I excelled, although I had dabbled in many. A few hours later, we were summoned. It was a tense and solemn moment, but having no emotional stake in the outcome I thought of it as a valuable adventure and a lark soon to end. Then I heard my name called as one of the winners and went numb.

We sailed—the thirty-two American Rhodes Scholars of 1956—on a gray noon the following October from a pier on the Hudson, Willie Morris and I and several others standing at the rail to watch the Statue of Liberty pass. "Goodbye, old girl," someone said melodramatically. We had gathered in New York a few days earlier; and on the eve of the sailing many of us, strangers to one another, journeyed down to Philadelphia by train for a starchy tea with the American secretary, Courtney Smith. Jane was with me as we waited to board the train at Penn Station.

"I can't guess who else might be going to Oxford," I said.

"I can," Jane said. "The ones in gray flannel suits." It was true. I was wearing one and so was Willie Morris, who was with us; and so were a number of others, strangers, all of whom detrained as we did at the Thirtieth Street station and took the local to Swarthmore.

Jane, with her intuitive gift, was good at such detection. A few days earlier she had also recognized Willie, who had asked us to meet him for a drink at the Taft Hotel on Broadway. We had been correspondents, he and I, as fellow student-newspaper editors before we learned that we would both be going to Oxford. He had called me from Mississippi and we had agreed to meet at the Taft at noon, two days before the sailing. I searched the room, seeing no one who looked the part.

"I'll bet that's Willie," Jane said. She nodded toward a bewildered-looking fellow in the very center of the huge and noisy lobby, gazing as if lost at the ceiling. She was right.

The sea voyage on the *Flandre*, a spiffy new French Line ship, began stiffly, with ponderous discussions of the voguish academic subjects of the time—existentialism, of course; faith versus reason; whether one could really appreciate Wordsworth's poetry before the age of forty—

that sort of thing. We were bantam cocks with our feathers fluffed, circling one another, testing our prowess. But the stiffness soon wore off and by the night of the *soirée de gala,* after four days at sea, the new American Oxonians were pelting one another in the *Flandre*'s beribboned second-class dining room with papier-maché balls soaked in champagne.

It all culminated in a brief shipboard scene between the two new Merton men, Selig of Yale and Schwartz of South Dakota. "Take that goddam thing off!" Selig commanded one night after dinner as we were heading for the first-class lounge to drink and watch the dancing, indicating the large Phi Beta Kappa key that hung from Schwartz's watch-chain. "Everybody has one of those." And as keys and other insignia of studiousness were shelved, so was the pomp and pretension, like hot air let out of a balloon.

For most of us—it would be quite different with a similar group today—England was virgin territory and the Atlantic crossing a novelty. In that, we were more fortunate, less jaded, than our successors. In the innocent 1950s, the Atlantic remained the cultural moat it had been for three centuries; and before the advent of cheap jet travel, the European experience had not been democratized and, if truth were told, rendered banal by tourism. Extensive English or continental travel remained a novelty for most of us. I had made forays with my parents and their friends into Mexico and Canada, but that was all; and even that was exceptional. I can still sense that pristine feel of the texture of new things, from the moment England's pleasant greenness came dimly into view through the sea mist. As we disembarked by tender in Plymouth harbor, I recalled one of Jim Godfrey's English-history lectures at Chapel Hill—or was it perhaps a Churchill speech I had heard on one of Charles Kuralt's recordings of great orators?—that it had been on these green heights that Sir Francis Drake had lingered serenely at his game of bowls as the Spanish Armada bore down in 1588. As usual, it was by the glancing light of bookish references that I tended to assimilate new landscapes and locales, deficient as I was in the gift of more creative friends like Willie (and later Peter Taylor) for seeing, as well as making, it new.

As the tender crept with our luggage toward the dock that mild mid-October afternoon, the harbor seemed magically illuminated by a quality of light I had never seen before, the distinctive slant of equinoctial sunlight at higher latitudes, filtered by the watery English air. Bill Williams, the warden of Rhodes House and our caretaker, was waiting for us. We took the train to Oxford in the fading light, some of us rushing to the dining carriage for our first genuine English tea: every inch the young Visigoths eager to sample the customs of Great Rome. I recall Neil Rudenstine's puckish grin when he tendered the waiter a pound note and received, in change, a large and heavy handful of those predecimal English coins—coppers, crowns, half crowns, for which no American pocket was ever stout enough.

In the mid-1950s, Oxford was still in the medieval habit of closing its gates and doors to the outer world at 10 P.M., turning a blank and silent face to anyone heedless of the warning bells that began to toll all over the city at that hour. After a brief reception at Rhodes House, we were delivered with our hand luggage to our colleges, glimpsing the brilliant green of the lawns and gardens as lights flashed on and off and porters answered our calls. I was deposited alone at Jesus, the only American Rhodes Scholar of the year at that college, and escorted by the white-thatched porter across three quadrangles and several flights of stairs to my rooms in the new building, high above Shipp Street. I have rarely felt more alone than I suddenly felt, thousands of miles from home and from Jane—and now, it seemed, separated from my companions on the *Flandre,* who were already on the way to becoming lifelong friends.

A Rhodes Scholar of the year before, Del Kolve, had thoughtfully left word that I should come to his rooms for a cup of coffee. I recrossed the desolate quadrangles to Del's room above the front gate. He was a friendly, studious man who would get a brilliant first-class degree in English the following spring, called a "congratulatory first" in Oxford; and today he is a Chaucer scholar of international rank. That evening he seemed a bit diminished by the surroundings, and his heavily anglicized accent made me wonder how long it might be—months? weeks? days?—before I sounded the same way. I commented that he seemed to have picked up the local inflections. Del laughed. He had been uncommonly receptive and impressionable, he supposed, because his Midwestern parents had been Scandinavian immigrants who had never quite learned to speak good English. I took his word for it. I didn't want to be one of those decayed old Oxonians of legend whose only souvenir was an outlandish way of speaking English. I needn't have worried. My southern drawl was impervious to all influences.

The morning light—the weather remained sunny and crisp, as it was to do for much of that first Michaelmas autumn—took me to the dining hall, already serving a scattering of early arrivals. I seated myself across from a friendly-looking redheaded fellow who introduced himself as Frank Lamont, a Canadian Rhodes Scholar from Winnipeg. In his turtle-neck sweater, he already seemed more acclimated than I to the Oxford ambience. I eased myself onto the long bench and turned to the scout, Bill, who was already filling my cup with coffee and hot milk.

"May I please have some water?" I asked. He shrank back with a look of mock astonishment, his eyebrows raised.

"Why sir, you cawn't wash in here!" he said.

I stared back, briefly wondering whether he really thought of Americans as barbarians who washed at the breakfast table. Then he laughed. Within minutes he returned, ceremoniously bearing a single glass of water on a silver tray, which he swept with a flourish to the table. Without further prompting, this was to become a daily morning ritual throughout my stay at Jesus College. As I approached the dining hall a few minutes before eight in the morning, I would detect cheerful and alert eyes and hand signals in the pantry. Just as I seated myself, in would come the glass of water perched high on a salver. It was my introduction to the civilized diligence of Oxford college servants, with their tradition as gentlemen's gentlemen. Perhaps I took to the institution a bit more readily than some of my more insistently democratic countrymen, who read American meanings into the distinctive English tradition of service without servility. My scout Phil had cheerfully awakened me with a knock at my bedroom door that morning. He was a dignified, rather stooped, and curly-haired man in his middle years who had been at the college longer than any of the other scouts. He had spent the war years as a skilled aircraft factory worker, but in 1945 rejected the temptation of higher pay to return quickly to the life of college service: a mark of the dignity with which he and others invested it.

In any case, plunged as I had been so unexpectedly into this adventure, I had much to learn about the college and about Oxford and the British. Jesus College traced its founding back almost four centuries to the first Queen Elizabeth, who had patronized its founding in honor of her Tudor ancestors. It had had from the outset a strong Welsh connection and was a gathering place for the gentry of otherwise Methodist Wales, as well as of a number of Welsh-speaking scholars whose lilting talk was indecipherable to an American ear. Like most other Oxford colleges, Jesus has now lost much of its historic regional identity; but it then abounded in Welsh names—Jones of course, Evans, Lloyd, Williams, with many Reeces, Prices, ap-Reeses—and sometimes it was hard to remember which Price or Reese was which. And while relatively wealthy and invariably, then and since, among the top half-dozen colleges academically, Jesus had no deer park or Wren architecture, unlike Magdalen and Christ Church; and it did not rank in amenities with New College or Trinity, where the so-called "hearties" abounded. My friends in New College were soon to be amused spectators of raucous junior-common-room arguments over the maintenance of that college's beagle pack, fiercely objected to by the socialists and as fiercely defended by the Tory fox hunters. All of this was of limited interest to an overseas visitor who had much to learn of the nuances of English social life, and who was to find the class-consciousness of the English awkward and sometimes boring. Fortunately, Yanks (and we were all called that, whether northern or not) enjoyed a sort of laissez-passer exemption from the usual social barriers and could mingle on easy terms with all sorts and conditions of men. And Oxford was emphatically still a man's world, as it had been two centuries earlier when the young and naive Edward Gibbon, the future historian, found himself "among the monks of Oxford, steeped in port and prejudice," imperturbably sunk in "dull and deep potations." In fact, however, democratization had been stirring in Oxford since the war. Universal government grants were available to applicants of any social background who could gain admission to a college. The historic grammar schools were now holding their own with the more prestigious "public" schools: Eton, Winchester, Harrow, and others.

> Here I am at last among Matthew Arnold's "dreaming spires." If that description is right, the spires are dreaming in extreme old age. . . . The dominant impression one gets on the first day is of the tremendous buildings, sunken over these hundreds of years into the black English soil. . . . I am high in the rear quadrangle of the college, and from my windows I can look out over the spires and towers of other colleges. My scout—

(valet—no one seems to know why or when they began to be called scouts)—is a middle aged gentleman who immediately assured me that he takes such good care of his "American chaps" that many of them return to see him yearly. . . . Phil awakened me in time for breakfast this morning and I walked over to the college dining hall—a cheery but oak-dark Elizabethan building in the front quadrangle on whose walls hang portraits of distinguished graduates of the college and the coats of arms of other colleges. . . . I haven't met my tutor, but have an appointment with him this morning. He seems to be a sort of legend . . . and was described to me by one student as a charming but fiery red-haired don who—as you read your essay at the weekly tutorial—dashes about his study pulling books from the shelves and throwing them on the floor. Of course, the idea is that you will read these books or know the reason why not and be able to explain either their thesis or your excuse to him at the next tutorial. (Letter to my father, mother, and brother, October 11, 1956)

My first duty, that first morning in Oxford, was to break the news to my designated tutor, the historian John Hale (the same "charming but fiery red-haired don" I had mentioned in my letter home) that I had changed my mind and planned to switch studies from Modern History to Philosophy, Politics, and Economics (PPE). The latter turned out to be of great practical value in journalism, especially the economics. But I missed the chance to study under Hale, who was on his way to becoming the preeminent scholar of the Italian Renaissance in Britain, perhaps in the world. Hale, however, had also been designated my "moral tutor," a quaint and nebulous office, a sort of personal supervisor, emblematic of Oxford's refusal to part with any traditional form or title. He was gracious about my change of mind and we soon became good friends. Hale was stage-struck, and at gatherings of the Henry Vaughan society, a college literary club named for the seventeenth-century poet and Jesus man, we read racy Restoration comedies with Hale zestfully speaking a variety of voices, male and female. The drink flowed on these occasions; and I have a dim memory of John Hale and me lurching together down St. Giles one evening after a hilarious bout with Wycherly's bawdy *Country Wife*.

PPE—which I had decided to read, instead of Modern History— meant economics, terra incognita to me; and economics meant Laurie Baragwanath, one of the liveliest of the livewires I encountered among the dons at Oxford. Baragwanath was a slight, wiry man with a shock of black hair that kept falling over his merry eyes; he lived in a tiny cottage in the country with his wife and baby and rode a very noisy motorcycle to the college every morning. He immediately invited me to walk with him in Christ Church meadows, where we strode rapidly along at about twenty miles per hour in the midafternoon light. In Oxford, I was to learn, ignorance was taken not as irremediable weakness to be lamented or evaded, but as a gap to be challenged head-on with massive intellectual overkill. When we returned to Baragwanath's rooms, he assigned me one of the more esoteric books in the literature of microeconomics, George Stigler's *Theory of Price,* along with a brace of articles from *Econometrica,* a journal abounding in appalling graphs and mathematical formulae that to my eye looked positively Einsteinian. These were to be swallowed, and preferably digested, in the intervening week and I was to read Baragwanath an essay on pricing and the maximization of profit. The issues and terms of art concealed in the deceptively simple-sounding topic eluded me, of course, and Laurie and I laughed our way all the way through my first formal brush with the dismal science.

I recorded all this at the time in letters to Jane:

> I went for a walk today with the economics tutor in the college, a fine, cheery don by the name of Baragwanath. What did we discuss? The South, Oxford architecture, cigarettes, Christ Church meadows—everything, in short, besides economics. Then finally he said: "Well, I suppose we'd better discuss what's at hand"—as if to say, or so his tone of voice implied, "I'd personally rather talk about the meadows." It seems that the conception of the intellectually conversant Englishman is something of a myth; and in fact it is rather bad form to discuss anything weightier than the weather and the scenery. Everyone . . . is seemingly too scrupulously polite to ask any question that might prove controversial or embarrassing to the other conversationalist. . . . I expected ere now to have been asked twenty thousand questions about the race situation in the South; but not one so far! (October 15, 1956)

> I am thoroughly enjoying philosophy and my philosophy tutor seems highly pleased with my work. Economics is, at present, another story. I am frightened of figures and graphs in the first place, and in the second, I've been flying through advanced economic theory and analysis at such a breathless rate that I couldn't assimilate all the graphs and formulae if I wanted to—and I don't. Fortunately, my economics tutor is sympathetic,

and somewhat dubious about graphs himself. We agree right down the line about needless graphs and about the turgid rhetoric most economists write; but unlike me, he believes in some graphs. In my tutorial today, I was busily reading an impassioned piece of prose about the derivation of supply curves from cost curves under perfect competition (!). Suddenly, Baragwanath jumped from his seat, bounced to his blackboard, and drew about half a dozen graphs. "I'm calling your bluff, Mr. Yoder," he said with a wide grin. "If the assumptions you're making in that essay hold, you will know what is wrong with these graphs." I stared at them, dumbfounded. Even if I'd understood them—which I didn't—I wouldn't have been able to produce anything coherent . . . at that stage. He had indeed called my bluff. I felt like James Thurber as he describes himself in "University Days"—the hours he spent trying to see some sort of virus through a microscope [and drawing pictures of his eye]." (November 13, 1956)

I was assuredly less spooked by economics, challenging as it was to one who had never read a text in the subject, than Willie Morris was by philosophy. By his comic account, his first tutor in philosophy—the subject of the day was the theory of knowledge and primary and secondary qualities—took a bizarre turn. His tutor listened patiently to Willie's essay, then asked for clarification.

"Now Morris," he said. "When we look across the room at your tweed overcoat hanging, as it is, on the back of the door, what exactly do we see?"

"The OPO label?" Willie answered. Within hours, he had fled to Modern History.

I had the advantage of a nodding acquaintance with classical philosophy, having taken several survey courses at Chapel Hill. But not with the peculiarly Oxonian analytic philosophy, which had spooked Willie and which at times struck novices as arid. Its preoccupations derived from the British empirical tradition (Berkeley, Hume, and Locke). It seemed to exclude from the realm of "meaningful" utterance the entire realm of poetic discourse. By its lights a line like Eliot's "April is the cruelest month" would be pronounced "nonsense," since months, an arbitrary unit of calendrical measurement, obviously could not feel or stir emotions. Unless, of course, you took it as some sort of botanical assertion, in view of the succeeding words about lilacs bred out of the dead land. Nearly any declarative metaphorical statement stood to flunk the acid test of the Vienna School: "The meaning of a proposition is the method of its verification," a favorite adage with my tutor. In the dry light of Oxford analysis, it seemed that only the propositions of hard science could be relied upon, and even some of those were suspect. Mike Hammond, a Rhodes Scholar friend in Oriel, and I had developed a playful nonsense colloquy.

"You realize, of course," I would say, faking a Viennese accent, "zat zere are no truths or morals; zere are only facts."

"Obviously," Mike would answer, parroting a nonsensical saying we'd once heard in a Paris sidewalk cafe. "It is only the mind that flaps."

My tutor in philosophy was a kindly and unworldly figure, David A. Rees, a caricature of the Oxford ascetic with a head of wiry hair that stood on end as if electrically charged and tiny granny glasses that veiled his stare of polite surprise as he struggled to parse some of the passages in my essays. "It was today that I read my essay on Descartes to the philosophy tutor. He interrupted me continuously for questions and comments, and his highest peaks of enthusiasm came when, several times, he exclaimed: 'Yes, yes, quite' " (letter to Jane, October 27, 1956).

Rees labored manfully to drill the subleties of analytic philosophy into me, but it was hard going and in the final schools (examinations) almost two years later, it was my dismal betas and gammas in philosophy that kept me out of the first class. Rees, however, was a friendly man who did as well as he could with unpromising material. He liked to joke about one Oxford student who had confused the pronoun "I" in some Oxford lecture with the "eye," the organ of sight, and had written accordingly in the final schools to the vast confusion of the examiners. It was he, also, who told me the Oxford joke about an absent-minded don who encountered a former student on the High Street one day in late 1945: "I say, Smith, do tell me: Was it you or your brother who was killed in the war?" Rees gently deplored the flamboyant style of my analytical essays, removed as they were in tone and diction from the chaste dryness in which fine points of epistemology were expected to be discussed. In the end, he lodged an understated protest, as I learned at the conclusion of the Trinity term, just before the long summer vacation, when we lined up outside the senior common room and went one by one before our tutors as they sat in stately array in their academic garb around their dining table. It was called the "don rag" and was a sort of report-card session in lieu of an actual report card.

The comments of my tutor in English parliamentary history, Ken

Tite, were encouraging. He had told me after the first essay or two on parliamentary history that I could have a First if I really wanted it: "I had a very exciting experience at my politics tutorial last week. I had told you that the tutor was highly laudatory about my first essay. When I finished the second, he seemed very, very pleased. 'Obviously, Mr. Yoder' (he said) 'that is first class writing and a first class essay with very substantial thought content. It is equally obvious to me that you can get a second standing on your head, and it would be a good idea for you to decide whether you want a first or not'" (letter to my parents and brother, February 3, 1957).

The principal, Mr. Christie, held various reports in his hand when I presented myself.

"Mr. Tite writes from Magdalen that you have 'a sense of history' and are doing excellent work. And you are making progress in economics, after a shaky start. But . . ." (he paused significantly and raised his eyebrows) "your philosophy essays are said to be . . . wordy."

"Wordy?" I asked. Christie looked to Rees, as if to say: the ball is in your court. Rees paused—I am sure he wished to spare me embarrassment. "Wordy. Yes . . . Hmmm . . . Yes . . . wordy in the sense of . . . *flowery.*" There was polite laughter. I tipped my mortarboard respectfully and exited, smiling. I have never forgotten the ring of that word "flowery" in my ears.

Oxford in the mid-1950s, as academic life returned to normal after the disruptions of the war years, was a high-flying place, then as now the most famous university in the world. For an American accustomed to the survey courses and lectures that then formed the staple of the American college curriculum, the Oxford B.A. degree seemed remarkably specialized—more like graduate than undergraduate study. I have mentioned how Laurie Baragwanath tossed me without apology into the murky waters of price theory. Sink or swim was the rule; swim, the expectation. One used primary sources, *loci classici,* and drew one's own conclusions—no second-hand or derivative analysis. Then, armed with the weekly argument—for the whole game was the development and honing of critical and analytical skills—one met his tutor face to face, reading the essay aloud to these learned and quick-witted gentlemen. The tutorial sessions were demanding but never stuffy or humorless. When a West Point Rhodes Scholar, Dick Sylvester, read a condescending essay on one of Shakespeare's comedies to his tutor at Worcester College, Colonel Wilkinson, the colonel began to sputter: "See here, Sylvester, Shakespeare was not *altogether* a fool!" Colonel Wilkinson's rebuke took its place in our collection of classical tutorial anecdotes—along with Herbert Nicholas's remark when Willie Morris ended his essay on the Reform Bill of 1832 with an agnostic flourish: "How close England came to revolution that year is a question we shall leave to the historians." "But my dear Morris," Nicholas said, "we *are* the historians." And so we were; we were the historians, also the economists, philosophers, literary critics, and linguists. It was the Oxford style, sometimes requiring a leap of faith, to treat the tutored as the intellectual peer of the tutor—at least for purposes of argument and instruction. And, there was something about reading one's essays aloud that exposed their gaps and ill-sewn seams and lapses of logic, not to mention the patches of thin ice one hoped to skate over. Thin ice was always noticed.

The tutorial system was epitomized for me one day in my second year as I prepared my course ("special paper," in Oxford terminology) in European Political History, 1870–1918. My tutor Philip Williams was an Oxford polymath in history and politics, whose authoritative book, *Politics in Postwar France,* had gone through several editions and was a bible of the politics school. It was rumored that when the politicians in turbulent Fourth Republic Paris could not recall some parliamentary precedent they would phone Philip, who usually had the answer at his fingertips. His fund of historical and political detail was astonishing and intimidating. One day after working through a number of thick books on the origins of the First World War I was reading an essay to him. My theme was that imperial Germany's rash decision to challenge British naval supremacy was mainly to blame for the war, Kaiser Bill's most provocative folly. When I finished reading, Philip nodded. "All right so far as it goes." (Translation: superficial.) "There are, however," he said, "at least six ways to argue the question." He proceeded to a lucid exposition of the other five arguments, as I hurriedly scribbled notes on the back and margins of my essay. I have forgotten the details. What I haven't forgotten is the point: that in historical analysis no "cause" ever suffices to explain a great event; that there are interacting elements in any chain of cause and effect; that historical causation is often "overdetermined," as Freud might have said; and that all historical explanation is at some level an artifice: A lesson I had already learned from Speck Caldwell at Chapel Hill.

> As to the educational side of Oxford: While I want to avoid direct comparisons between this system and ours—for after all there is a world of difference—I can say that this system has given me a greater intellectual humility than the other . . . that it has inculcated the spirit of caution, of discontent with one answer, of the disconcerting realization that everything is complex; that it has taught me the difference (I think, at least) between logic and illogic; sense and nonsense. About the facts I will not comment, suspecting that the home-grown system is really better at cramming your head with detailed trivia if you prefer that process to the process of having it opened up, having the cobwebs and dusty corners blasted out."
> (Letter to Charles Kuralt, November 2, 1957)

After the rat race of American college life, Oxford seemed almost defiantly serene. Most of us had been campus big shots—five of us student-newspaper editors: Willie and I, Mark Ball, Bob Picken, and Cliff Thompson—but the feverish busy-work had abruptly disappeared and at first no substitute offered itself but an endless round of teas and sherry parties. One day some friends were trying their best to stage an authentic tea for English friends in New College, everyone scrambling to fetch some missing ingredient. Watching the activity in befuddlement, one of the Englishmen politely asked: "I say, is this what you Yanks call a *barbecue*?"

Ed Hudgins, who had gone from Chapel Hill to Merton as a Rhodes Scholar in the early 1930s, had warned me that I would find Oxford remarkably leisurely. He recalled that he had waited for two weeks following his own arrival, expecting all the while to be marshaled and drummed into some intense drill, only to be left entirely alone. Finally a small card appeared one day on the college lodge bulletin board, inscribed in a small and shapely hand: "Mr. ——— (his prospective tutor) would be pleased if those gentlemen intending to read jurisprudence under his supervision would call at their convenience." It was the signature Oxford style; and many of the dons in his day and mine must have been quietly amused at the spectacle of quondam American campus big shots running compulsively in place on their imaginary treadmills.

> In sum [I wrote to Jane on October 15, 1956] what I've been doing since I last wrote is social and not academic at all. Every day is checkered

with coffee, tea (always at 4), sherry parties (venerable institutions) in which people gather casually and enjoy seeing each other. Among the Rhodes Scholars, there is quite a circle of tea-tours. Yesterday I had tea with Willie . . .; today he and a friend from Princeton and a friend from the college across the Turl (a street) came to my room for tea. It may all sound at best incongruous . . . but in Oxford, it's all perfectly natural, uncontrived, and without the slightest ounce of affectation. Can you imagine sitting down for tea at 4 in the Deke House at Chapel Hill?

Lonely as I sometimes was—though less annoyed than some of my American friends by the silence of the English when meeting a stranger: clearly the mark of a more crowded and private society than our sprawling country—I invested a good bit of my spare time visiting new friends from the *Flandre* crossing. There was Don Sniegowski, who'd played baseball and studied English at Notre Dame, across the street in Exeter. There was Ed Selig of Yale and Merton College, who'd won the coveted Scholar of the House prize for his senior honors thesis on the cavalier poet Thomas Carew and was now revising it for publication. He and I began a series of fall afternoon tennis matches on the lovely grass courts, where he teased me about my "drawl balls." His booming voice and declamatory style had already won him, permanently, the nickname "senator." We were to travel Europe together and become fast friends. And of course there was the congenial crowd at New College—Willie, Van Ooms of Amherst (soon to be my unofficial tutor in economic theory), Neil Rudenstine, Rocky Suddarth, and John D'Arms: close friends then and now.

The college food was so drab—I ate what seemed to be tons of brussels sprouts that fall and winter—that we often dined out in town, at a shabby upstairs restaurant called the Town and Gown on the High Street, where waiters in worn and now shiny formal tailcoats served a filling meal of beef, chips, onions, and peas for about three shillings. And there were, of course, the pubs—the King's Arms being a favorite, as was the Turf Tavern, down a twisting alley-way called Hell's Passage, close under the old city wall, near the place where I froze and almost impaled myself one night on the spikes. Later, we would discover George's tea room in the attic of the Oxford Market; in our second year, it was to become an institution.

You have asked about the food—and specifically what foods we get at most meals. The great staple food of the English table is potatoes, and more potatoes, mashed, baked, boiled, etc., but always potatoes. Meats are usually roast beef, fowl, or some sort of fish. Vegetables usually brussels sprouts, carrots, peas or cooked cabbage. Inevitably, there is a soup course before each meal, but I find the soups practically unpalatable and usually decline when I can do so gracefully. The English have much more imagination about desserts. They serve a different pudding almost every day. Some of the puddings are closer to what we would call ginger bread. I miss most of all the old Southern specials like turnip greens. Willie Morris and I agreed the other day . . . that what we'd most like to have to eat is a heaping dish of turnip greens and vinegar, accompanied by good corn bread. All in all, the food situation is not really bad. (Letter to my parents and brother, November 18, 1956)

Our counselor and hand-holder was E. T. Williams, known to his friends as "Bill," secretary to the Rhodes Trust and warden of Rhodes House, the same quiet fellow who had met us at the dock at Plymouth. Like all tutelary figures, he was much speculated about by Rhodes Scholars. An air of mystery lingered about him, and some ignorant but not entirely pointless speculation that he was the secret head of the secret intelligence service. Slumped in the easy chair of his Rhodes House office with his reading glasses typically pushed up on his forehead, he invited gossip; and his spare and elliptical conversation, as he glided from topic to topic, demanded and rewarded close attention. He seemed to know what Rhodes Scholars were thinking even before they knew it themselves. It was rumored that he had had a war of great distinction as an aide to Field Marshal Montgomery, the top British general of the war, and, word further had it, had been the youngest brigadier general in the British army. All this (except for the business about secret intelligence) was true enough, as we eventually learned. But since he spoke little about himself, beyond an occasional cryptic allusion to his time with the British U.N. delegation, details were not easy to come by, and I had not been bred to pry. Bill Williams was resolutely averse to all self-referential talk, then and later. In one of our many exchanges of letters—this was decades after I had left Oxford—he remembered how his nanny had held him up to a window so that he could see an illumination, perhaps for the Armistice of 1918. When I wrote back with enthusiasm to say that it sounded as if he was gathering string for a memoir, and I was glad, he replied that nothing could be farther from his mind. For some reason, he seemed almost to cherish an anonymity which his distinction and intellect denied him. When he died in the summer of 1997, he left his body to medicine (one of his keen interests) and to the dismay of hundreds of protégés and admirers, left word that there was to be no memorial service. But Bill Williams was not made for anonymity, and some day someone will do justice to his remarkable life and personality. Some snide obituary writers in the London papers slighted him in death, noting his brilliant promise and distinction (for instance, as editor of the *Dictionary of National Biography* and as an operator of legendary influence in Oxford), but implied that he had not quite lived up to his early billings and had, in fact, drunk more than was good for him. This suggestion was mortifying to his wife Gillian, so much so that she rebuffed a friendly note by Willie Morris (certainly one of his favorite people) that had mentioned his possibly serving whisky to Rhodes Scholars. One positive giveaway of the warden's secret distinction came early for me, just after I had taken my degree and returned to the U.S. One day, the book editor of the *Charlotte News,* for which I was then writing, handed me a review copy of Montgomery's war memoirs. In the index I discovered a glowing tribute to Bill Williams:

> I cast my eye over the intelligence organization at my headquarters. I discovered there a major in the King's Dragoon Guards, by name Williams. . . . He was an Oxford don and had a brilliant brain; as we shall see later it was a conversation with him that gave me the idea which played a large part in winning the Battle of Alamein. He was not the head of my intelligence staff but I was determined that he soon must be. . . . In a conversation one day . . . he pointed out to me that the enemy German and Italian troops were what he called "corsetted"; that is, Rommel had so deployed his German infantry and parachute troops all along the front, the latter being unreliable when it came to hard fighting. Bill Williams's idea was that if we could separate the two we would be very well placed, as we could smash through a purely Italian front without any great difficulty. This very brilliant analysis and idea was to be a major feature of the master plan for the "crumbling" operations, and it paved the way to final victory at Alamein. . . .
>
> Bill Williams was the main source of inspiration; intellectually he was far superior to myself or to anyone on my staff, but he never gave one that impression. He saw the enemy picture whole and true; he could sift a mass of detailed information and deduce the right answer. As time went on he got to know how I worked; he would tell me in ten minutes exactly what

I wanted to know, leaving out what I did not want to know. . . . In the Second World War the best officers in the intelligence corps were civilians; they seemed to have the best brain for that type of work, trained in the "rules of evidence," fertile and with great imagination, and Bill Williams stood out supreme among them all.

I felt as if I had struck gold. I wrote a review of the book, including a lengthy reminiscence of the warden. I recalled how he liked to tease American Rhodes Scholars, whose company he clearly enjoyed, about the political conservatism of Eisenhower's America. "I am a very right-wing Tory," he would say, adding after a theatrical pause, and a little dance-like step, "far to the left of anything you have in the U.S." "He is," I wrote, "at his best with a glass of something and a good cigar." My piece was reprinted in the *American Oxonian* and enjoyed a long shelf life, for it found its way into almost everyone's remarks about Bill Williams at almost any American occasion. I can still see Bill Williams rolling his eyes in my direction with an "Oh, no, not again" expression one night when my laudatory words were used to introduce him at the 1965 Rhodes reunion at Swarthmore. Indeed, my words followed him about like a perhaps not entirely welcome little dog. But I think he secretly liked what I had written—or at least did not dislike it. When Willie showed him a copy, he wrote: "Willie has given me a cutting of your piece, in which you portray me as an intoxicated reactionary. Thank heaven my poor mother did not live to see it, as she was a dedicated member of the Women's Christian Temperance Union."

I was horrified to learn unexpectedly of his death during a jolly dinner with Alistair Horne at the Garrick Club. Alistair had been working with David Montgomery on a memoir of his father, the great World War II commander. I asked how Bill was getting along—I knew they had talked at length about the book. "Oh, dear," Alistair said, "Bill died some weeks ago." I promptly wrote Gillian a long letter from my London hotel, still asking myself just what it was about Bill Williams that had so intrigued me as a young man, and had made him a force and influence in my life for almost forty years (and I was far from alone in that). At a mere glance, one might have taken him for a Tory country gentleman who happened to have strayed accidentally into the academic world. But that was persona, perhaps a shade compensatory. His father had been a Congregationalist parson, so his origins weren't exactly establishmentarian. The warden could be both warm and abrupt, sometimes on the same occasion. I once innocently outraged him by trying one night to defend Eden's clumsy Suez adventure. He and I and Gillian, and one or two others, were having a quiet pre-dinner drink on a summer evening at The Mount, the Balliol country retreat in the Cotswolds. It was hot, and the flies were buzzing freely in through the screenless windows when I began to hold forth. I said that I thought "history" would vindicate Eden's strategic judgment, if not his secretive tactics. Bill reddened, speechless with suppressed outrage. I don't recall his comment, but it was barbed and it prompted me to change the subject quickly. When Oxford declined to give Margaret Thatcher an honorary degree—the only British statesman thus rebuffed since Edmund Burke—I wrote to ask him why Burke had been high-hatted; I assumed it had something to do with his views on the French Revolution. Bill's answer was amusing, but with a stinger. The explanation of the rebuff to Mrs. Thatcher, he wrote, was that scientists (who resented her cuts in academic-research grants) "discovered the Sheldonian"—the Wren auditorium where the faculty vote on such matters. He added, pointedly, that I could easily have found the answer to my query in the Burke entry in the *Dictionary of National Biography*, which, of course, he had edited and may have written. He would have none of that sentimental bonhomie that often marks American-style friendships. His style was high and dry, and one of our last visits was typical. I was in Oxford to interview Isaiah Berlin in connection with a book I was writing. Bill instructed me to meet him in the Balliol garden. He was sitting there on a bench in his dark three-piece suit, though it was a warm summer day. As I approached, not having seen him in five years, he greeted me laconically. "Sit you down," he said, pronouncing it *doon* in the Scottish manner—no "hello-how are you-glad to see you" nonsense. This was the dry side; but it was deceptive. He loved funny stories and was a marvelous raconteur. In July 1985, when I was on my way back from a Parisian adventure, we had agreed to meet for dinner at the Randolph. The television had been full of diagrams elaborating endlessly on Ronald Reagan's colon surgery. Bill came bouncing into the lobby wearing a big grin. "You'll never guess what a funny thing Gillian just said," he began: " 'Don't you just hate Reagan's guts?' "

That June day following my lengthy "viva" (oral exam, after the written schools) I hastened excitedly to Rhodes House to tell him that I had been questioned for an hour almost and, clearly, a first was a possibility, but only if I had talked my way into it. (I hadn't, as it turned out—see below.) We walked up and down in the Rhodes House garden for half an hour as he eagerly drew from me a detailed account of the questions and what I had said in answer—his interest in his charges was vital and intense. I knew that he liked me as I liked him, a point of some value after I began serving on American Rhodes selection committees and read the caustic evaluations he sometimes wrote about Rhodes Scholars who failed to meet his standards. He was lenient with academic mediocrity but acid on questions of character, especially with those who exhibited two characteristics he despised—complacent ingratitude and what he called "sharp elbows."

During the six-week vacations that separate fall from winter terms at Oxford, and winter from spring terms, the natives tend to burrow at home for heavy reading. For us, vacations were seasons of wanderlust. As the first Christmas in England approached, we were invited to Rhodes House to meet Miss Macdonald of Sleat and her friend Lady Ryder, whose Dominions Fellowship Trust arranged visits to stately homes and families all over the British Isles. Neil Rudenstine and I applied for Scotland and promptly received two generous invitations.

But before Scotland, there was London to explore for the first time.

During our December stay with the hospitable A. E. Priests in their boardinghouse in Bayswater ("the last outpost of gentility," my friend Timothy Preston had called it), Willie Morris and I lucked into a spectacle. We were in the strangers' gallery at the House of Commons one day when Sir Winston Churchill himself tottered in, supported by a cane, and briefly sat, nodding, just down from the treasury bench. He seemed to be there to offer moral support to his beleaguered successor, Sir Anthony Eden, whose botched attempt to recover control of the Suez Canal would shortly lead to his resignation. I tried to recapture the scene for several newspapers in North Carolina:

> The galleries all around were full. The air of anticipation—as Commons opened at 2:30 P.M.—was not due to the questioning of Mr. Jones, the minister of fuel. Everyone waited for another figure. . . . At 3:15, the grilling of Mr. Jones had been going on 45 slow minutes. The familiar lanky figure of Mr. Eden appeared suddenly, as if it had risen bodily from

the shadows behind the throne-like Speaker's box. Eden paused, as if getting his bearings in an alien place, then sauntered in a half-lope out into the full light of the hall. The tories broke into cries of "hear! hear!"—and sustained them politely as Eden passed down the length of the table, past the dispatch box where the fuel minister was still holding forth, to his seat. . . . The Labor Party benches across the House were silent. . . . In the final cavalier gesture, Eden lifted his spindly legs and propped his black shoes on the table beside the dispatch box. With a practiced flip of the wrist he put on his glasses and began to study his order paper. The impression, as I watched him, was unmistakable. Here was an old hand, one for whom the adversities of world events are nothing strange, and one whose battle scars have given him the power to see even the most serious struggles of men and affairs with a certain irony and detachment. ("Mr. Eden's Return," *Greensboro Daily News,* December 29, 1956)

In early January, Neil and I took the overnight express to Scotland. The first of two hostesses, the Hon. Muriel Lindsay-Carnegie, met our train at the depot in Aberdeen in her tiny car. She apologized that "petrol" was short and that she had not been able to send her driver with the Rolls-Royce, a huge antique that was to be seen in one of the garages. There was something a bit incongruous about rolling up to a magnificent country house in a Morris Minor, or whatever her smaller car was. It was like arriving at a castle on a tricycle, and incongruity of sizes reminiscent of *Gulliver's Travels.* Later, as we were having coffee after lunch in the library, Mrs. Lindsay-Carnegie took a call. Eden had just resigned. "I wonder what that beast Gaitskell (Hugh Gaitskell, leader of the Labor opposition) will do now," she said, not minding if we overheard—no mistaking her political flavor; but it went with the house. Politics was for the most part muted at Kinblethmont, where the every-day emphasis was on every imaginable variation of the theme of hospitality. We could even choose between Indian and Chinese tea at the lavish breakfast table, and there was a bakeress whose only job, it seemed, was to cook the steaming scones and spectacular pastries for a sumptuous daily tea. And whether the guests were many or few, we "dressed" for dinner. It was during one of the lengthy after-dinner rituals at Kinblethmont, when the men lingered with port glasses and cigars while the ladies withdrew, that the custom of separation—a fixed practice in the England of that time—was explained. Muriel Lindsay-Carnegie's nephew and heir, Captain Ramsay, who was living with his young family in the nearby dower house, explained that before indoor plumbing, a chamber pot went the rounds of the dining room with the port, brandy, and cigars. It was, he said, to spare ladies the indelicate sight of that after-dinner ritual that the custom of separation had arisen.

We have been royally greeted by Mrs. Lindsay-Carnegie and it is very satisfying to be in a home for a change. Mrs. L-C's house is old English—I should say, Scottish—country manor, set out in the hillsides of Angus. It is beautiful country, reminiscent in many ways of western North Carolina. The house is huge and Mrs. L-C believes in old-fashioned entertainment. Last night, she gave a formal dinner and dance for us here, a sumptuous affair, with all the lassies in their evening dresses and the laddies in their tartan clan kilts, buckled shoes and besilvered jackets. We danced the Scottish reels—somewhat like our square dancing, with overtones of baroque minuets. They are not complicated dances, and we found them great fun, even for novices. The Scottish people themselves are no different in accent or custom from the English; but they are much livelier, friendlier, more talkative, and they dispense with the trying reserve which to an American is the most difficult thing to become accustomed to with the English. I would compare what we have received here to a good dose of southern hospitality. Most of the people . . . depend upon sheep and beef-cattle farming for their incomes, and judging by their houses, education, and manner, they do very well at it. You can hardly open a door in this huge old house without finding some kind of maid in it. Mrs. L-C employs, by our count, a cook, some half dozen maids, a chauffeur, a gardener, a forester, and goodness knows whom else. But she is completely unaffected and gracious. . . . Unlike the English, the Scots seem genuinely delighted to have strangers in their midst. (Letter to my parents and brother, January 6, 1957)

Dear Mrs. Yoder, I feel I must write to let you know how much I enjoyed having your son Edwin to stay with me. He is such a very nice lad, so easy to amuse and got on so well with all the people he met here. I was only sorry that owing to petrol rationing, I wasn't able to take him & his friend Neil Rudenstine as far afield as I should have liked, but I did take them to see Glamis Castle, where the Queen of Scots used to live & to one or two other places & I think they enjoyed the little . . . dance in Arbroath, where they danced mostly our Scotch reels! which really are great fun. Edwin seemed very well & very happy whilst he was here and I hope he will come back again. (Muriel Lindsay-Carnegie to my mother, January 18, 1957)

The dance, in the parish hall—and for the benefit—of Mrs. Lindsay-Carnegie's church in Arbroath, followed a lavish buffet dinner at Kinblethmont, with the "county" turned out in their spectacular highland costumes. Neil and I, in plain black tie, were drones. The reels called for much yipping and yelling, and I found myself wondering whether the famous "rebel yell" that struck such terror into Yankee hearts during our Civil War might have echoed long-lost clan cries in Scotland. We did visit gloomy, empty Glamis, with its Macbeth associations, a huge pile through whose vaults we twisted our way to a small inner apartment, somewhere on the upper floors, where a small, sandy-haired man whom Muriel Lindsay-Carnegie addressed as "Jamie" offered tea. He was, she explained, the queen's cousin; and I wondered whether he were a sprig of the long-deposed Stuarts. At Glamis, and not only there, relics of familiar history surrounded us. The entry hall at Kinblethmont displayed two conversation pieces. A large photograph showed Mrs. Lindsay-Carnegie's brother, Viscount Arbuthnot, pledging his fealty as the senior peer of his order at Queen Elizabeth II's coronation four years earlier. Near it in a glass case was what a label identified as Bonnie Prince Charlie's red wig, though surely not the only one.

Of course, no country house visit could be complete without after-dinner card games. In lieu of bridge—for my game was shaky at best—I introduced Muriel and her friends to a card game my parents liked, "set-back," a simplified cousin of bridge and whist. As in poker, jokers are wild, and the game places a strategic premium on the poker face. Muriel Lindsay-Carnegie, who delighted in the game, seemed not to grasp this point. She would eye her foes with suspicion as she tentatively laid down any high trump, saying, "You wicked lad, I'll bet you're going to play the joker." No need to guess whether it might be in *her* hand. She liked the game so much that when she drove into Arbroath for tea with her sister, the Hon. Nancy Arbuthnot, nothing would do but that she, too, should learn this new game from the wilds of North Carolina. So the cards were broken out at the tea table, under which Miss Arbuthnot's two huge dogs constantly surged and seethed as the two sisters reveled in the game. Neil and I struggled to keep a straight face as the dogs threatened to overturn everything, but the two ladies were too deep into setback to notice.

At the end of the week, Neil and I entrained for the highlands. I hated to leave. For years, Muriel Lindsay-Carnegie and I exchanged

Christmas greetings, her card invariably reiterating her kind invitation to come back again—isn't there a poignant Scots song of farewell, "Will Ye Na Come Back Agin?" Alas, I never did; and since the North Sea oil boom in that part of Scotland, I occasionally remember the week at Kinblethmont, and its gracious mistress, and wonder what that world is like today—probably changed beyond all recognition.

From Arbroath, we went by train and bus to Inverness, arriving at remote Glenurquhart in pitch darkness during a driving wintry downpour. We could see almost nothing. All we could hear, as the bus growled off into the night, was the torrential rush of a stream in spate just across the road. As Neil and I stood wondering what next, a cloaked figure materialized out of the darkness and asked if we were Mrs. Jollyman's American guests. John Simpson, the local Anglican parson, was Mrs. Jollyman's host at most dinners. We were to see much of him during that week and later, when he visited in the U.S. Simpson drove us up to the house, with its welcoming lights and warmth. "Shewglie" was spacious and, though by no means as grand as Kinblethmont, perhaps older, with a sixteenth-century date inscribed above the portal. Much of the dinner-table talk at Glenurquhart was of the Loch Ness monster (or monsters). "There's something str-r-an-ge about that loch," Mrs. Jollyman would say, with her trace of a burr. Every morning after breakfast we were, in effect, handed our walking shoes, and Neil and I went one day in search of the strangeness.

> We are continuing an enjoyable, but remote, life in the highlands. Our present hostess, Mrs. Jollyman, is an elderly widow . . . She keeps this large house and farm some 20 miles from the nearest town, which is Inverness. The emphasis here is upon relaxation, good food, some study, and Mrs. Jollyman's billiard table. The dinners (and all other meals) are delicious, and as at Mrs. Lindsay-Carnegie's they are formal affairs; so my tux continues in useful service. Mrs. Jollyman's house is in the middle of a broad valley or glen, and Neil and I have tackled the mountains on both sides in extended hikes each day. It is rugged and unspoiled scenery and the way to see it is on foot. This is all Macbeth country. (Letter to my parents and brother, January 14, 1957)

> Neil and I walked out to [Urquhart Castle] from Mrs. Jollyman's. . . . It first went up in the 12th century, out of the old redstone one sees so

much of in Scotland, was gradually expanded, became a citadel of royalism during the civil war, was blown up by some of the Crown troops for fear that the Jacobites would get it, later made the ancestral home of the Grant family. Now it mellows just above the still waters of Loch Ness—with its monsters and underwater caves so much storied and feared in the north of Scotland. The Loch Ness monster—as perhaps you've heard—is not really singular, but plural, and there are two types—the serpent and the dolphin—both seen by too many sane people to be entirely fictional. (Letter to Jane, January 21, 1957)

We were back in Oxford by late January for the beginning of the winter (Hillary) term. The English winter had settled in—brief days preceded by a feeble sunrise and ending in darkness by four in the afternoon, with foggy nights in which the ancient buildings took on an enchanted air—when you could see them at all in the mist. The streets glowed under the lamplight in a persistent drizzle that somehow *transpired,* without seeming to fall. One night, as I passed the Sheldonian Theatre on my bicycle, under the glare of its weather-effaced Roman emperors, the Oxford police wrote me a ticket for operating my bicycle without a tail light. I duly appeared before three city magistrates, who fined me a pound (about $2.80). The junior dean, Mr. Rogerson, scolded me for appearing without legal representation. "How careless you Americans are with your money," he said, one of the few outbursts of anti-Americanism I encountered, anywhere, during those two years in Britain. (The only other stereotyped complaint, not infrequently heard, was that *you* [Americans] had sat out the first years of the war, an offense for which, of course, I was not responsible, having been but five years old in 1939 when these friendly old ladies who complained thought we should have jumped in against Hitler. I agreed, after the fact.)

It was in that first winter term that the chapel fiasco occurred. Dr. Whitley, the chaplain, had asked that every member read the Scripture lesson at matins. Being then in my witless free-thinking stage, I politely resisted his requests until further evasion began to seem rude. A date for my reading was set at a brief morning prayer service held just before breakfast on weekday mornings, heralded by the clanging of the unmelodious chapel bell. On the day appointed, I overslept in the winter darkness. It was vanity, in part. I had never used an alarm clock, nor, since I usually woke up with the sun, needed one But there is little sunlight in Oxford at 7:30 on a winter morning; and I had failed to tell my scout

Phil that I needed to get an early start. The tolling of the chapel bell jarred me into consciousness. I realized in a panic that I had five minutes to wash, dress, throw on my gown, and present myself for sacred duty. When I dashed, breathless, into the chapel, Dr. Whitley was just ending his opening prayers at the chancel steps. Seeing me emerge from the gloom of the narthex, he eagerly beckoned me forward. I advanced with what seemed to me remarkable gravity and composure and mounted the stairs—to the pulpit. No Bible there. I looked down and saw the chaplain pointing across to the lectern. Finally finding the right place, and seeing the pointer set at a passage from the Old Testament (a dry interlude, I seem to recall, from the chronicles of the more obscure kings of ancient Israel), I began to read in a loud and confident voice. I read and read, and read, and read, but no stopping point had been indicated. I heard Dr. Whitley cough meaningfully from his seat, and when I looked up he had risen to his feet and was waving his arms crisscross like a railway signalman. Perhaps he would have blown a whistle, even in that hallowed place, if he had had one. The meaning was clear: *Stop!* I stopped. Afterward, as we walked together into the dining hall, Dr. Whitley was gracious.

"You read expressively," he said, pausing thoughtfully, "but at somewhat unnecessary length."

The winter term was conducive to study. But the persistent chill stirred a southerner's longing for warmer days. The spring vacation was approaching and four of us formed a partnership to buy a car and drive it to Paris and Rome. My Chapel Hill classmate Shelton Alexander, in Paris on a Fulbright scholarship, had promised to find lodging for us there; and off we merrily went, one April day, in an antique touring car we had bought in London called the "John Foster Dulles." We did make it to Paris at least, and beyond Paris to Avignon and Nice, but not in that car; and in Paris the small Hotel Pavillon, on the rue St-Dominique, was to become for some of us a home away from Oxford then and on many days thereafter. But our arrival was not untroubled.

The John Foster Dulles of which I write was not the secretary of state of that name but a car named for him—a 1927 Buick touring car bought in London, in the spring of 1957, with the aim of driving from Oxford to Rome by way of Paris. . . . The episode began with a casual remark. The way to take a spring vacation in style, said an English friend, was to buy an old London taxicab—the old square boxlike kind—which could be had for about 50 pounds. You could drive it around the world and then get what you paid for it.

Thus originated a consortium of five, of which Van Ooms and I were designated purchasing agents. Ooms and I spent an early March Saturday prowling the back lots of Bayswater for this bargain. No one had heard of a used taxi for sale. What was to be found . . . was a 1927 Buick touring car, slate blue with buff fenders, belonging to a Captain Buckley-Johnson. The captain would sell it for 55 pounds. He seemed almost eager to do so. He would even undertake certain repairs; we could send for it in a couple of days. Done, we said.

It was on the shakedown cruise that the car first disclosed a temper. Willie Morris and Dick Baker were ferrying the car from London to Oxford. Puffing up the Chiltern Hills, the Dulles's radiator boiled over with a great effusion of steam and noise. Morris, at the wheel, took his usual comic view. . . . Baker, who took the rational view of cars, was angry. This for 11 pounds? He announced his withdrawl from the consortium and fastened himself in his rooms at Christ Church.

On the day of departure, Baker now appeased and the radiator mended, ceremoniously christened with a Coca-Cola, the John Foster Dulles stood poised at the ancient gates of New College. At mid-afternoon, five merry tourists chugged southeast into the green English countryside. Not far into Berkshire, suddenly, with a loud blast, a rear tire expired. Only cows looked on. But as if miraculously, a little man from the Royal Automobile Club roared up by motorcycle, dismounted, saluted, and bent himself to patch the tire. He asked no questions; he demanded no fee. Was there no limit to English civility?

We rumbled on, darkness falling over the countryside, but our spirits rising. Rome, now, or bust! It happened just as we were passing through a small village of Surrey, looking for a pub. A certain sinister scraping sound was to be heard as the Dulles negotiated a sharp corner, then a horrid bumping sensation.

"Now look what's happened," exploded Baker in a tone of bleak accusation, regretting that he had not defected after all. "The wheel's come off!"

The wheel had not, in fact, come off. But no matter, another ancient tire was in shreds. A garage man announced that tires for that sort of Yankee car—he eyes us as he might have eyed five men astride a harnessed mastodon—had not been sold in southern England since before the war, if ever.

We spent the night—it was April, and warmer than we had a right to expect—perched at a strange angle in the leather seats of Captain Buckley-Johnson's machine. We were perched at an angle because the car was hoisted at the rear end of a towing truck. In the dim light all one could see on either hand were derelict cars. . . . To some of us, it was obvious that not all the mechanics or Royal Automobile Club dispatchers in the Kingdom could have doctored this car as far as Rome, or even Dover. Like an old dog that knows his master's boundaries, the Dulles had adapted to a territory. The boundaries could not be breached. . . . This was not the view of Baker. In his view, we had bought a wreck. The wreck had performed just as a wreck might be expected to perform and that was that. . . . I was not there when Captain Buckley-Johnson learned, late the next day, that he still owned a 1927 Buick touring car, slate blue with buff fenders, but an insufficiency of tires. They say he reacted as an officer and a gentleman. ("Wouldn't You Rather Have a (1927) Buick?," *Washington Star*)

The comic episode of the "John Foster Dulles" didn't stop travel, but it did dispel the illusion that we could tour Europe luxuriously and cheaply by car. A few of the Rhodes Scholars drove cars, but mostly they were the affluent West Pointers, Dick Sylvester and others, who enjoyed the handsome advantage of active-duty allowances in addition to their Rhodes money. These gilded colleagues also had purchasing privileges at U.S. bases, where whisky and other costly goods were to be purchased for a fraction of their heavily taxed English prices. But most of us were quickly becoming accustomed to the sparer life of post-austerity Britain.

And that brings me to a few reflections on the inwardness of being a "Yank at Oxford" in those quiet years, an experience far removed from that depicted in the sappy Robert Montgomery film of that title. It was, I think, Col. Robert McCormick, the isolationist publisher of the *Chicago Tribune,* who led detractors of the Rhodes scholarships from the outset. He professed to fear that saturation in English life and learning would subvert the patriotism of Americans, anglicizing corn-fed midwestern boys, turning them into effete and lisping dandies. Or something like that, a peril in any case. Cecil Rhodes, the founder of the scholarships bearing his name (to whom I remain deeply indebted, whatever his flaws), had fostered, or at least failed to discourage, that and other speculations about the dangers of Oxford. In the early drafts of his will, before sensible counsel prevailed, Rhodes seems to have contemplated a secret transnational order of Anglo-Saxon males who would somehow rule the world, pulling its strings benevolently, to be sure, by the lights of late-nineteenth-century English imperialism. No doubt the Oxford experience, powerful as it is, has at times deracinated Americans exposed to its subtle blandishments. But the risk of culture shock was otherwise than as McCormick imagined. It had little to do with political loyalty and far more to do with a certain aggravation of self-consciousness. With his stilted speech and manners, Abimalech V. Oover, the "anabaptist from Pittsburgh," Max Beerbohm's grotesque caricature Rhodes Scholar in the novel *Zuleika Dobson,* gets closer to the central phenomenon.

As we became more acclimated to Britain, still licking the deep wounds she had suffered in World War II, and to an extent shared the mild deprivations of that time, the effect was a kind of sympathetic estrangement from home. By contrast with that recovering Britain, laboring under currency controls and occasional trade and foreign-exchange crises, where bombed-out neighborhoods could still be seen all over London as one passed along in double-decker buses, Eisenhower's America seemed spiritually remote, gaudy, self-satisfied, and self-indulgent—a far-off Babylon entranced with consumer goods, manipulated by advertising, and, worse, intimidated by political demagogues like the then-fading Sen. Joe McCarthy. Consumer durables—refrigerators, for instance—were rarities in Oxford. It was an experience to pass through the city market on the way to George's tea room (a lunch-time gathering place, where the food was cheap and "crumbles," a mixture of ice cream and gummy fruit pastry, were the *pièces de résistance*) where hare and other game hung in the open-air food stalls, chilly enough to keep them fresh. If you kept milk, for coffee and tea, you simply set it on the window ledge outside your sitting room; that was private refrigeration in Oxford. Cars were small and few, in contrast to the gas-guzzling, high-finned monsters Detroit was pushing. When Willie Morris returned to Mississippi on a family emergency, he entertained us all by writing back that American cars were now so huge that people *lived* in them. Such were the excesses, as we saw them, of "the Great PX." The mild estrangement was intensified by scare-books of cultural warning like William H. Whyte's *The Organization Man,* which portrayed an America bewitched by corporate cultures that rewarded mindless conformity and punished individuality of character.

Between serious books for my course, I have been reading a book called *The Hidden Persuaders*. You may have heard of it; it is written by an American journalist, Vance Packard, and it is all about the new trends in advertising technique . . . more frightening in implications than *The Organization Man*. Apparently, big-time advertising has forgotten any thought it ever had of playing up the genuine (or even fake) merits of a product in ads. Instead, the trick now is to minister through ads to the hidden impulses, frustrations, desires, snobbery, fears, etc., which are lodged in our semi-neurotic civilization. The advertisers do what they call "depth research" into the hidden reasons why people buy or do not buy a certain toothpaste, ride or fly from place to place, vote as they do, and so on. The whole assumption . . . is that people do not act on rational grounds and that if they did they probably wouldn't be willing to reveal them. . . . Thus people buy a certain kind of toothpaste, not because they want their teeth to be clean or because they want to guard, simply, against decay; they buy it because it advertises itself as "the toothpaste for those who brush their teeth only once a day"—having found out that most people only brush their teeth once a day and have all kinds of deep and hidden fears because of it. . . . People don't travel aground because they fear a crash; they . . . fear what might be said by wife, family, or friends if they should be *involved* in an accident. They secretly . . . picture the little wife saying: "The fool, he could have gone by train." . . . Now the plane advertisements show a happy family . . . waving goodbye to the grinning passenger—who will "be back by nightfall." (Letter to Jane, February 1958)

I have forgotten who first began to speak of the spiritually distant homeland as "the Great PX," but the label stuck. It was again Willie, with his talent for defining our experience, who discovered in Henry Miller's novel *Tropic of Cancer* a characterization of 1920s America as "the fetus with the fat cigar," and that, too, seemed congruent with what we were hearing and reading from home. Seen through the lens of British manners, moreover, the American tourists who flocked to Europe in mounting numbers every summer (though nothing to match the hordes who jam every square foot of Oxford in the tourist season today) seemed loud, uncouth, and whiny. We guests in this subdued and understated country tried to blend into the background and avoid the stigma of these clamorous strangers with their shrill, nasal midwestern voices, demanding, abroad, what they imagined to be the superior amenities of American life. Whatever our problem was, if problem is the word, it was far from the deracination that Colonel McCormick professed to fear.

The experience of English life and learning was to teach us, or remind us, how indelibly American we were. It heightened one's sense of Americanness—or, for those of us who came from southerly places, of our southernness. The English still entertained a romantic idea of the South. We who came from there were supposed to be culturally different from other transatlantic outlanders, as in fact, to a degree, we were. For the first time in my life I found myself developing a regionalist sensibility, devouring previously unexplored books by William Faulkner and Vann Woodward that nourished and reimagined that sensibility. Willie and I were beset by undergraduate publications to "explain" the South's current racial crisis, in Little Rock and elsewhere, where for the first time since Reconstruction the federal government was using armed force to vindicate the constitutional rights of black people. Forty years later, this sense of southern distinctiveness, of historical experience and temperament, has eroded in the general banalization of American culture. But this was the remarkable paradox of the Oxford experience. It reversed the poet's familiar question: "Who can England know, who only England knows?" We were not uprooted but forced to a restless exploration of once unconscious roots. Most of us developed a permanent admiration, even love, for British character and institutions, which in those last dying days of the Anglo-Saxon ascendancy in America were already ours by heritage. But we left after our two or three years more confirmed than unsettled in our national identities.

My poor old head is, as they say here, a bit delicate this morning. Last night was the term's meeting of the ancient society of Antler (my newly joined dining club). If you have read a novel I recommended about Oxford, *Zuleika Dobson* by Max Beerbohm, you will remember the Junta. Well, about all the Oxford dining clubs are like this: You put on your dinner jacket, meet in someone's room for sherry; then, last night, we went out into the country to an old place called Studley Priory, which has been turned into a hotel–private dining room affair, where in great elegance, amidst candle light and old portraits we feasted on such delicacies as Lobster Mornay and Chocolate Rum Baravoise and washed it all down with much white wine. The object, if there is one, is to try to out-repartee everyone else and as the evening progresses and everyone gets mellower and mellower, the babble increases to unbelievable proportions. Pendleton Campbell, who is half Scots and half Kentucky, kept trying to tell me about the Shamrock Hotel in Houston and I kept trying to tell him that I thought most of Texas was probably vulgar, not realizing that the American branch of his family has been in Texas for some time. Fortunately, I don't think the hostility implicit in what I was saying really registered, because from time to time our voices were drowned out in the general din. After dinner, port, coffee, and two cigars (!) we drove back into town to one of the boys' rooms and continued sipping and talking. There was an abortive attempt to elect new members, which no one really took seriously, and it was finally agreed to leave that for soberer moments. All told, it is a bit expensive, but it only happens once per term and is fun; and I'm glad I joined. (Letter to Jane, November 22, 1957)

Oxford was nothing if not studious, but its style was to wear learning lightly, almost off-handedly, avoiding the drearier forms of pedantry, which the English with serene insularity identified as a Teutonic intrusion. Doctorates represented solitary research and were regarded, with distaste, as sops for the more pedantic Americans and Germans, inferior substitutes for the tutorial rigors of the Honors B.A. degree. It was bad form to talk about one's own academic specialty; the trick was to be witty and well informed, and if possible provocatively amateurish, about someone else's. Even among undergraduates, arrayed at dinner along benches perpendicular to the high table, one could be "sconced" (compelled to guzzle a giant tankard of beer) for any number of gaucheries. Oxford was famous, or notorious, for knowing how to stage a good time. Drinking and dining clubs abounded; and in the opening scene of Evelyn Waugh's novel *Brideshead Revisited,* the main character, in the elegant formal livery of his dining club, vomits through an open window into someone's ground-floor room and explains that it was not the quantity but the variety of the wines. And there was the memorable line from Waugh's acid Oxford novel, *Decline and Fall,* about the English upper classes "baying for the sound of broken glass." It was true; they did bay for it in their cups and I saw many a wine glass hurled with delight into fireplaces. Oxford social clubs lacked the solemn and secret mumbo-jumbo of American Greek-letter clubs, professing no purpose other than to gourmandize and raise hell at stated intervals—mild hell, it should be added, such as the English temperament allowed.

In the Michaelmas term of my second year, I found myself invited to join most of the college clubs, including the famously rowdy Elizabethan Society, the "Lizzie." Since spirits were too heavily taxed for swilling, the Lizzie's celebratory medium was the flat, lukewarm English bitter beer, in oceanic quantities. After a couple of hours of drinking, the Lizzie would parade noisily through the quadrangles in a sort of conga line, one hand grasping one's tankard and the other grasping the shoulder of the man just in front, bawling out bawdy songs. These celebrations tended to get off the ground in the later hours, toward midnight, when soberer members of the college were trying to sleep. I have forgotten, if I ever learned, the lyrics of most of the songs, and by today's standards of universal vulgarity they would seem mild. But a few fragments linger (sung in a mock-Cockney accent):

> It almost broke the family's heart
> When Lady Jane became a tart—
> It was a source of sore regret
> As she fucked her way right through DeBrett.

Or:

> Il Duce gave the order for to march against the foe,
> And it's off to Abyssinia that the organ-grinders go.
> They are splendidly accoutered in every sort of way,
> But they all left their testicles, behind, behind, behind!

I approximate the third and fourth lines of the latter drinking song, long forgotten, because the sense of it suggests the utter absence of ethnic sensitivity or hypocrisy—sometimes called "political correctness"— that marked British undergraduates two decades after Mussolini's shabby attack on Ethiopia exposed the toothlessness of the League of Nations. While they admired Italian culture and loved to ski in the winter Dolomites, and study art and sculpture in Florence in the spring when they could afford it, the British were then still bitter that their quondam allies had piled on in Hitler's war. So they bawled out lines of blatant caricature without self-consciousness. Today the bawdy songs would seem laughably Victorian, but a new kind of prudery prevails, and I wonder whether anyone would dare insinuate that Italians (their military forces, anyway) were ball-less organ-grinders.

Among my Oxford mementos is the handsome bound menu for the annual feast of "Ye Elizabethane Societie . . . holden on ye eighth daie of March, 425 A.C. *et anno regni Elizabethae II septimo*" (that is, the

425th year of the college, and the 7th year of Elizabeth II's reign). Oxford is, or was, proud of its royalist past, and toasts to the sitting monarch are respectful and heartfelt. That was true of the toasts to the young and beautiful Elizabeth II on that March evening in 1958, when we had feasted on "sole-fysshe wyth lymmon" and "a fyne turkie-cocke wyth ye newfound rootes of ye Indies and ye cole-flours." But about the great patron of the college, the first Elizabeth, the customary Lizzie toast was brazenly irreverent: "To the ever-green memory of our Virgin Queen: God bless her, balls and all."

My initiation into this carousing had taken place on a fall evening in the preceding term. The rite of passage was to drink beer right up to the Plimsoll line, in just short of lethal quantities, the initiation culminating in a sconce of beer poured over one's head to loud cheering. I somehow managed to make it back to my digs at 22 St. Margaret's Road in North Oxford, just how I don't remember. Having arrived there and toiled up two levels of the stairway toward my attic room, I was overcome with the need for a brief rest before the final climb. It was there, peacefully slumbering on the landing, that Truman Schwartz, one of our housemates, found me the next morning when he emerged from his room to brush his teeth. I can't recall that the Lizzie committed any dire outrage on those silly evenings, other than harassing some of the more monkish members of the college by banging with sticks at their "oaks" (outer doors) in the dead of night and threatening to "debag" them, that is, remove the baggy thick-wale corduroy trousers that were standard daily undergraduate attire, a suitable defense against underheated rooms. It would have been odd if any of the intended victims of this mild harassment were still dressed at such an hour and I don't recall that anyone was rash enough to open his door. The ingrained English respect for privacy made forced entry unthinkable. In later years, the Lizzie had become increasingly boisterous, and I was not surprised to learn at a college reception in 1983 that it had been suppressed.

Most Americans had already taken undergraduate degrees and were granted "senior status" at Oxford, exempted from the usual preliminary exams, and allowed to sit, as I did, for the B.A. degree in two years rather than the customary three. But after spending the first year and a half savoring the special ambience of Oxford, and European travel, we typically woke up one morning in the second year facing a dire day of reckoning just over the horizon: eight three-hour exams all in a row in four days.

My tutor in English parliamentary history had held before me the flattering possibility of a first-class degree. This blandishment was soothing to the ego, and of course I wanted to give a good accounting of myself. But after thinking it over I decided that a calculated push for a first would be a distortion of priorities. When I began tutorials in my special paper in European political history under Philip Williams, he assured me that the fates were in the stars anyway. "I can predict almost from the first paragraph of the first essay whether someone will—or could—get a first," he said. I suggested that this was a fairly deterministic view of human intellectual capacity, and he agreed. "After all," he said, "where else than in the schools at Oxford are the essential demands of high intellectual performance under pressure so well replicated? Those who do well in schools will, in most cases, do pretty well afterward." And since Philip gave me encouraging alphas on my "collections" (practice exams), I assumed that he included me in the charmed circle of those fated to do well.

My other specialization was classical political theory, Hobbes to the present, and to be tutored I went once a week to the New College rooms of the elegant Anthony Quinton, later principal of Trinity College and now a life peer. Tony was a plump, jovial, smiling fellow, stylishly dressed, looking the part of a Tory squire whose keen mind, however, belied that impression. He seemed to like my essays, with the exception of one bombastic piece on Hegel (widely deplored in Oxford as a fount of authoritarian doctrine). Tony cheerfully dismissed my effort as "claptrap." And so it was, I now suspect.

Whatever one's intentions, or capacity, however, a sense of doom does predictably tend to strike Rhodes Scholars around Christmas of the second year. Schools—those twenty-four demanding hours of examinations in less than a week—loom six months ahead. And while failure is unlikely, it seems in darker hours a possibility. Not surprisingly, my letters home indicate that hard and more systematic study was actually making headway against all the pleasant diversions of Oxford: club meetings and dinners, parties, continental travel, and just hanging out in the pubs.

I am again writing from the library—where I seem to be spending the majority of my working hours. Everyone, including yours truly, is hard at work for exams—which are now only just over four weeks away. The results of my informal tutors' exams were quite favorable, and at last I am beginning to make some real progress in economics. It is pleasant to think that in a few short weeks I will be able to get off this intensive work schedule, stop cramming, and begin to enjoy Oxford again. Not that I'm not still enjoying it, even under slave conditions. (Letter to my parents and brother, May 8, 1958)

At least I was beginning to get the hang of economics under Laurie Baragwanath's patient tutelage. We had moved on from the impenetrable mysteries of price theory to Keynesian macroeconomics, which involved interesting questions of public policy, and I was far more at home. Keynes, whose *General Theory of Employment, Interest and Money* was the landmark text of the era, was a lucid and witty writer, far easier to read than the dry-as-dust, mathematicized, microeconomic essays I had plodded through in various journals. I felt increasingly at home with Keynes's view that the so-called classical economists had been wrong in assuming that there was a natural "equilibrium" in free-market economies, and that recession was therefore a self-curing ill. The persistent Great Depression constituted a devastating argument against those complacencies, although, in the manner of stubborn but anti-quated generals, the classical economists clung to their theories, fact be damned, just as certain neoclassical successors do today.

Examination time in Oxford is a formal and ritualized affair. It is also, as intended, a mental and physical test. Philip Williams, ever the acute strategist, took the view that last-minute cramming was pointless. Rest and recreation in the days just before schools would be far more productive, he told me, since stamina and a clear head would trump any marginal accretion of information. "Your arguments, beyond a certain point, will matter far more than your information," he said. Accordingly, after months of ten-to-twelve-hour study days, I closed the books a week before schools and repaired to the tennis courts, the movie houses, and the pubs.

I felt rested, focused, and confident when I put on my "sub-fusc," bought the customary red boutonniere at a flower shop on the Broad Street, and took my seat in the Schools on the High Street at 9:30 A.M., June 5, 1958, with scores of other PPE candidates. The weather was gorgeous, and that boosted one's morale. Monitors, known as "invigilators," paced the aisles but I was too busy to notice. There were three hours for four questions, chosen from among seven or eight, questions ingeniously worded, though one could usually detect in them a variation on some set subject: the Reform Bill of 1832, or the Keynesian multiplier effect, or problems of perception, or the wisdom of high central bank rediscount rates. I recall one typical question: " 'In Latin societies, the purge, the pronunciamento and the coup d'état are the functional equivalents of the cabinet shuffle, the election manifesto and the polling in more sedate nations.' Comment." In typical Oxford style, this was an invitation to attack or defend a provocative analogy, whether one considered it an outrageous defense of authoritarianism or a wry comment on the formalism of democratic institutions, or a touch of both. Well armed with clever arguments, and a few pertinent facts, a candidate might relish dilating for forty-five minutes on such a question; it could even be fun! The tension resided in the stakes; for no less than a degree, representing two or three years' work, would ride on such performances.

I crossed the last T and dotted the last I on the last of eight papers at 12:30 P.M. on a radiant June Wednesday and emerged with my Canadian friend and study-partner, Fred Drummie, and other PPE candidates onto the High Street: free at last! Champagne corks were popping, a post-schools tradition, and Truman Schwartz was waiting for us with our own magnum. From there, we trooped on to the King's Arms for lunch and further celebration; and by midafternoon we were making quite a racket in the High Street. A familiar face from among the Jesus dons cast a sidelong glance of mingled amusement and disapproval, and we piped down.

At last the heavy hand and the shadow have been lifted, and I feel like a free agent again. There is a hangover, though; getting through, and knowing that I can count what is left of my Oxford career in hours, is not an unmixed kind of knowledge; certainly, I am not exhilarated. But I am relieved—and especially happy to be able to sit down and write . . . without feeling there's a gargoyle or something peering over my shoulder . . . The exams? On only one paper, economic theory, as I expected, do I think I did badly—which is not a bad average out of eight. . . . Not that I really give a damn, now that they're over, and now that I know that at least on occasions I gave the examiners something to read which is not the work of a complete moron. . . . I feel that it will be a while before full human sensibility returns. I feel all dried up . . . Our tutors threw a big celebration party last night in the Senior Common Room for those who'd just finished PPE schools. The grog flowed, of course, everything from sherry beforehand, through Rhine wine with the fish course, to vintage Madeira afterwards; and the party lasted till after one o'clock, when they quite unprecedentedly let us out of the college with private keys. (Letter to Jane, June 13, 1958)

The Madeira was exactly as old as I was; it had been laid down to age in the college cellars in 1934. After a round of parties, Van Ooms and I took off for Paris and Tours for a week's bicycle tour of the Loire Valley chateaux, drinking quite a lot of the "natural wine" of the region and sleeping the grateful sleep of survivors of a long campaign.

Two weeks later, tanned and rested from the Loire Valley sojourn, I presented myself once again, and for the last time, in academic dress before the PPE examiners. We gathered in a large room at the schools. The spokesman for the examiners, after a few brief pleasantries, said: "You are now free to go, but would the following ladies and gentlemen kindly remain." With a stab of mingled pleasure and apprehension, I heard my name called and after a short wait found myself seated before this formidable and learned panel. I noted with relief that they looked not at all solemn, but they gave no hint of their purpose. It was only later, when Laurie Baragwanath sent me my marks, that I saw just what had been going on. My mixed array of marks made me eligible for a first if (a big if) the examiners could discover any real depth of learning beneath the specious glitter of my essays. I was wrong, as it turned out, about the economic theory paper. I had done better, not worse, than expected, and when he saw my marks some weeks later Laurie Baragwanath was pleasantly astonished. One of the economists led off with a couple of questions about perfect competition, which I dispatched, I thought, with ease.

Then the examiner in English parliamentary history took over, and the conversation took a more problematic turn.

"Mr. Yoder, you write in your essay on Joseph Chamberlain's radical phase that he was an advocate of land reform. How do you 'reform' land?"

It was an intriguing question, a touch too intriguing, and I had given absolutely no thought at all to the matter.

I stalled, trying to collect my wits. "Well, it wasn't 'forty acres and a mule,'" I said, a lame, but I thought amusing, allusion to post–Civil War Reconstruction in America.

The examiners laughed obligingly but waited for a serious answer.

"Chamberlain's slogan was, I believe, 'three acres and a cow,' and was suggested to him by his campaign manager, whose name escapes me. Jesse something, I believe. I guess that was the essence of it, some sort of redistribution of land."

"Obviously. But whose three acres?" my interrogator pressed genially. "Where would they come from and by what lawful process would they be 'redistributed'?"

I hadn't a clue, and I knew better than to try to bluff.

"Sorry, sir, I just don't know."

The examiners changed tack, and I had the feeling that my by now disheartened advocates among the examiners were fishing for a subject in which I knew enough to be dazzling. My learning in English parliamentary history clearly had its shallows, and so did much of what I had learned in two years. A first-class command of the period would have included at least a modicum of information about land reform, and the damned cow as well as the three acres.

"Thank you, Mr. Yoder," the chairman finally said, after almost an hour. I rose, bowed, and left. When I looked at my watch I was surprised to realize how long I had been before the examiners. It was almost an hour but had passed so quickly. What could it mean? I began to think that maybe I had talked my way into a first; and buoyed by wishful thinking I hotfooted it down Parks Road for an excited post mortem with Bill Williams, the warden of Rhodes House, our shepherd and guardian. He and I paced up and down in the garden, canvassing the questions and answers one by one. I think he shared my optimism. As it turned out, it was misplaced; but in the great scale of things my high second was only one, and perhaps among the least, of those valuable legacies I took from Oxford and prize to this day.

As the day of departure approached, Oxford in late June stood quiet and empty. Some of our English friends treated us to a last supper at the Welsh Pony, a favorite pub. Ed Selig and I, with tickets to sail for New York a few days later on one of the last Atlantic crossings of the doomed *Ile de France,* piled into a taxi and headed for the train to London. It was one of those sunny summer evenings, when long shadows and brilliantly highlighted patches of lawn and flowers etch an unforgettable pattern. I recalled the powerful emotions John Henry Newman felt as he left Oxford for the last time, all but driven away for his religious views, remembering the snapdragon on the walls of Trinity. Poor man, he never returned. I was more fortunate, but it would be sixteen years, with a new world intervening, before I saw Oxford again.

GREENHORN DAYS

A Table in the Corner of a Newspaper Office *Henry Adams, in his great auto-biography* The Education of Henry Adams, *said it definitively, and I used his words as an epigraph for my book on the successor in Washington journalism who so much resembled him, Joseph Alsop. I repeat it here as an overture to my own greenhorn efforts: "One profession alone seemed possible—the Press . . . still the last resource of the educated poor who could not be artists and would not be tutors. Any man who was fit for nothing else could write an editorial or criticism. The enormous mass of misinformation accumulated in ten years of nomad life could always be worked off on a helpless public, in diluted doses, if one could but secure a table in the corner of a newspaper office." In Adams's case, it was entirely untrue in detail: He was a superb reporter and critic, minutely well informed—his great reporting is still well worth reading; and he could certainly have been an artist, as he showed in his later foray into political fiction and in his magnificent study of medieval architecture and thought. And he had other options. But what he said was true in the large. Being a newspaperman in my day as in Adams's, in mid-twentieth- as in mid-nineteenth-century America, was a way to write if one wanted to write, while putting a crust or two of bread on the table.*

Notions of journalistic apprenticeship are changing, and those described in the ensuing chapter are perhaps a bit antiquated. It was my good fortune to serve my own apprentice years under superb mentors and on publications that appeared on a human scale. When I was teaching college students a few years ago, I had the impression that many of them wanted to start at the top, on large and impersonal "national" newspapers (or in the equivalent television newsrooms). But when asked for advice I continue to recommend starting at smaller publications under editors who have something to teach and the time and patience to teach it. The recent scandals and misadventures at prestigious publications—stemming from the premature hiring of immature reporters—tend to support my view.

When I look back at the beginnings of my long career as a commentator, the word that springs to mind is "brash." There is always a certain brashness in the assumption that an audience is waiting out there for one's instruction on public questions. Yet there is a redeeming side of the coin. Few—fewer now, probably, than forty years ago—examine the news closely or, if they do, analyze it systematically. As the great

Walter Lippmann argued in justification of the pundit's presumption, *somebody* must do it professionally; and by virtue of taking on the assignment one admits: It might as well be me.

When I took my first full-time editorial-writing job at the *Charlotte News* in September 1958, my only body of work (apart from the *Daily Tar Heel* adventures described above) consisted of a dozen or so dispatches I had written from England (and France, at the time of Charles de Gaulle's return to power earlier the same summer) to North Carolina newspapers: The *Raleigh News & Observer,* the *Greensboro Daily News,* and the *Charlotte News.* Those dispatches had drawn some attention, some of it flattering, especially the screed that I think of as my neo-Confederate manifesto. As I have said, one curious aspect of the Oxford experience was to kindle a novel southern self-consciousness. The mid- and late 1950s happened to be a fertile time for such ventures in self-identification—especially if one qualified as a "southern liberal" or "moderate." As I once wrote, attempting to capture the spirit of that time and the forces that shaped my own regional consciousness:

> The first, for me, after discovering W. J. Cash's *The Mind of the South* as a college sophomore (a fateful age to do so), was foreign travel, distancing the experience of growing up southern and suggesting that the assimilationist pressure of "Americanism," then . . . so much in the air might be eccentric to the larger world's experience: a point soon to be memorably made by C. Vann Woodward. . . . Woodward's essays quickly became and remained a touchstone for defining one's regional imagination. Like a mineral trace they run in our blood and marrow now, carrying the notion that the southern experience of history had been touched with distinctiveness and was rather un-American when it came to the point: that it involved guilt, not innocence; pessimism, not optimism; the experience of social tragedy and intractability, not easy progress; defeat, not victory; poverty, not riches. . . . The time and setting, moreover, were just right. The late 1950s and early 1960s—when so much of national importance was happening in and to the South—assured a cresting of interest in what it was like to be southern. We southerners were studied hard, everywhere, like savages brought in from a newly discovered continent in the Elizabethan Age.

The phenomenon was bookish, obviously, and smelled of the lamp. But Willie Morris and I were reading and discussing southern history and fiction in spare hours—one of those useful distractions from course work that Oxford permitted and even encouraged—and finding that it opened new windows of sensibility. I had summed up my sentiments in a sort of manifesto, attempting to make the case that the new situation was like the famous Chinese ideograph for "crisis" in which symbols of both challenge and opportunity are joined. In the face of the new racial ferment and change, southern grace and manners might be combined with a more enlightened racial policy; and agrarian nostalgia with more progressive economic policies. Echoing Woodward, I made claims for the distinctiveness of southern historical experience that I believe in still, however attenuated they may be now. In my concluding sentence I resoundingly declared: "That is why I am, and will remain, a Confederate." The piece was widely printed back home, and one reader of this *cri de coeur* from exile, C. A. McKnight, responded by offering me a job. McKnight was editor of the *Charlotte Observer* and before that of the *News,* the *Observer*'s evening competitor; he had also directed the Southern Educational Reporting Service in Nashville, a clearinghouse for reliable information about school desegregation. Visiting in London, McKnight summoned me to lunch in that great city's vast clubland, plied me with roast beef and wine, and asked if I'd like to be the paper's roving southern reporter. I said that I would like it very much. But perhaps McKnight had second thoughts. He dithered over the details, and the idea finally faded away.

Meanwhile, a more definite invitation came from McKnight's Charlotte rival, Cecil Prince, editor of the *News,* who had taken a kindly interest in my writing since *Daily Tar Heel* days. His associate Perry Morgan had just won a Niemann Fellowship and would be off to Harvard in September. Cecil asked if I'd like to fill in. "I've had worse ideas," he wrote. So having completed my English education, I returned to the Great PX and reported on Labor Day weekend to Cecil in the ancient radio broadcast studio—still with perforated ceilings—that served as the *News*'s ivory tower. I liked to think that I was following, as Cecil and Perry had done, in the footsteps of the great Wilbur J. Cash, author of *The Mind of the South.* Was this not the very chamber in which, so I imagined, Cash as a *News* editorialist had written so many passionate articles and editorials? And even some of the unforgettable passages of his unforgettable book? The rundown old *News* building on South Tryon Street abounded in old hands who had known Cash a quarter-century earlier. Many claimed to have been his intimates and drinking buddies and had tall tales to tell. For instance, it was said, when the United Press ticker brought word of the September 1938 Munich Agreement, in which British and French statesmen had capitulated to Hitler's threats and handed over the frontier areas of Czechoslovakia, Cash fell to the floor in a sort of catatonic fit. Certainly he was a passionate and far-sighted detractor of Nazism; but the fit, if it actually happened, may not have been altogether political in origin. Not long after the publication of his great book in 1941, Cash, on a Guggenheim Fellowship in Mexico City, began to imagine that he was shadowed by Nazi agents. One day he said goodbye to his new wife and hanged himself in a bathroom at the Hotel Reforma, one of several analysts of the South in that era to take their own lives. It was as if staring into the eye of this basilisk of southern tragedy and confusion were dispiriting and might even prove fatal—a conceit later to be given wide currency by the political scientist V. O. Key. Cash's suicide had become part of the romance of my neo-Confederate identity. It did not occur to me or, as I recall, to the *News*'s storytellers, as it probably would today, that this magnificent stylist (and habitual drunkard) may have exhibited the symptoms of what is known to psychiatry today as bipolar disorder. Perhaps what he really needed was therapeutic attention, but he lived in the day when emotional disorder was thought to be vaguely shameful and about which even brilliant people tended to be secretive. And it would have meant a catastrophic loss to imagination had Cash been subjected to the hot therapy of that day, frontal lobotomy.

My first professional mentor, Cecil Prince, was an elegant man, in his three-piece tailored suits with passport pockets, and a suave and graceful writer, with a neo-Confederate streak of his own. The romanticism of the newest New South hung in the air, and Cecil was one of its master interpreters. Within a year, he would win the national Sigma Delta Chi editorial-writing award with a piece entitled, "This Could Be the Southern Century." I first read it while on vacation, in the Brooklyn Heights townhouse of my old Chapel Hill friend and colleague, Charles Kuralt, who had just left the *News* to join CBS in New York. Charlie knew Cecil well. We were sitting at the breakfast table when the mail brought the previous day's *News*. He read the editorial and drily commented: "This is Cecil's yearly award entry and it will win." He was right.

Cecil welcomed me indulgently; and he and his hospitable wife, Bubbie, saw that Jane and I were elegantly entertained in their modernist house overlooking a wooded hillside and brook in the suburbs. As time passed, Cecil's tutelage took on features of the discipline he had acquired as a sergeant in George Patton's Third Army during World War II. He edited out my more flamboyant (and sophomoric) flourishes and insisted that I take the rules of editorial craftsmanship seriously. My work wasn't exactly slapdash; but I wrote easily and rapidly and had yet to learn the value of revision. The low point came one grim Friday afternoon when I was eager to tear off to the mountains with Jane; Cecil made me rewrite all three of the pieces I had dashed off earlier in the day. He knew I was in a frantic hurry to be off for the weekend, and that was no doubt why he made me do it. Even with these occasional frictions, however, I was lucky to be there under his tutelage, spouting off on every imaginable subject at a hundred dollars a week: reportedly the highest pay the *News* had ever offered a greenhorn writer. I gradually began to get an idea of what the game was really about. As survivors of the ivory tower know, there are two abiding axioms of editorial writing: The fervor of one's expression tends to vary inversely with one's distance from the situation—"there's nothing like knowing too much about the subject that more quickly spoils a strong editorial," my eventual Greensboro colleague and mentor Bill Snider used to say. And editorialists are often unsure what they really want to say—newspaper deadlines being daily and unforgiving—until they "run it through the typewriter," another Sniderism.

Right off the bat, however, my grass-green labors were handsomely ratified by the first prize in the yearly editorial-writing competition sponsored by the North Carolina Press Association. The key exhibit, of three, was a piece entitled "Virginia's Retreat" (also reprinted in the *Washington Post,* the first of my appearances there), a consideration of the reversal of Sen. Harry Byrd's "massive resistance" anti-desegregation policy. Byrd's doctrine, whose intellectual godfather was James J. Kilpatrick, the feisty and eloquent editorial-page editor of the *Richmond News Leader,* was more than a bit antiquated—Perry Morgan, who felt strongly about it, often observed that the only historical detail Jack Kilpatrick had overlooked was the outcome of the Civil War. Massive resistance invoked state sovereignty, even in its tattered state, and interposed it as a supposed constitutional obstacle to "forced integration." Massive resistance had disastrous effects for Virginia schoolchildren, black and white, but mainly black. Several Virginia towns and counties closed their schools rather than obey court orders to desegregate them. Viewing the damage, a new governor pledged to continue Byrd's policy soon reversed it. Our editorial applauded the change but struggled to frame our response sympathetically. The prize came at a handy time. The *News* was losing money and threatened with closure—it would be bought, a few months later, by the Knight Publishing Company, which already owned the *Observer.* When news came of the award, Brodie Griffith, the paper's colorful general manager, told me that I had "saved his job." Vain as I was, I was not so vain as to believe *that.* But I was certainly pleased.

I was flying high, but back home in Alamance County my draft board had been waiting impatiently through six years of student deferments and let me know that my number would be up with the next draft call. It seemed an unfair interruption for a married man with a baby on the way; but the board meant business. The least inconvenient alternative seemed to be the six-month-and-six-year reserve program offered by the North Carolina Air Guard, and I seized it. I left in February for five months of basic training at Lackland Base in San Antonio (where a number of friends, including Rocky Suddarth and John Poole were under arms). One day a letter from Cecil informed me that our faltering newspaper had been saved from oblivion when the Knight Company bought it (after a near-disastrous fire in our ancient pressroom). Cecil rather melodramatically described "a considerable flow of tears from our hardy little band of irregulars" and bade me "return to us untainted by militarism." By the time I came back to Charlotte that spring, the *News* had moved up Tryon Street to the *Observer* building's third floor.

Cecil thought that it would be good for me and my writing to do some shoe-leather reporting and he was undoubtedly right. So I moved out into the newsroom, sharing a double desk with Emery Wister, the popular movie and entertainment editor of the *News.* Emery, an amiable deskmate, was celebrated, fairly or not, for colorful malapropisms. He had supposedly referred in a movie review to the Exodus as "the story made famous by Cecil D. DeMille"; and he had described the parking lot at the new Charlotte auditorium-coliseum complex as having "seating space for more than two thousand cars." In the newsroom, I learned more about writing on deadline—especially on the day when Col. Elliott

Springs, a famous South Carolina aviator and textile manufacturer who designed his own Springmaid Sheet advertisements, died on our first deadline. I sat writing furiously as Brodie Griffith fed me information about the colonel's adventurous life—he had been a member of the famous Lafayette Esquadrille during World War I—and as I finished each paragraph it would be ripped from the typewriter and handed to a copy aide who literally dashed with it down to the composing room.

But then, just as I was getting the hang of shoe-leather reporting, disaster struck, of a wholly unexpected sort. Cecil, having been honored at the national Sigma Delta Chi convention, entered the hospital for routien kidney-stone surgery—this was before ultrasound techniques made incisions unnecessary. The surgery went well, but a stubborn infection developed, persisted, and worsened. Cecil reentered the hospital critically ill and died within hours, the victim of one of the frightening staph "hospital" bugs. For the first time in my life I knew death close at hand and it was unsettling. I wept uncontrollably as we carried Cecil's heavy coffin down the steps of Christ Church toward the waiting hearse. Pallbearers, I told myself, should show sterner control but I failed. As I've said earlier, my parents believed that children should be spared the darker side of things and their gentle regimen did not permit or encourage underaged attendance at funerals, even of close relatives.

The practical effect of Cecil's sudden death was to leave me in sole charge of the *News*'s editorial page at the tender age of twenty-four, performing alone, under Brodie Griffith's supervision, until Perry Morgan returned in the autumn. I must say a word about this uncommon newspaperman of the old school. Griffith, fondly known to all as "Mr. G," was said to be the best tutor of young newspapermen in the two Carolinas; and indeed he was a generous and bracing supervisor. A South Carolinian who had learned his trade, and written English, in newsrooms rather than classrooms, he frequently related, with a laugh, that an early editor had told him, "Brodie, you punctuate *geographically*." He affected the countryman's lingo (Bourbon and branch water, his favorite drink, was "Baptist punch") and often remarked that "some people"—I suspected he sometimes meant me, as well as some of the pompous people he specified—"are educated beyond their intelligence." I was now in charge of the day-to-day formulation of *News* editorial policy, under Mr. G's authority. Never overbearing, he exercised that authority with a remarkably casual hand. He clearly liked to hire whippersnapper editorialists with what they, at least, deemed advanced views, give them their heads, occasionally yanking at the reins when enlightened enthusiasms got out of hand. For all our callowness, I believe he saw the future in us, and in his way approved.

We occasionally clashed, but always politely, for he was a very civil man. But the outbreak of the first dime-store sit-ins, in 1960, was such an occasion. At the Greensboro Woolworth's polite, well-dressed black students from North Carolina Agricultural and Technical College unexpectedly sat down one day at the lunch counter (where only white customers usually sat) and asked to be served. If their money was welcome elsewhere in the same store, why not here? White youths gathered to taunt, making a rowdy scene of what was otherwise decorous. (President Eisenhower hardly helped matters when he spoke airily of the sit-ins at a press conference as "disorders"—the disorder, in fact, was caused not by the demonstrators themselves but by these ill-behaved young white boys.) When news came of the first Greensboro sit-in, I wrote a lead editorial, thinly disguised as an interpretation, saying that the new tactic marked a significant shift from the courtroom to direct action and would doubtless spread to other cities. (The Montgomery bus boycott of several years earlier formed a precedent, though in its nature it involved *not using* a segregated facility.)

On most mornings, a regular ritual unfolded at eleven o'clock when the first ("bulldog") edition of the paper came up from the press room. Mr. G, after a quick scrutiny, would often walk from his nearby newsroom cubicle into the editorial chamber and offer a comment, complimentary or droll, on the editorials. He declined as a rule to preview them, whether as a matter of principle or because he wished to have plausible deniability when the complaints flowed in: perhaps a bit of both. But on this day, he hurried in, visibly agitated.

"Ed," he said, "this lead editorial on the sit-ins must be yanked. Do we have something to put in its place?"

"No, sir," I said truthfully. "What's the matter, Mr. G?" (I suspected that I knew what the matter was.)

"This ain't nothing," Griffith said, dropping into his *faux-rustique* lingo, "but a bunch of young bucks making trouble for the merchants. They'll be doing it here before long, too. We're making too much of it." In commercial-minded Charlotte, making trouble for merchants was a grave offense; and perhaps in Mr. G's mind, my prediction that the sit-ins had a future might be read here and there as an invitation.

"Why don't we try to fix it?" I suggested. "Can you tell me more specifically what you object to?"

Griffith, never unreasonable, scanned the objectionable editorial again. He paused. "Well," he finally said, "I guess it's not all *that* bad." He suggested minor changes and the editorial ran through all editions, essentially as written. It was hailed by some readers as farsighted and I think Mr. G was not displeased that the *News* had taken a respectably receptive view of the sit-ins. The Greensboro episode did prove to be far more significant than Mr. G's remark about "young bucks making trouble for the merchants" anticipated. It became the harbinger of a spreading movement and led shortly to the organization of Dr. King's Southern Christian Leadership Conference. And as I believe I reminded Mr. G, the *News* claimed in its yearly "platform" statement to believe in equal treatment for all, so long as it was "voluntary." The sit-ins sought voluntary compliance; there was then, as I shall explain, no other recourse.

One of our preoccupying issues—certainly one of mine—was the weird surge in the late 1950s of right-wing conspiracy-theorizing, illustrative of what the historian Richard Hofstadter would call "the paranoid style in American politics." When he coined the phrase, Hofstadter was writing of the Goldwater candidacy of 1964. But by comparison with the stranger conspiracy theorists, the Arizona senator at his farthest stretch (advocating, for instance, the abolishment of Social Security and the Tennessee Valley Authority) was a model of sobriety and historical grasp. The most interesting but sinister-sounding fount of this thinking in the early 1960s was an organization called the John Birch Society, founded by a Massachusetts candy-maker, Robert Welch, originally from eastern North Carolina. The Birch Society claimed multiplying cells everywhere, a genuine underground movement, which struck its detractors as dangerous. Welch had graduated from Chapel Hill at the age of sixteen, and apparently thought of himself as a political genius. I obtained the Birch literature, including its bible, the so-called *Blue Book,* a screed by Welch whose paradoxical theme it was that communist sympathies were heavily distributed in the higher reaches of American society, among those, in effect, born with silver spoons in their mouths. This persistent subtheme of the Red-hunters perhaps owed its origins to the Alger Hiss spy and perjury case of a decade earlier. Hiss, distinguished in government service—he had advised Roosevelt at Yalta and helped design the United Nations—had enjoyed every privilege the nation accorded, including social position—his family was, or had been, in the Baltimore *Social Register*. He had even clerked for the demigod of American jurisprudence, Justice Oliver Wendell Holmes Jr., at the Supreme Court. His accuser, Whittaker Chambers, who "named" Hiss as a member of spy cells in Depression-era Washington, offered a vivid iconic contrast. By then an editor and valued writer at *Time* magazine, Chambers was a rumpled, rather seedy-looking fellow who in his sensational memoir *Witness* made no secret of his former allegiance to the Soviet Union. In this he exemplified a host of former Communists who now made it their business to trumpet the dangers of their former enthusiasm, although Chambers was far more intelligent and charitable than most of this number. Those who believed in Hiss's innocence—as I did for a time, but only for a time—found it hard to imagine that so upstanding a young man as Hiss could be lying and so unprepossessing a man as Chambers could be telling the truth. In a representative moment of their first confrontation before members of the House Un-American Activities Committee, Hiss demanded to see Chambers's teeth. Hiss was beginning to back away from his earlier denials that he had never known Chambers. If, he explained, Chambers was a man he remembered as George Crosley, the identification would be confirmed by Chambers's bad teeth. (It turned out that Chambers had had them fixed.) This was one of many iconic moments in this strange case and it was perhaps this thematic template—another case, perhaps, of Blifil against Black George—that led Welch and the Birchers, by strict logic, to suppose that if Hiss had spied, notwithstanding his good fortune, almost anyone could be a secret Comsymp; and even President Eisenhower was vaguely indicted by Welch as a director-general—witting or not—of the conspiracy. It may have had to do with Eisenhower's insistence, as supreme Allied commander in Europe, on the controversial "broad front" strategy. The failure to throw out long spearheads into eastern Germany and central Europe arguably eased the Russian penetration of those areas and the Soviet capture of Berlin; and there was, of course, Eisenhower's friendship with his Russian counterpart, Marshal Zhukov. Circumstantial evidence!

The complexities of history rarely interfere with the musings of conspiracy theorists, who ignore simple but obvious explanations and stretch for more lurid conclusions by a process of elaborate deduction from flawed premises. For many reasons—callowness was doubtless part of it—I found Welch and his writings outrageous and poured much indignant editorial rhetoric into dissections of the *Blue Book*. I mention this now forgotten matter at length because of a strange sequel, shortly to be described.

Some months after Perry Morgan returned to Charlotte to head up the editorial page, I had a call from Carl Jeffress, publisher of the *Greensboro Daily News*. The third man in the *Daily News* editorial department, Holley Mack Bell, was joining the U.S. Foreign Service and Jeffress wanted to know if I would be interested in replacing him. *Would I ever!* Greensboro, my native city, and the *Daily News* had a special meaning. The *Daily News* had been our family's morning paper throughout my childhood. My notions about editorial writing had been shaped by its graceful, moderate, and literate commentary—a tradition exemplified by such writers as Gerald W. Johnson and William T. Polk and their successors. Its editor, H. W. Kendall, called this tradition the "apostolic succession" and traced its ethos to the legendary first editor, Col. Earle Godbey. The *Daily News* had been founded early in the century as the Greensboro "industrial news," a paper of Fusionist outlook—that is, of Populist/Republican sentiments, progressive as such views went in the Tar Heel politics of that era, following the "redemption" of the state by conservative Democrats. My grandfather, active in Fusionist politics, considered the *Daily News* editorial page the only one in the state worthy of the attention of a serious man; and when the paper was acquired by the Jeffress family in the 1920s, its new publishers made a gentlemen's promise to be "fair" to Republicans. This was not a common practice now that Reconstruction was being steadily mythologized, and denigrated, as a time of black rule, carpetbagger plunder and corruption. Moreover, southern Republicanism of the early twentieth century was light years distant from its later manifestations in the post-1960s South, where the GOP became a catchment for Democrats estranged by the national party's embrace of civil rights. But the *Daily News* did have a remarkable independence of party lines. Some years later, when I was editing its editorial pages, a fellow parishioner at Holy Trinity Church earnestly remarked to me of the paper one Sunday morning: "It's like the German army; you may not like it but you have to respect it." He was pleasantly shocked that the *Daily News* had endorsed the Republican candidate for the U.S. Senate.

The city of Greensboro, with its old Quaker community, thought of itself as "the friendly city," and the boast was not empty. With five colleges, it had a strong academic community that reinforced its urbanity, liberality, and literacy. It was also a city of uncommonly accomplished and learned lawyers; among them, Edward Hudgins, Maj. Lennox Polk McLendon, Hubert Humphrey, McNeill Smith, David M. Clark, and others would become close friends. Henry Wiseman "Slim" Kendall, the editor of the *Daily News,* was a wiry little man looking more like a small-college philosophy professor than a newsman; he couldn't have weighed more than a hundred pounds. He welcomed me to what I quickly sensed was my natural, almost foreordained berth as a young journalist; and that feeling never flagged through fifteen happy years. Slim Kendall's view was that those who wrote for the editorial page should think for themselves—even if, as some claimed, the *Daily News* sometimes seemed to contradict itself, depending on who was editorializing on any given day or subject. My friend John Sanders of Chapel Hill described our editorial policy as "enlightened equivocation." "Think for yourself," Slim Kendall quoted Colonel Godbey's First Commandment, "but try to think sanely." His favorite anecdote about the colonel was that Godbey had once been threatened with a libel suit by a certain mediocre North Carolina politician of whom he had written: "X, who has announced his candidacy for governor, subject to the forthcoming Democratic Primary, is qualified to be elected dog-catcher." A retraction was demanded. The colonel told the newspaper's lawyers that he would not retract. "If I had said that he was *not* qualified to be dog-catcher, then perhaps *that* would be libelous. But I didn't."

Kendall entertained admirable passions and principles from which he never wavered. He considered the treatment of prisoners a gauge of the quality of a civilization. His support of North Carolina's work-release program for state convicts had been influential in shaping it and overcoming natural fears that it might be dangerous; and the program was widely admired and copied around the country. Every morning, Slim advanced to the exchange table just outside our editorial cubicles and scanned the county weeklies in search of misdeeds by local law-enforcement officials, the cardinal offense being the careless handling of drunks and vagrants leading to jail suicides. He was equally passionate about the convenience and safety of the motoring public. His sources in the state highway department and the state patrol were extensive; he knew when the slightest mischief was afoot in Raleigh and nailed it editorially. He adamantly opposed toll roads (there were, in consequence, none in North Carolina). But he reserved his hottest wrath for the "trucking boys," as he called the influential motor-transport lobby, who constantly sought easements on weight limits and truck lengths from the ever-pliable North Carolina General Assembly. The truckers' "hospitality suite" at the Sir Walter Raleigh Hotel, where legislators were plied with strong drink and free meals, was a special object of his scorn. Eventually, years later, the trucking lobby finally prevailed and double trailers, which Slim Kendall had viewed as the end of (highway) civilization, were permitted in North Carolina. But not on his watch.

Slim had other prepossessions. He kept a beady eye on a prominent legislator from eastern North Carolina who as a county prosecutor had once described night-riding Ku Klux Klan hoodlums as "rural pranksters," a phrase Slim neither forgot nor allowed the readers of the *Daily News* to forget. Nor had he forgiven the *Raleigh News & Observer,* or its proprietors, the Daniels family, for trying to chase a distinguished historian, J. Spencer Bassett, out of North Carolina. The episode was many years in the past but still green in his memory. Bassett had written in a *South Atlantic Quarterly* article that Booker T. Washington was "the most distinguished man, saving only General Lee, produced by the South in a hundred years." Josephus Daniels, the old red-shirt Democrat who then owned and edited the Raleigh paper, had initiated a crusade to get Bassett fired. He caused the historian's name to be spelled "bASSett" in *News & Observer* editorials. That Bassett was on the history faculty at Trinity College (later Duke University), Slim's alma mater, compounded the offense. I learned of the lingering intensity of this recollection for Slim Kendall one Saturday morning when I read that the U.S. Navy was, at last, naming a ship—a small one, if I recall—for its least favorite civilian head, Josephus Daniels. (The teetotaling Methodist Daniels, as Woodrow Wilson's secretary of the navy, had dried up the shipboard officers' wardrooms.) Shouldn't we, I asked, congratulate the Daniels family on the honor—say a collegial and congratulatory word? Whether or not Slim actually held his nose, that was his response to my suggestion. I persisted. Finally, he agreed; but our collegial gesture was limited to a word, almost literally—no more than fifty, anyway. It probably set a record for editorial brevity in the *Greensboro Daily News.*

Slim's cordial and graceful associate, Bill Snider, was a fine prose stylist who had served as private secretary to two North Carolina governors. He knew North Carolina's history, political traditions, and customs intimately and had a fund of funny stories about the governors he had served, chiefly Greg Cherry, known as "the iron major." High literacy was not Cherry's forte, and when Bill wrote an elegant address for him to be delivered before the joint University of North Carolina faculties, and including references to the then-popular work of Arnold J. Toynbee, Cherry, who also liked his toddy, misread the historian's name throughout as "Tony-bee." Bill and Slim conducted an authoritative editorial page that was read with attention and respect statewide, at least until the Jeffresses sold the paper to Landmark of Norfolk which soon began to pinch pennies and in the end shrunk the paper over a term of years to near inconsequence, a mere ghost of its former self.

The only irritant, quite minor, was Slim's insistence that all three of us produce, every workday, a stick of "Paragraphics," one-sentence wisecracks or doggerel about the day's news. Slim wrote them with ease, Bill Snider less so. I had no aptitude for them, although I still recall one. A Latin American caudillo named Janio Something had been overthrown and fled the scene of his depredations. My paragraphic read, in its entirety: Janio/Ranio.

I had been lucky enough to arrive at the right place at the right time. Print still reigned, the news was not yet infused with "infotainment," nor would the present din of glib talking heads on television and "talk" radio have been confused with serious commentary. People who had something to say about the passing scene or public issues customarily wrote letters to the editor; and the *Daily News* letters column, "Public Pulse," was widely read. There was one rather silly pratfall, which became a learning experience. In a signed "Tar Heel Talk" column (which each of us wrote once a week), I got on a high horse about some matter now long forgotten. The blunder was my throwaway reference to "Louisa May Alcott's *Uncle Tom's Cabin.*" How it happened I don't know, perhaps because the rhythm of Alcott's name matches that of Harriet Beecher Stowe and journalistm, as I've said, is always written at speed on narrow deadlines. Whole squadrons of elementary school children were recruited by their teachers to write polite letters setting me straight and they arrived by the bushels. Friends teased, far and wide. I was presented by our cartoonist, Bill Sanders, with a framed "Oops Award" in which I was shown under attack by Ms. Stowe with a furled umbrella. The moral, of course, is that if you take a very high and hectoring tone, you'd better double-check your references. For many years my Oops Award hung on the wall of my office as a reminder of the fallibility of commentators.

Soon, there came a last echo of my encounter with Robert Welch and the John Birch Society, both comic and infuriating. Some months after I settled in, Slim Kendall called me into his spacious corner office one morning and shut the door.

"Beg your pardon," he began, "but I have to ask you an awkward question." I wondered what on earth this wise, decent, and considerate man had in mind. "Certainly," I said.

"Did you leave Charlotte on good terms with the *News*? You weren't in any sort of trouble, were you?"

The question stunned me. "No, sir," I said emphatically. Slim pushed an anonymous letter across his desk, saying it was not the first. I read it with astonishment. It said, in so many words, that the unsigned writer thought it vital to warn Slim Kendall that the editorial writer he had recently hired—me, of course—had been "fired from his previous job at the *Charlotte Observer*." Slim knew, of course, that I'd been at the *News*, and he had every reason to believe the letter was a smear. But he wanted to make sure, and also, I suppose, to warn me gently that somebody out there among our readers was no friend. The letter was demonstrably malicious and false and I offered to phone my former boss, Brodie Griffith, who would vouch for my good standing when I left the *News* several months earlier. "Let's forget it," Slim said, ripping the letter to shreds. No more was said of the matter.

One night some weeks later I accompanied my friend John Maurice Evans, who was then teaching English at Woman's College, UNC, to a meeting of the campus History Club. The scheduled speaker was the so-called "area coordinator" of the John Birch Society, a man from High Point named Arthur Lyon. It would be entertaining, we thought, to hear his take on the menace captained by Dwight D. Eisenhower and other agents or dupes of the Comintern; I accepted the invitation with alacrity. The small auditorium in Elliot Hall was jammed with townspeople, faculty, and students, all no doubt expecting to be amused. The area coordinator droned predictably enough about the unfitness of Americans to understand the hideous danger they faced and about how the young hero John Birch, for whom his organization had been named, had died at the hands of the "Chi-coms." He dwelt in clinical detail on the precise number of stab wounds Birch had suffered—such gratuitous and often gruesome details being, in my observation, an earmark of conspiracy theories. The spiel, however, was above all boring and my attention began to wander. But then the area coordinator suddenly said something that caught my attention.

"Incidentally, the chief apologist for the Comsymps in this part of North Carolina is one Ed Yoder, an editorial writer for the *Greensboro Daily News,* who was fired from his previous job at the *Charlotte Observer.*"

I saw red. So this was the source of the rumor Slim Kendall had questioned me about! I shot up from my seat in the back of the room like Banquo's ghost. "I happen to be Ed Yoder," I shouted, "and I happen to know that everything you just said is a lie." Heads swiveled and the meeting soon disintegrated in a murmur of shock. By the time I reached the front of the room, intending to confront this sneaky character assassin, he had fled into the night, his natural medium, I suppose. But at last I could pinpoint the defamation: It was Welch's retaliation for what I had written about him and his "seditious trash," as I had hot-headedly called it in a letter to Welch himself which he took care to copy and circulate. I had been brash; that was my single tactical mistake. After hearing the story, Slim escorted me to the offices of the newspaper's lawyers, where Beverly Moore drafted, and Richard Wharton signed, a stiff letter to the area coordinator putting him on notice that if he repeated the slander legal action would follow. We obtained, and enclosed, a warm letter from Jim Knight, the publisher of the *News,* assuring one and all of the regard in which I had been held at my previous paper. I heard no more of the matter, and little more of the Birch Society. It turned out to be running on empty. In the 1962 California election, soon to follow, none other than Richard Nixon, once Eisenhower's resident expert on the Democratic Party's softness on communism and responsibility for the "loss of China" to Mao Tse-tung—*even Richard Nixon!*—attacked the Birch Society in his campaign for governor. Nixon had for some years exemplified what Adlai Stevenson called "white collar McCarthyism." But in its Birch Society mode, the Red smear, never fair or respectable, had become too loopy to be a useful tactic in the party wars. Nixon, with his seamy past, was accused by his victorious opponent, Pat Brown, of being a Birch Society errand boy and the accusation stung. Too much was too much!

The Birch Society receded from view, but I emerged from this encounter with a lesson yet to learn. In my innocence, I supposed that adherents of conspiracy theories of history were merely misinformed and could be reasoned out of their often bizarre but elaborate views by argument and evidence. But as I now see, paranoid thinking, whether about domestic subversion or invisible gunmen on the grassy knoll in Dallas, is a style and tendency of temperament, a way of perceiving the world that has little to do with argument or evidence as most of us define them. In fact, many of the right-wing conspiracy theories of the late 1950s and early 1960s smacked of a displaced reaction to the intensifying racial crisis. Segregationist rhetoric of the extreme stripe often barely veiled the underlying view (or at least the allegation) that southern black people were very happy in their peonage and with the indignity of "Colored Only" signs in public places, and would have remained placidly submissive but for their manipulation by "outside agitators," themselves suspected of serving communist influence.

Exactly illustrative of this displacement was a piece of legislation suddenly proposed by Jesse Helms (then a Raleigh television commentator) and railroaded without hearings or debate through the General Assembly in the last hours of the 1963 session. Its key provision banned "known communist" speakers from the campuses of state colleges and universities. The so-called Speaker Ban Law's target was Chapel Hill, its unmistakable inspiration the civil rights demonstrations there and in Raleigh, in which substantial numbers of faculty members had enlisted.

As I wrote years later, in a reminiscence of my friend Al Lowenstein, the chronic activist:

> As an instructor at N.C. State in 1963 . . . Lowenstein organized civil rights demonstrations to beard the North Carolina legislature in its den at the Sir Walter Raleigh Hotel. The tippling legislators glared and seethed as Al Lowenstein's young hosts chanted and marched before their doorstep in the warm springs evenings. The good result was that some—a few— accommodations opened their services to blacks; the bad result was that

the legislature passed a mischievous gag law banning "known communist" speakers (of which there were, of course, very few) from state college campuses.

The *Daily News* declared editorial war on the law the morning after its sneak passage and we must have published dozens of editorials and signed columns denouncing it over three or four years. But the challenge of getting it off the books proved harder than we could have foreseen. It stood for three years, somewhat modified by the 1966 legislature, ultimately falling on First Amendment grounds before a declaratory judgment in the federal courts. But not before doing grave damage to the good name of North Carolina and its state university system.

Our experience with civil rights demonstrations in Greensboro was happier. With its large liberal community (and, as some historians would have it, its tradition of civility) the city was a natural target for "open accommodations" demonstrations, as it had been three years earlier for the first dime-store sit-ins. It has been observed that only the civil and generous British, as rulers of India, would have responded in a conciliatory way to Gandhi's *Satagraha,* his passive-resistance movement for Indian independence. Others, even among the more civilized colonial nations, might have greeted it with brutal repression.

In the same way, I felt that something of the same quality of civic responsibility leavened public and official attitudes in my native city to an uncommon degree when the desegregation challenges of the 1960s began; and the *Daily News* played a role in maintaining those attitudes. Every evening throughout the spring and early summer of 1963, Jesse Jackson, then president of the student body at North Carolina A&T, led biracial groups of chanting demonstrators westward up East Market Street to Jefferson Square where the demonstrators sat down for fifteen minutes to make their point. All traffic, of course, stopped. Under the admirably professional Capt. William Jackson, who coordinated the daily protest with the other Jackson, the Greensboro police collaborated in an orderly balletic ritual of petition. Soon, most places of business, if previously segregated (chiefly restaurants and movie theaters), opened their doors on equal terms to all, though there were a few holdouts. As the law then stood, unwelcome customers—even if victims of blatant racial discrimination—could be, and in other places sometimes were, jailed or prosecuted for criminal trespass. Many states and localities had trespass laws tailored for that purpose. It was then believed that the Fourteenth Amendment's Equal Protection Clause, which had been invoked against school segregation, was not intended to prohibit "private action" that was not state imposed or sponsored, although the said trespass laws could not be enforced without the cooperation of local police. And that was nothing if not state action. The problem did not arise in Greensboro, which with the help of enlightened city officials like Mayor David Schenk chose to solve the problem by encouraging the merchants to open closed doors—and this more than a year before Congress, disgusted by the brutalities of Birmingham and Selma, passed the 1964 Civil Rights Act. Under Slim Kendall's temperate direction, *Daily News* editorials supported the open-accommodations movement, while our letters column served as a forum where writers of every view could blow off steam. Our regular correspondents on civil rights issues included a local Quaker pastor who wrote eloquent and interesting letters, cautiously signing himself "the Rev. Anonymous." He told us privately that his congregation was divided and that he felt obliged to treat all his sheep equally. Hence the anonymity. We always insisted on knowing the identity of letter writers, and that they be signed, but there were occasions, as in the Rev. Anonymous's case, when exceptions could be made. As doors began to open in Greensboro, the debate over the federal Civil Rights Bill warmed up, with much national debate over the theoretical threshold at which a small business might still practice racial discrimination without legal molestation—the "Mrs. Murphy's Boarding House" issue, as it came to be called. It was an angels-dancing-on-pinheads debate and it seems another world now. I doubt that even the Mrs. Murphys of small boarding establishments—in significant numbers, anyway—would think today of discriminating by race. The *Daily News* endorsed all ten titles of the Civil Rights Bill, with the exception of Title VII, which empowered federal agencies to withhold funding—a coercive device that might be needed but for which I had, and retain, a lingering distaste.

As I look back on these greenhorn years of the late 1950s and early 1960s, and the nearly forgotten battlegrounds I've described, I feel no regrets. We operated in what some may view as a relative small, even intimate world; but that was part of the charm. It was an educational experience in the broadest sense. Under the tutelage of editors and writers like Cecil Prince, Slim Kendall, and Bill Snider I learned more than journalistic skills; I learned about state and local government, their traditions and personalities; and I learned that political and administrative talent is not infrequently found in inconspicuous places. It was, I now believe, a better way to start out than in the anonymity of metropolitan journalism. For with notable exceptions—my friends David Broder of the *Washington Post* and Robert Novak, the syndicated columnist, for instance—many hotshot New York and Washington journalists (to say nothing of the hot-air artists now so thick in the TV studios) know little of local politics and personalities and underrate the vitality and usefulness of the federal system. In fancy newsrooms and ivory towers federalism is often dismissed as a bothersome anachronism at best, an obscure mystery at worst, of little but obstructive consequence. I learned better at the feet of my mentors and, I believe, became a better journalist for it.

STAR WARS

Sleepwalking into Washington *Washington is today regarded, I suppose, as a mecca for journalists. That was true even half a century ago. I almost went there when I was starting out, in 1959. Alfred Friendly, then managing editor of the* Washington Post, *offered me an attractive deal. I would join the metro staff. Then, after a year, if the experiment worked out, I would have my choice between the national staff—covering some aspect of federal government—and the editorial page, where the genial Robert Estabrook presided. He also had agreed to the plan. I accepted the offer and prepared to move. Then, to Friendly's indignation, I changed my mind for a variety of reasons and lingered in North Carolina, which he had called "the best newspaper state." I never regretted my second thoughts (it certainly was good for my tennis game) and it would be another decade and a half and more before I finally said yes to a Washington newspaper proposition. Even then, I did so reluctantly. My decision crystalized only when my old friend Robert Mason, then editor of the* Virginian Pilot *in Norfolk, told me I would be a "damned fool" to refuse Jim Bellows's offer. He was right. Even so, I had no idea what complexities awaited me, sleepwalker that I am and always have been in such decisions.*

Which raises an interesting question of Destiny. Some lives seem to be well planned along predictable lines almost from the cradle. Mine, in this as in other adventures described in this book, has been a marvel of randomness and sudden good fortune. My guardian angel has been kind to me. The "complexities" I mention above had to do, as the following chapter indicates, with the way in which human quirks of character and temperament affect the fortunes of great institutions. Indeed, for the writer who would understand American journalism at its loftier elevations, that is perhaps the most valuable lesson of all; and I learned it the hard way.

My six-year adventure at the *Washington Star*—the "falling Star," as wags liked to call it—began with a phone call. One day in March 1975 George Will called. "How would you like to be rich and famous?" he asked.

My response was that if either had been a professional priority, I would not be a newspaper editor in Greensboro, North Carolina. "A fellow named Allbritton has come to Washington," George explained. "He is buying the *Star* and looking for an editorial-page editor. I'm not leaving my basement. I recommended you. You are opposed to busing little children, aren't you?"

I had read about Joe Allbritton, a Texas banker and specialist at the rescue of failing enterprises, who proposed to take over the fragile *Star,* the capital's oldest surviving newspaper. It had been around since 1852, dominant in the city most of those years; but self-appointed experts on newspaper economics were making book that its days were numbered. Allbritton had certified to the Federal Communications Commission (which had to approve his takeover, since the Star Company owned television licenses as well as a newspaper) that he was worth at least one hundred million dollars (which Texans, I am told, refer to as a "unit"). That was all I knew about Joe, but I would soon learn a lot more. If my friend George Will had added—or known—that my duties would include those of priest and counselor, hand-holder and adviser, and even amateur confessor, I am not sure I would have responded as I did. But I would have missed a rich experience if I hadn't.

The *Star* building was a gloomy place, set improbably in the slums of southeast Washington, south of Capitol Hill: an outsized gray building, covering most of a city block, and reflecting the expansive, not to say megalomanic, ambitions of its establishmentarian owners, the Kaufman, Noyes, and Adams families. They had built this new plant in the 1950s, before the *Star*'s financial troubles began. To one side stood a shabby liquor store; to the other, penniless slum kids swarmed, waiting to be hired by the newspaper deliverymen. Card and dice games were always in progress between editions, and in this very place, I was told, a black newspaper handler had been shot dead in a gambling quarrel only a few weeks earlier. To the east and south, all the way down to the Washington Navy Yard, spread streets of dispiriting, decaying housing projects: monuments to the unrewarded optimism of "urban renewal." In some ways, things were as gray inside.

Jim Bellows, the genial and brilliant editor, took me to meet Allbritton for the first time one blustery March day. In the Montpelier room of the Madison Hotel, a pricy watering place for lobbyists and lawyers across from the *Washington Post* building, waited a short, round-faced man, not much over five feet tall. His full face had a boyish freshness about it. Allbritton extended his hand. "Your name was . . . ?" he asked. I wondered if this were a joke. "Yoder," I announced, "Ed Yoder."

Allbritton had come to the *Star* by a set of curious chances. He had been the main money-raiser for Ed Muskie's presidential campaign in 1972, his first venture into national politics. Three years later, when the owning families of the *Star* sought new blood, they heard of Joe through their adviser Clifford Folger and James Reston of the *New York Times*. Allbritton, a son of small-town Mississippi, had made a fortune reversing the fortunes of money-losing corporations. Still at heart a country boy from a tiny Mississippi hamlet, he had felt the allure and romance of Washington. Joe posed as a sort of Daddy Warbucks figure, constantly coming and going in his private jet. One day he would be in London visiting banking friends in the City, the next in Kentucky buying racehorses, the next in La Jolla, California, resting (if he ever rested) for the next project. He ran on nervous energy, and the telephone was almost an extension of his arm.

We liked and understood one another instantly, as southerners in exile sometimes will. I had just turned forty; the pay was good; and my children were approaching the age of serious educational expenses. It seemed a good time for a midlife transition. I liked the excitement and sense of adventure Joe radiated, his gambler's instinct.

From its high-cotton days in the 1950s, when the proprietors had designed a printing plant—overambitiously—for a circulation of millions, the *Star* had, in twenty years, sunk into chronic deficit. It was beset by the same marasmus that afflicted afternoon newspapers nearly everywhere, great and small, famous and obscure: television, auto commuting, cocktail parties, the turning of the nation's work force from industrial to service jobs. The old management had made its mistakes, as well. The top editorial and business-side jobs were monopolized by the owning families. Only one "outsider," Benjamin McKelway, had become editor of the paper in more than a century. One ancient general manager, a member of the Kaufman family, gained an unfortunate reputation for anti-Semitism, and had alienated major advertisers. The situation was worsened by the fact that he was stone deaf. At board meetings, an aide had to sit beside him writing the proceedings on a slate.

Joe Allbritton had a desperate fight on his hands. His plan was to use proceeds from the television station to see the *Star* through the advertising dearth while he modernized and rebuilt it with Bellows's expert help. But that was contingent on the agreement of the FCC, which had just promulgated a decree against so-called "cross-ownership" of major media properties in the same market. Joe sought a waiver of that rule and should have had it. But the FCC preferred to dither in its doctrinaire folly, and its dithering helped to dig the *Star*'s grave.

As for Bellows, the editor, I was fascinated to discover that unlike most newspapermen I knew he was not a political animal. "If you believed the papers," he liked to say, "you would think life is politics." Essentially, Bellows was a man of style and intuition and, like Allbritton, an authentic genius. What he wanted on the editorial page was reflected in Pat Oliphant's brilliant, iconoclastic, naughty, and sometimes bigoted cartoons. He wanted journalistic handsprings that people would sit up and notice. Their political tendency—except for certain topics like women's rights—were a matter of relative indifference to him. Sprightliness, he thought, was the only high card the *Star* could play in trying to overcome the *Post*'s huge lead in the race for survival. And there was another thing—the *Star* must shake its unfortunate reputation for being Richard Nixon's patsy. Jim Bellows's obsession with that was to be a source of friction between him and Allbritton. What really delighted Bellows was anything fresh and unorthodox. The editorial he really raved about was one I knocked out for fun in about ten minutes on Hubert Hamphrey's decision not to run for president in 1976, written in mock–King James Bible English. "Save this one for the Pulitzer file," he scribbled on it.

Around town, there was immense curiosity about the Allbritton-Bellows plans, and hence about my views. Arthur White, a *Time* correspondent in Washington, had phoned me in Greensboro to try to get a fix on my politics. He and some bilious ultraconservatives seemed to believe it was the *Star*'s natural role to be conventionally reactionary. I had small interest in and less commitment to any ideology, and neither did Bellows or Allbritton. In their standard forms, then as now, ideologies seemed to me predictable, shallow, jejune, and unhistorical—and irrelevant besides. I told Arthur White that I was an Adlai Stevenson conservative and a Sam Ervin liberal. He probably thought it was a put-on, but it was true. The formula did not satisfy him. He continued to press me in prolonged phone calls. His sources told him that I was actually a—gasp—"southern liberal"! I pleaded with him for nearly an hour one night not to use that term in the magazine, inasmuch as Joe deserved not to have his new editorial-page editor pigeonholed. Our job, I knew, was to create credible contrast between the *Star* and the *Post,* but not at the expense of strain or abandonment of principle.

* * *

Late on the night of October 1, 1975, a few weeks after my arrival, striking press operators at the *Post* burned its presses, severely crippling our powerful rival. It limped along, a shadow of itself, printed, I believe, in Winchester, Virginia, on the presses of Sen. Harry Byrd Jr. Katharine Graham immediately appealed to Joe Allbritton's sense of chivalry, to the spirit of the unofficial club of beleaguered publishers. She insisted that Joe owed it to American journalism and civilization to print the *Post* on the *Star*'s presses. There was, as she knew, plenty of capacity there. Joe balked. And, according to reports that quickly got around Washington, Kay Graham grew very angry. "Standing on this very doorstep," Joe told me one night soon afterward—the Allbrittons had leased the handsome John Sherman Cooper townhouse in Georgetown—"she told me, 'Joe, I ran Richard Nixon out of town, and I can do the same to you.'"

Whether she had used those very words I have no idea, but Joe persuaded himself that she had. Joe's view of the *Star*'s dilemma was faintly tinged with paranoia, at least as I saw it. He believed the *Post* was actively working to finish the *Star* off. I was confident that its better spirits, including Kay Graham, realized that the *Post* would be hurt if the *Star* closed. Joe accused me of naïveté. "Mr. Yoder," he would say, "You have led a sheltered life." That happened to be true enough.

Joe, of course, had practical reasons for refusing to print the *Post*. There was no agreement, as there had been during the New York newspaper strike, to collaborate in resisting union demands. None had been suggested. Some of the striking pressmen worked at both papers; they might sabotage the *Star*'s presses also. *The Post* could survive a shutdown. The *Star* couldn't. Yet when word got around that Joe would not help Mrs. Graham, the journalistic establishment rallied to her side. Joe Allbritton, it was said, was a new boy among publishers who didn't understand the unwritten rules of the club. Joe was stung, but he cloaked his resentment in flippancy. He would "weep about it all the way to the bank," and there was even some brave talk that this might be the great turning point. As in the mid-1950s, there would be a reversal of the economic positions of the two papers. For Joe, and for the rest of us, the worst blow was a stinging column in the *New York Times* by Scotty Reston, perhaps the most prestigious father-figure in American journalism. "Burn, Baby, Burn," it was called; and Reston came near accusing Joe of treason to the trade. "The *Post*," he wrote, in what was clearly an echo of Mrs. Graham's view, "felt that the *Star* played the role of the fearful bystander." Joe's dilemma, then, was whether to "come out against the sabotage . . . or concentrate on his own immediate interest." Not a very pleasant choice for a man like Allbritton with a southerner's sense of honor.

The Reston column, with its intimation that the *Star*'s new management condoned sabotage, stirred us all. We had to spike the insulting insinuation that we at the *Star* found press fires an unacceptable weapon of union pressure. I was designated to write an editorial, which we called "Trouble at the *Post*." The caption was bland, but it was no doubt examined in every newspaper front office in the land. "The *Star*," we said, stating the obvious, "takes no satisfaction in the *Post*'s difficulties." (This was true in a way but perhaps only about 80 percent true.) "The journalistic community of this city is at one on the basic issues— and above all on the quite fundamental issue of violence, vandalism and arson. . . . Violence is not collective bargaining; it is a travesty of it." High, sanctimonious, sonorous words. I am not sure they were believed, but they had to be said. The *Post* soon broke the strike and soon retrieved the lion's share of the advertising.

Joe had promised that the *Star*'s editorial policy would be mine to set. He would, though very rarely, suggest a subject for editorializing. But he kept a friendly distance. Still, there was one colossal exception to the hands-off rule; and the story became, for a time, a subject of intense speculation in Washington newspaper circles.

It began on the July Fourth bicentennial weekend in 1976. The Allbrittons gave a hotdog roast in their rear garden on N Street. Their guests milled about, admiring a gigantic tomato plant their son Robert had grown. Joe took Jim Bellows aside. Would he please keep a space open on the front page for Monday week? Bellows asked why. "I'm not going to tell you," Joe said with a laugh. "You would try to talk me out of it." Jim reported the exchange to me at the office. I knew nothing of Joe's plan.

No more was heard of the matter for about a week. Then all hell broke loose. Bellows called me at 7 A.M. on a Monday. His voice was agitated. Joe, he said, had sent an "editorial" via his aide Steve Richard, with instructions that it be printed on the front page that day. The editorial called for the renomination of Gerald Ford, who was under heavy challenge from Ronald Reagan. Jim had learned of the piece when the night editor called him at 5 A.M. He had immediately countermanded Joe's order. Joe had then fired the night editor for insubordination. A nasty confrontation was brewing.

The issue in Jim Bellows's mind—as in mine—was one of professionalism, not substance. Neither of us had read the editorial. It was, however, most irregular—unheard of, in fact—for a publisher to railroad an editorial onto the front page, of all places, without consulting his editors.

The atmosphere in the halls of the *Star* building was that of an armed camp. Joe, it appeared, viewed Bellows's balkiness as insubordinate, an outrageous obstruction of his proprietary right to say whatever he wanted, whenever he wanted to say it, in his own newspaper. Joe, a novice in publishing, was a quick study indeed. But he was better acquainted with the hierarchy one finds in banks and law firms. The story, moreover, hit Bellows at one of his fracture points. He worried that the *Star* had been over-credulous about Nixon and Watergate; he was eager to distance the paper from its historic flavor of Republicanism. And quite apart from the irregular procedure, this editorial seriously threatened the strategy.

In origins, the project had much to do with Joe's Houston connections. Jim Baker (later the first George Bush's secretary of state, at the time Gerald Ford's delegate recruiter for Kansas City) was working furiously to stave off the Reagan challenge. Reagan's unexpected victory in the North Carolina primary had revived a campaign that seemed nearly finished, and now the race had turned tight. Reagan had found a rollicking issue in the Panama Canal treaty negotiations; he had raised the "giveaway" cry to great effect. Meanwhile, Joe had grown to like Ford. He and his wife Barbie, along with the Rockefellers, had been guests of the president to watch the July Fourth bicentennial fireworks from the Truman balcony. It was then and there, Joe later said, that he had felt what a tragedy it would be if Ford lost. Now, with the derailment of his editorial, the tension in the *Star* building thickened.

On Tuesday morning, the day after Bellows had kept the editorial out of the paper, Joe's faithful dogsbody Steve Richard, an easy-going Louisiana Cajun, sauntered into my office. Joe was absolutely beside himself, he said. "One little thing, just one little thing, and he might just close this newspaper down." I swallowed hard, hoping he exaggerated.

What did he mean, "one little thing," I asked in what was probably a tight voice. Oh, said Richard, for instance some gaffe in the way the paper covered Queen Elizabeth's bicentennial visit, then in progress. Joe was on the dinner list at the British embassy. He did not want to be embarrassed.

The editorial that had by now caused such an uproar was lively but amateurish. It was rumored to be a committee product, the result of a collaboration among Joe, Steve, and Harry McPherson, the former LBJ aide and speechwriter, who was Joe's friend and did the *Star*'s legal work. Harry McPherson was and is a superb writer, and the piece didn't seem quite up to his rhetorical standards. It opened with a marvelous J. Frank Dobie story from Texas: "Many years ago . . . a railroad decided to dispose of two antiquated engines by a more dramatic method. . . . It advertised that on a certain summer day, on a plain in Texas, it would start the engines rolling toward one another from a distance of several miles, and let physics take its course. . . . A town sprang up near the track—named, with Western simplicity, Crush, Texas." Kansas City, the piece continued, could be the site of a similarly ruinous collision between Ford and Reagan, a "colossal crunch," in which the GOP would be too shattered to make an effective fight in November. It would be Goldwater and 1964 all over again. Ford had earned the nomination; Reagan should yield gracefully.

The irony, of course, was that at the moment two locomotives called Allbritton and Bellows were speeding toward a crushing collision over an editor-publisher misunderstanding. The further irony was that there was nothing in the proposed editorial with which Bellows or I disagreed. The *Star* had been saying much the same things, and its distaste for Reagan was no secret. The problem was that Joe did not appreciate the procedural punctilio of his balking editors.

By Wednesday, the clouds were even darker and lower. I called Berl Bernhard, Harry McPherson's law partner and a polished Allbritton handler, and urged him to intervene. It was time for mediation. Berl, I am glad to recall, succeeded. At about eight o'clock that evening Berl called to say that there would be a meeting at Joe's house. Within minutes, I was rushing to the house on N Street, wondering what came next. As I walked in, it was a relief to find that the mood was friendly and relaxed. We met—Joe, Jim Bellows, Berl, Steve Richard, and I—in the library of the Cooper house, a high-ceilinged room, eggshell blue, lined with books, overlooking the garden where the first chapter of this strange episode had unfolded a week or so earlier.

Joe opened the discussion. "Ed," he said, "I didn't want to bother you about this editorial. The editorial page isn't under my jurisdiction." Bellows interrupted. "Joe, everything is under your jurisdiction. This isn't a jurisdictional issue. It's an issue of procedure." Joe seemed puzzled. He looked at me. What did I think?

I told him there was no disagreement on the Reagan-Ford nomination issue itself; no one wanted Reagan nominated. It was his prerogative, moreover, to set endorsement policy; everyone agreed that was traditionally the right of a publisher. But editors needed and expected consultation. They were entitled not to be surprised. And a front-page editorial carried heavy connotations. "Joe, it's the nuclear weapon of editorial journalism," I said. In addition, a newspaper's intervention in a heavy party-nomination fight was unusual, if not unheard of. Some would think it implied a commitment to support Ford in the fall. And there was the risk that Ford would blow it. Was it wise for the *Star,* in its fragile state, to bet all the marbles on Ford?" "It would be like lending half the capital of your bank to an unreliable borrower."

Joe laughed; our hearts rose. "Now you're talking my language," he said and agreed the front page was probably the wrong place for the editorial. That left only the question of whether we should print it at all. Berl was for it, perhaps because he sensed that Joe wanted it printed. Joe spoke with fervor about Ronald Reagan. He had seen an appalling speech by Reagan, he said, and if he were nominated there might be another landslide like the Goldwater debacle twelve years earlier. In the end, we went ahead. I rewrote the editorial, keeping the story of the Crush, Texas, locomotive collision in the lead.

A few days later, Joe summoned me to his office. He showed me a graceful little thank-you note from the president of the United States. When Ford squeaked through at Kansas City, some of his supporters seemed to believe that the *Star*'s editorial had turned the trick, a myth that in any case did no damage to the *Star.* Joe was treated with elaborate courtesy, assigned quarters at the Crown Center hotel on the same corridor as the president's party. Joe hired a fire-engine-red Mercedes stretch limousine and threw a big party. Then he flew off to Kentucky to buy race horses, pressing me to keep the red limousine and move from my shabby hotel across town to the vacant quarters at the Crown Center for the remainder of the convention. I told him it would ruin my reputation as a serious journalist and refused. I wish I hadn't.

II

The most harrowing crisis, however, broke with little warning in February 1977. At 5:30 one Monday morning, Joe called the night desk from Los Angeles. He directed that his name be removed, immediately, from the *Star*'s masthead. As in all the *Star* crises, the local Washington television crews soon took up their vigil, like scavenger birds, at the *Star* building's front entrance. Soon, the *Post,* the *New York Times,* and other papers were humming with speculation, some of it malicious or silly or both. It was the beginning of two weeks of odd and unwelcome publicity.

In a *Washington Post* story by Steven Klaidman and Douglas Watson on February 11, the usual shopworn rumors were rehearsed: Joe was preparing to sell the *Star* to the right-wing Michigan publisher John McGoff, who had tried to buy it earlier. Or he was trying to "frighten" the labor unions, with whom contracts were now being renegotiated. The McGoff rumor was a perennial horror story. McGoff's primary foreign-policy enthusiasm was said to be the Afrikaner nationalist regime in South Africa. So far as I know, there was no truth in the rumor. Mary McGrory, who seemed to have inside information, was quoted as saying that Joe wanted to make himself chairman of the board, not publisher, because he viewed his role as "financial."

When Joe returned from the West Coast, I gingerly suggested—with Jim Bellows's approval—that he finesse the rumors by making a joke of the masthead matter. I even drafted a jocular news release. Joe did not act, but he sent word that if his name went back on the masthead it would be as CEO, chief executive officer, a familiar title in banking and business but entirely strange to journalism. I suggested a memorandum. It had to do with the traditional relationships of publishers to their newspapers. I went back to the Hearst-Pulitzer days and ended up recommending a model out of Walter Bagehot's famous book on the English constitution. A publisher, I suggested, works a bit like a constitutional monarch, with the right to be notified and to warn. It was an elaborate project. I sent it to Joe, but there was no answer, written or otherwise. Months later, I asked him one day whether it had been helpful. "Not very," he said.

Now, however, Joe was in a worried and stormy mood; and with each of these reversals, as in the Ford editorial episode, he was, as I think about it now, probably storing up what he saw as well-warranted frustration. He must have viewed himself as a savior balked at every turn by obtuse, ungrateful, nit-picking editors; a prophet without honor at his own newspaper. His mood was further exacerbated by what he thought of as a slight at the annual Gridiron Club dinner. One day during this unsettling period, Bert Lance, Jimmy Carter's (briefly) all-powerful director of the Office of Management and Budget, came to lunch. He was talking about some issue that had nothing to do with the *Star*. "If any subordinates gave me that kind of trouble, I'd fire them." Joe nodded vigorously at this endorsement of the managerial guillotine. Bellows, Mary McGrory, and I exchanged nervous glances.

Mary—who had recently won a Pulitzer Prize and was at the top of her form—was the *Star*'s premier personality; everyone deferred to her, including Joe. Her loyalty to the paper and her strong-mindedness were unimpeachable. Not long after arriving, I heard a trademark McGrory anecdote. Richard Nixon had come for lunch and was doing a walk-through of the newsroom, shaking hands here and there. All work had ceased in deference to the president of the United States. But there was one exception. In the distance, from Mary's small cubicle in the northeast corner of the newsroom, a typewriter could be heard defiantly clacking away—an audible earnest of her refusal to be drawn into phony cordiality with a president she held in contempt, who had put her on his infamous "enemies list." When in late 1974 rumors spread that Joe's early talks with the owning families were collapsing and soon might leave the ailing paper without its Texas rescuer, Mary had written Joe: "Say it ain't so, Joe." He had responded: "It ain't so. Joe." It was a clever exchange between two very verbal people who liked one another. Brilliant, funny, caustic, Mary divided the world between cops and robbers, morality and immorality. How this schematic view of the world flowed from her subtle mind and wit was not always apparent. Mary was Mary, *sui generis*. During the February crisis, as often before, we were driven into confederacy, both liking Joe and enjoying his confidence. I liked her taste for good-natured conspiracy. I became, in the code we employed, "Light Horse" (sometimes "Lightfoot"), since she pictured me as a recalcitrant Confederate. She was "Stonewall." When the crisis finally lifted, at least for a while, it was at a carefully staged lasagna luncheon at Mary's, where Joe was drawn into group singing of the familiar Baptist hymns he liked.

For reasons that had perhaps been inevitable all along, Joe and Jim Bellows soon came to a parting of ways. Jim went off to Los Angeles to try his hand with another failing newspaper, the *Herald-Examiner,* and Joe was now the undisputed driver of the *Star*'s creaky machine. He clearly relished the sensation; his mood brightened immeasurably. A few days after Jim's departure, Joe summoned Jim Smith, the business manager, Sid Epstein, the managing editor, and me to his office. The three of us sat down in this make-believe-English drawing-room office. After brief pleasantries, Joe tossed out a bombshell. "Gentlemen," he announced, "unless you object I propose to name myself editor and publisher—at least for the interim."

There was an awkward silence. I finally suggested, swallowing hard, that maybe Joe ought to think that one over. I asked if I could send him yet another of my many memoranda. I once again found myself offering advice which probably seemed to Joe impertinent. But he never refused it.

I laid it on the line: "Anyone who advises you that the editor's title is something to be put on like a hat is giving you unsound advice. . . . In my view you need a professional editor at the *Star.* . . . Owners of newspapers who assume the editor's title were and are regarded within the trade as whimsical eccentrics and amateurs. Indeed, their papers were often regarded . . . as the toys of rich men (or women) and their weight and influence discounted accordingly. . . . A second major problem lies in the combination of the two titles . . . [which] may imply an unsavory merger, as well, of business and advertising affairs with news and editorial comment. If you wish to run a serious and reputable newspaper, as I am confident you do, this is a confusion to be avoided absolutely."

I have no idea how Joe reacted to this blunt advice, but being counseled not to do what one longs to do is never pleasant. Joe's actions constituted the only answer I got. He did not go through with the plan, even temporarily. There was no sign of strain, however. As December passed and the new year came, we settled into a working routine that seemed smoother than ever. He delegated control of the editorial pages and policy to me, and most of what I heard from him, when he was in town, was friendly badinage about Thomas Jefferson. I had a print of the "lost" Stuart portrait on my office wall. Joe affected to be anti-Jefferson, a partisan of Hamilton and Burr. He loved to laugh about the pendulum on the clock at Monticello that was too long and had to be recessed into the basement through a hole in the floor. For Joe, that summed Jefferson up.

Only once in this period did Joe get really hot about an issue. One day, just back from a New York meeting, he sent word that I was to see him immediately in the *Star* dining room, where Joe and his son Robert were sitting for a formal portrait.

"What are we saying about the B-1 bomber?" he asked when I dashed in, looking sidelong at me without turning his head. (Jimmy Carter had just announced that he was cancelling production of the new air force plane.) "We have said the president is right," I responded, wondering if the view would be ridiculed as Jeffersonianism run wild. Instead Joe beamed. "Splendid!" he cried. I later learned the story. At a New York board meeting that morning he alone had defended Carter's decision. The boardroom fat cats had heaped abuse on Carter, disgusting Joe and rousing him to the president's defense (though he had no personal use for Carter at all). It was a lucky coincidence that I had not embarrassed him.

Or was it? Beneath the veneer of Texas opulence and English taste (in art and horses and friends) a vestige of Joe's boyhood Mississippi populism lingered. As a very rich man from Houston he was often relegated to the pigeonholes reserved by media stereotypes for Texas millionaires. Indeed, during the February crisis of a year earlier I had been astonished to read one day in a national newspaper that Joe was upset and acting funny because he was outraged by the *Star*'s insults to big oil and gas.

The facts, as I well knew, were ludicrously to the contrary. In Texas, Joe had been asked by the state assembly to chair a three-man state commission, whose job it was to break a momentous impasse. The three were to decide whether a new, very expensive offshore oil tanker terminal in the Gulf would be a public facility, financed with bonds, or a private one, financed by a consortium of oil majors. Joe had cast the deciding vote for a public facility. But big oil had had the clout to persuade the legislators to overrule its own commission. That and other Texas power plays by big oil had left Joe with a bad feeling about imperial oil. He had no use for oil barons.

In fact, the irony was that his editorial-page editor—which is to say I—was distinctly more sympathetic to the oil companies than he was, and that sympathy was occasionally reflected in *Star* editorials. One day after an editorial had appeared on some then-current energy issue, in which the oil majors had been mentioned at least dispassionately, Steve Richard came by my office. "What are we doing in bed with the oil companies?" he asked. I hadn't thought of it that way. It was then that I learned the story of the off-shore terminal commission.

On February 2, 1978, hinting that big events were afoot, Joe flew off to New York for a meeting. Later that afternoon his secretary, Virginia Church, called. She urged me to stick around the office, because Joe would have important and exciting news. Maybe I should have read the signs, in retrospect so clear, that a sale of the *Star* was in the wind. But I hadn't. I was as surprised as everyone else when George Beveridge, the assistant managing editor and ombudsman, called about 7:30 to say that Joe had sold the *Star* to Time, Inc. *Time,* it turned out, had had an eye on the paper for a long time. The Post Company's *Newsweek* was *Time* magazine's main competitor. The *Post* had a highly visible presence in the capital. *Time* longed to raise its banner there too. Soon, the *Star* had a new cast of managers, and Joe was gone.

To this day, Joe Allbritton and I remain cordial friends. But Joe spends most of his time in banking. And while he still owns television and newspaper properties, I have the impression that he stays out of daily management. We meet for lunch or at parties from time to time, but we have never discussed the exciting days at the *Star*. I have no idea how the events I have recounted looked from his perspective. I am inclined now to think that he minimized the difficulties and exaggerated the rewards and satisfactions of being a Washington newspaper publisher. Maybe he had in the back of his mind a picture a bit too much out of *Citizen Kane,* though of course without the ruthlessness and irresponsibility. Like many other occupations, newspaper publishing has undergone the managerial revolution.

As for the great Ford editorial flap, which may have been the experience that tipped Joe against newspaper publishing, consider the ironies. Gerald Ford, with whatever nudge of help from our support, won the

Republican nomination—narrowly—at Kansas City but lost the election—again, narrowly—to Jimmy Carter. Carter, despite some impressive accomplishments, never learned how to be presidential and in 1980 lost the presidency to Reagan: the *bête noire* we had so much feared four years earlier. There was no repeat of the Goldwater debacle, no decimation of the Republican Party. It is, looking back, a lesson in modesty for those of us who deal in the writing and merchandising of opinion. When I feel myself tempted by the illusion of infallibility, I think of those far-off exciting days and laugh.

III

One day in late April 1978, Sid Epstein, George Hoyt, and I were summoned to New York for a 3 P.M. meeting. The flight, by private jet with private bar and fruit basket, was quick and pleasant. At the Time-Life building, all the brass had assembled—Henry Grunwald, Hedley Donovan, Jim Shepley, and Andrew Heiskell. They had an announcement. Murray Gart, a corporate editor and former chief of correspondents, would be named editor of the *Star* "next week."

Sid Epstein and I burst into disconcerting laughter. Our hosts looked startled. We quickly explained that if the decision had been made it had better be published the next day in the *Star*—unless they wanted to read the news first in the *Washington Post*. No journalistic secret could be kept for days in Washington. As I walked into the *Star* building later that evening, I met Barbara Cohen, the national editor. She had seen us scurrying out of the doors after lunch. "So what's the deal?" Barbara asked. "Let me guess. Murray Gart's going to be editor." I could only smile awkwardly as the elevator doors closed between us.

Gart, whom I had met, was trim with a hint of portliness, black-haired, and dark-eyed. He wore glasses with heavy black rims and the standard-issue blue *Time* executive's suit. As I soon learned, he also had vociferous detractors at *Time*.

His principal problem, apparently, was a gift for borrowing trouble. It started with a redecoration project. In place of the almost barren look of the Bellows era, workmen were soon laying new carpets in the editor's office, installing chintzy chairs and sofas, and fixing a colossal world map on the east wall. It seemed a kind of imperial statement. The desk itself was a door-sized marble slab. Gart told me it had belonged to Luce, and that Luce had used it to "carve up editors." Soon the hall door that Bellows had kept open was always closed, and subeditors needed an appointment. It did not escape notice that Gart also had a chauffeured car, unusual for an editor.

When regimes change, editorial-page editors are in an exposed position. Gart soon signaled that he intended to take a hand in the editorial routine. A few days after he settled in, he sent for me to make an editorial suggestion. We should support Andy Young's view that "disinvestment" was not a wise U.S. policy in South Africa. I agreed and wrote the piece. But the timing was dubious. Not long before, Steve Biko had been murdered in police custody, and it seemed the Boer government was bent on a blindly suicidal policy. It was a strange time to editorialize against disinvestment. But Murray was given to occasional impulses. He tended to miss the irony of some of his enthusiasms. One day as he and I were being driven back from lunch downtown, Murray volunteered that he had recently asked the mayor of Washington why the city could not be a "model city" for the nation. I thought there was a grim answer to the question in the wasteland that surrounded the *Star* building. But I said nothing.

Murray was a hard man to top on any subject. One day at the 10 A.M. editorial conference which he had instituted, I made an indiscreet allusion to my friendship with Justice Lewis Powell of the Supreme Court. He immediately said, "I'll have to check that [we were discussing some judicial point] with my friend Potter Stewart." Across the table, Jonathan Yardley suppressed a grin.

All this was trivial enough. What soon began to get on everyone's nerves was Murray's tinkering with copy. He was a good copy editor, but he tended to get to the editorial page after hours, often necessitating changes in the makeup. It was routine to get an anguished call from Jeffrey Frank, who handled those chores. Murray would have changed something, and asked Jeff to get my approval. It was no doubt the leftover newsmagazine habit. *Time* was notorious as an editor's playground and a writer's nightmare, where reporting from the field tended to be mangled by editorial tinkering and political adjustment on the way into the magazine. Murray seemed to be importing an impulse for boiling the personality and spontaneity out of the copy, when my own idea was to allow divergences of taste and view for the sake of encouraging the flavor of personality and idiosyncrasy.

Among Murray's policy interests, two were especially keen—the Middle East and Jimmy Carter's performance in the White House. "We ought to toss our hats in the air," he would occasionally say of some Carter move—at that stage he was enthusiastic about the former governor of Georgia. We clearly differed about the function of editorials. Murray wanted the *Star* to paint boldly, with a broad brush, in dramatic strokes. I preferred tatting for most purposes. Sweeping declarations are traps, often leading directly to the inconsistencies that make editorial policies look whimsical.

A typical Gart project was to be an editorial campaign for Warren E. Burger's resignation as chief justice. Burger had now served for a decade, said Murray, and we should tell him he'd had his day. Burger, a hearty, not overqualified jurist, was not among my favorite figures. His long suit was bonhomie, and around the Supreme Court the view was that he was a bit out of his depth. But the arbitrary ten-year milestone was hardly an occasion for a resignation crusade; most Supreme Court justices, if not all, serve as long as their health lasts, and some have served into their dotages. The most likely result of a call for Burger's resignation would be to delay his departure, if one were intended. Murray persisted. He asked our excellent Supreme Court reporter, Lyle Deniston, to draft a piece. Lyle's piece turned out to be providential, for in trying to give body to the idea even Lyle came up empty-handed. His failure really confirmed the whimsicality of the idea. The enthusiasm passed.

Murray's great enthusiasm was the Middle East. He wanted the *Star* to line up behind an "entity" or "homeland" for the Palestinian Arabs, a project that left me cold. Murray could barely contain his dislike of Menachem Begin, Israel's prime minister. Begin, to be sure, was an acquired taste; but I had acquired it. At Begin's accession, a year or so earlier, *Time* had described his name as "rhyming with 'Fagin'" and the pun had caused an uproar. Many readers considered it slyly anti-Semitic, and I was afraid that *Time*'s anti-Israel tone would rub off, by association, on the *Star,* which had always been sympathetic to Israel. But Murray pressed. Soon after he arrived he gave me a copy of what he called the "*Time* Plan" for a Middle East settlement. He had helped to shape it, he said, and he spoke of it as reverently as if it had been a state paper as important as the Balfour Declaration. In the typical mixmaster English of Timese, this "plan" examined the Palestinian dilemma at a low level of subtlety. Among Israel's friends in Washington, it was regarded as a nonstarter. I feared the issue would bring Gart and me to an early showdown. But we were saved by Anwar Sadat. In Sadat's bold initiative, and the Camp David meetings, we found common ground. It allowed us to detour around the larger questions on which we were sure to differ.

In other areas, however, petty tiffs continued. I thought of myself as an accommodating fellow, but I did not respond well to close supervision. Not since I had worked as a very junior editorialist of twenty-four under Brodie Griffith at the *Charlotte News,* and we had wrangled over the significance of the early civil rights sit-ins, had I had to work with a hovering editor. For the first time in more than twenty years, I found myself entangled in corporate journalism, and I hated it.

The most mortifying episode was the China editorial incident. In late 1978, the Carter administration announced that it would soon end U.S. defense ties with Taiwan and establish full diplomatic relations with the People's Republic of China. In view of Time Inc.'s long and notorious alliance in the days of Henry Luce with Chiang Kai-shek and the China Lobby, I was surprised to find Murray enthusiastic. "Long overdue," he said.

I agreed in principle but with reservations. Once again, the U.S. seemed to be jerking the rug from under a dependent it should never have created in the first place. But if you invested in a client state as heavily as the U.S. had invested in Taiwan, wisely or not, you incurred certain moral obligations. Moreover, some of the remarks filtering out of the Carter adminstration hinted that facile notions of realpolitik—the formation of a "triangular" relationship among the U.S., China, and the Soviet Union—were involved.

Worse, the story had broken on Friday night. Tuesday would be late for an editorial reaction, and I hated weekend office hours. But I went down Sunday morning and wrote a Monday editorial. It applauded "normalization," but dwelt at some length on the collateral risks of this sudden switch. "What conclusions about American friendship and patronage," it asked, "will be drawn by other Asian nations (and other nations generally) from the denunciation of the . . . defense treaty? It would be surprising if they were favorable." I left a copy of the editorial with a doorman at Murray's Connecticut Avenue apartment. The sunny late-autumn afternoon passed, and I assumed he had no comments.

That evening at a dinner party at Joe and Polly Kraft's, the new China policy was the topic of the occasion. Several other guests asked what the *Star* would say—I suppose the well-known Luce connection made the question more interesting than usual. I rashly previewed the editorial I had written earlier. About 10 P.M., as everyone was milling about in after-dinner fashion, I was called to the phone. It was Murray, and he sounded tense. Sorry, he said, but he couldn't go along with the editorial; it was much too negative in tone. He would have called earlier, but he said he had only just seen the editorial an hour before. "We ought to toss our hats in the air," he said.

I felt my face flush. "Since you don't like it," I said, "do you mind calling the night desk and killing it?"

"I think you should do that," Murray said. After another tense exchange or two, he insisted, and I agreed to call. It was awkward; I rued my indiscretion in having previewed an unpublished editorial. Depend on Murray, I raged to myself, to veto an editorial at the eleventh hour. At home, I railed with anger and embarrassment. This was intolerable, absolutely the last straw.

By morning, however, I had cooled down and so had Murray. But he still wanted surgery on the editorial and, when I reached the office, had already written out proposed revisions. Where I had asked what other countries might think about the dependability of American friendship, his suggested change read: "It would be surprising if [the reactions] were unfavorable. Only in special circumstances—Israel is an example— are other nations important to U.S. interests likely to allow [the change] to outweigh the obvious benefits of return to a more normal state." As he often did, Murray had turned a point nearly 180 degrees and had taken a dig at the Israelis besides. I reluctantly folded Murray's emendations into my text. The editorial finally appeared on Tuesday. To me, it read like a mishmash, braiding together two essentially incompatible attitudes. But maybe I was wrong. We received a number of compliments on the editorial.

Murray continued to be civil, and in the social events after hours he was always cordial and friendly. He also kept raising my salary and putting me in for fringe benefits. But in working hours, sharply worded memoranda flowed on. The battle extended to our array of op-ed page columnists and even to design. For reasons I couldn't grasp, Murray insisted that we use all of James Reston's columns, even though they would usually reach *Star* readers many hours after they'd been available in the *New York Times;* and in Washington most key people read the *Times.* Murray also disliked two columnists I had recruited, Michael Novak and John P. Roche. Novak, a Catholic theologian, had been the *Star*'s writer in residence, and his popular writing had led to a syndicated column which had a considerable following. Murray wanted to cancel it, though he declined to explain his distaste. It was perhaps the overt religious flavor. Murray would press Bob Berger, our op-ed editor, not to use it; I kept insisting that it be used. There were more tart memos. I had persuaded Roche, a professor of political science and a former aide to Lyndon Johnson, to switch his column from the *Post,* which never used it, to the *Star.* He had obliged; it would certainly be embarrassing if he began to get the same treatment at the *Star* that he had suffered at the *Post.* We finally settled on a quota system for the columnists, but Novak and Roche both got slight display. This rankled.

Murray also had hired a shaggy artist from New York, a former department-store ad illustrator, to redesign the paper's topography. His great West Side shock of frizzled hair prompted Mary McGrory to nickname him "the Russian wolfhound." The wolfhound closed in, with lolling tongue, on the editorial pages with splendid designs entirely defiant of the principles of functionalism, pretty but confusing to readers. Here, too, I managed to stall until Murray finally ordered the change to be executed.

As Jimmy Carter sank from sight and the Reagan years began, Murray became increasingly preoccupied with other matters. But sometimes the overmanagement impulse re-emerged; and a trivial incident of editorial meddling almost caused a severance of ties. On the day after John Hinckley Jr. shot Reagan and several others outside the Washington Hilton, Jeff Frank wrote a lead editorial about handguns. It deplored the easy access of criminals and kooks to concealable weapons. It was a more than passable piece of work. I left the office thinking it would be our lead editorial. Murray spiked it, with the odd result that on a day when everyone's mind was on the shooting of the president the *Star*'s lead editorial had to do with Conrail! The main excuse for this intervention was that Murray favored mandatory sentences for any crimes committed with handguns. It was a well-known nostrum for evading sensible gun control, concocted by the handgun lobby. I told Murray so. He did not relent.

I became regrettably rude and reckless in the next memo. "It seems to me," I wrote, "that you are dealing with our editorial operations much as Carter did when he was trying to handle even the scheduling on the White House tennis court. . . . I cannot function as a cipher and do not wish to do so. It seems to me that the *Star* can have only one editorial page editor at a time. You must decide who that editor is to be." The missive was uncivil but honest. Had I known what Murray must have known by now about the thin ice under the whole *Star* operation, I wouldn't have bothered him with this surly ultimatum. But this time even his thick armor seemed to be pierced. A few days later we sat across from one another in the late afternoon. He peered gloomily across the marble-slab desk. I had become "personal," he complained. I denied it; and indeed my feelings were not personal at all. It all had to do with the abrasions of day-to-day office routine. I had, I said, been accustomed to working with and for people who were easier to reach. Harsh language seemed the only way to get his attention.

"Nobody ever accused me of being a charm-school graduate," Murray said disarmingly. He couldn't and he wouldn't "abdicate" his responsibility to edit the whole paper. It was his job. If his system crowded me, I should propose some way to make it work better. I left for a dinner engagement with the faintly sick feeling that nothing had been resolved. But I needn't have worried. The impasse was about to be overtaken by a final catastrophe.

Early one bright July morning, the phone rang at 6 A.M. "Can you be at a 7 o'clock meeting in my office?" Murray asked. It was clear that something had gone wrong. An hour or so later I arrived to find all the other editors gathered in Murray's office. No one spoke. Murray looked stricken, Jim Shepley looked sad and fidgety. The *Star*, Shepley announced, would close in two weeks unless a buyer could be found. Time Inc. had now invested more than eighty million dollars in the rescue attempt, thirty million dollars more than it had budgeted for the first five years.

Would anyone buy it? someone asked. "I could sell it to an oil company," Shepley said, "but I'd rather close it." When the others trudged out of Murray's office a few minutes later, I lingered. We sat sadly on his office sofa for a moment. Murray held out his hand. "Let's just forget all the problems, let bygones be bygones," he said. I readily agreed. All the irritations and sharp memoranda of the past three years now seemed as distant and irrelevant as fights for the sunniest deck chairs on the *Titanic*. We had become fellow victims of a lost war. We parted friends.

On Friday, August 6, I wrote the last of my signed columns, packed a few remaining books and files in the car, and read the last page proof of the last editorial page. I walked down to the newsroom and into Mary McGrory's little cubicle. It seemed the best place to say goodbye to this institution which had stretched and strained me, of which Mary's gallantry and faith had been an unfailing beacon. We embraced warmly but wordlessly; words would have been redundant anyway. Then I walked out into the hot late-summer weather. The next day, after 129 years, the *Star* published its last edition.

MEG GREENFIELD AND THE PERILS OF PUNDITRY

A Friend in Power *"A friend in power is a friend lost." Henry Adams reached that wry judgment, so he says, when his close friend John Hay became secretary of state. It is often difficult to be sure that Adams literally believed what he wrote; but as usual he was right in principle. And the principle is in a way illustrated in the following chapter. The episode speaks for itself and certainly doesn't lend itself to dispassionate analysis.*

I regret only the incidental asperities here, for I have absolutely no grounds for complaining that life is unfair. It certainly hasn't been to me. My professional life has been invariably fortunate, as I have said, and I have no idea why the pleasant trajectory of my career in commentary flattened out during the years when I wrote a syndicated column. Of course the competition was keen, and I am as reluctant as the next man to think that this faltering, if that is what it was, had anything to do with the limits of my capacity. But the reader is free to examine the evidence presented here—with a certain bias, to be sure—and to draw his own conclusions.

Meg Greenfield and I met at George Will's dinner table on a hot June night in 1975, a week or so after I moved to Washington. In my unalloyed vanity, I would have said at the time that there had been no more stellar gathering of journalistic stylists since Walter Lippmann dined alone. I had admired Meg's sprightly writing for the *Washington Post* and *Newsweek* and, still earlier, for *Reporter* magazine. We quickly spotted affinities which I'm sure Will doesn't share, not that it matters. We had both been "madly for Adlai" (Stevenson) in 1952; and both of us answered to the patronizing label of cold-war liberal, being both anti-Stalinist and anti-McCarthy. She was then in her blue-stocking mode, at least in appearance, usually dressed in black shifts, with little makeup, and smoking like a chimney: a persona she was shortly to abandon.

I knew and liked her as a personal friend, as a rival (she would soon become editorial-page editor of the *Post,* consequently my competitor), and, after the *Star* closed in August 1981, as a patron when she became a client of my syndicated column. Civility prevailed throughout, although in the latter relationship I was sometimes reminded of Henry Adams's rueful comment quoted in my headnote.

Regarding her not only as a friend and colleague but as something of an enigma, I was eager to read the memoir *Washington,* whose secret existence was revealed only after her untimely death of cancer in May 1999. Might there be some revelatory clues? Some; but for Greenfield-ologists not enough. *Washington* has substantial virtues and distinctions, but self-disclosure—in the usual fashion of me-me-me memoirs—isn't among them. Whether the final chapter on friends and family, which she projected but did not live to write, would have filled these teasing gaps no one can say. I suspect not.

The alert reader will learn more than a bit about this intriguing woman—Meg Greenfield, the granddaughter of Russian Jewish immigrants, the summa Smith College English major and would-be novelist, the post-college European knockabout and Greenwich Village political activist who more or less stumbled into journalism. But they are such fleeting glimpses as one might gain through the lighted windows of a moving train.

As usual, however, the ingenuity of her writing compensates. Meg Greenfield was a writer's writer, as unconventional and often as compelling as her model George Orwell, the "incomparable journalist" as she calls him. Her writing was, at its best, quirky, subtle, factious, with a preternatural range of peripheral vision for nuance. Like many fine writers, she perhaps underestimated her strength—the witty way (and often lethal, too—her friend Joe Alsop called her "the cobra," and I believe she relished the label) in which she grappled with specific persons and situations. In the memoir, she describes her painful tangle with Sen. Alan Simpson over his freewheeling slander of Peter Arnett when Arnett was reporting for CNN from Baghdad during the Gulf War. She offers it as an example of the duty not to be soft on friends that journalistic integrity demands; but its actual charm is the glimpse it affords of the Greenfield who wrote with such telling trenchancy and specificity when she was not speculating with almost mandarin subtlety about paradigms and prototypes (as she often preferred to do). Like Antaeus, she needed anchorage on the solid earth to do her best work, though she seemed at times not to see this.

I once saw her at work, in action at her best as an editorialist. She was in Dallas for the Republican convention where the turncoat former Democrat Jeane Kirkpatrick denounced her former party on grounds that Democrats were compulsive detractors of their country, at least in foreign-policy issues. "Somehow, they always blame America," was the refrain. It drew loud cheers from her Republican audience. I watched Meg address herself the next day with great concentration to the event. She was using a small portable computer in the *Post*'s convention bureau, and of course one could read the (anonymous) result the following morning in the *Post*'s editorial column. It was a masterpiece of stinging editorial commentary, whose barbed theme was that Madame Kirkpatrick had delivered a great speech but to the wrong audience. It would have been more appropriate to say it directly to the Democrats, rather than sling mud over the fence from a safe distance—or words to that effect. I envied the piece; Meg had gotten the matter just right.

Of course, it is no secret among newspaper people that the anonymous editorial is intrinsically leaden, carrying the burden of a presumed institutional authority. It is a rare editorialist—Vermont Royster, long of the *Wall Street Journal,* was surely the best—whose personal touch endows this faceless form with art. Meg Greenfield was as surely another. Her infrequent unsigned editorials in the *Post* might as well have been printed in a different-colored ink. They leapt out of the gray sea of type, touching an inherently dull journalistic form with Swiftian fire and bite.

On the other hand, her signed pieces—written to a set length for the back page of *Newsweek* and reprinted on her op-ed page—often struck me as inflated and abstract, as do occasional musings in her memoir. I think that must be seen as the defect of a virtue. She loathed simple-mindedness with the fury of one who saw life in all its fine shadings and ambivalences and was determined to take account—in advance, prophylactically, as one might say—of every quibble that a rational and fair-minded reader might offer to practically every assertion. Inevitably, the elaborate Jamesian qualifications multiply, at times, to a point that dulls the effect.

Except for the final chapter, where Meg Greenfield speaks specifically of her adventures as director of the *Post*'s editorial pages, many of her attitudes toward political and journalistic Washington were already familiar. Her extended metaphor for the capital is the high school, with its adolescent insecurities and preening, its good and bad kids, its protégés and hall monitors. Like the more usual "company town" the metaphor is useful but has narrow limits. She was at her most Greenfieldian in describing how her editor at the *Reporter* magazine, Max Ascoli, abruptly dispatched her to Washington in 1961 as a fill-in editor, and how in this "existential" exposure to the capital she shed the preconceptions of the parlor political reformer. She began to see, more quickly, I suspect, than she now admits, that Washington abounds in overrated dunces, windbags, showoffs, liars, hypocrites, time-servers, and cynics, while many deserving cases of diligence and dedication to the public interest go unobserved and uncelebrated. But she also understood, as bright newcomers do, that Washington is also full of smart and perceptive people, playing many roles, and condescension is not a useful strategy. Washington journalism, she writes, forced her to add a "predicate," that is, a firm conclusion, to previously airy and formless attitudinizing about public people and issues. Suddenly, it wasn't enough to say "Oh, Dulles" as if the point would be obvious; you had to get it right, you had to dig.

If one were to venture a speculation about the animating principle of Meg Greenfield's journalism, it would be that the novelist she had aspired to be as a young woman lived on somewhere beneath the surface of the columnist and editor. This Tolstoyan sensibility, though submerged, was disturbed by the brutality and heedlessness that too often pass for political and journalistic discourse. On the basis of her fascinating but unfinished book, it is clear that after some forty years, Meg Greenfield was saddened by the prevailing trends in politics and the press. She, no fool, saw that by a sort of journalistic Gresham's Law, the dreadful superficialities of television (which she resolutely avoided) tended to drive the complex out of existence, or at least out of circulation. Struggle as she might to qualify her verdicts, they were unmistakable.

But she was no common scold and *Washington* is a connoisseur's book with the bouquet of a well-aged vintage, the testament of a brilliant writer who learned hard truths about the defects of modern mass democracy and journalism, expressed them with surpassing originality, and longed with diminishing hope to set them right.

Such, modified to fit present purposes, was my written judgment when the memoir *Washington,* edited by Michael Beschloss, appeared almost two years after her death. I knew immediately when I heard of it that I would have to read the book and come to terms with it. Colin Walters, book editor of the *Washington Times,* offered me the opportunity to review it for his paper—certainly it was out of the question to do it for the *Post,* which contented itself with a perfunctory review by Pat

Moynihan. I asked for a week to consider; and after some soul-searching decided that I could avoid animus and give it a fair appraisal. But I knew that some mutual friends and colleagues would be familiar with the mixed history underlying anything I might write about Meg or her book; and that in some ways I might be considered wholly unsuited for the task. So I inserted—I hope with a suitably artful touch—that little reference to the strain between Henry Adams and John Hay, trusting that the few who might care would get the point. For the truth was, I had written an earlier and perhaps more searching appraisal of my relationship with this complex woman, whose involuntary destiny it became to play a substantial, and from my point of view questionable, role in my professional life.

It began with a phone call. When Meg died, a very old friend who was well aware of the tangled tale, called to offer me his condolence. It was intentional irony; for he knew that I had struggled with ambivalent feelings about Meg for a long time (not romantic but professional, I hasten to say) and that they had been intensified three years before when I learned she was gravely ill. What, I kept asking myself, is the obligation of charity, and human sympathy, when one feels that a stricken sufferer has done him significant injury? To complicate the matter, the sense of injury is subjective and qualified in invisible and unknowable ways by considerations to which one has no access. Indeed, it might go beyond that. Psychiatrists are fond of a term they use to describe a disordered relationship to the outer, objective world, and to other people, which may be so subjective as to border on illusion—"ideas of reference," they say, which might be reduced, for instance, to the mistaken illusion that we are more important in the thoughts and calculations of others than is or could be the case.

There was no doubt of my unconscious feelings. They were unmistakably registered in a vivid dream, some years ago. I was on vacation at Wrightsville at the time, with more than the usual leisure to brood about the state of the syndicated column I was writing for the *Post* syndicate, which she used fitfully and capriciously. In the dream, I was sitting on a scholarship selection committee before which Meg appeared as a candidate. I recall at least two feelings very clearly. One was the discreditably triumphant sense that if she thought *I* would vote in *her* favor, she had another think coming. The other was that while her mild facial features were fully recognizable, her face was encompassed by a bizarre hairdo of writhing serpents. In other words, she appeared in the dream in the persona of a Gorgon-head, a Medusa. As we laughed at the breakfast table at the beach over this improbable apparition, my old friend Martha Evans, a student of Freud, noted that snakes are symbolic of the *vagina dentata:* the demasculinizing female. That too seemed to fit the case. What I felt, professionally, was a kind of symbolic castration.

To one with no emotional investment in the matter, all this would probably seem melodramatic, inasmuch as the issue was a strictly professional relationship with few overtones of the personal—none at all, so far as I knew. I resisted the suggestions of friends that her failure to use the column as often as I thought it should be used stemmed from some sort of writerly jealousy, and I still think I was right to do so.

It began—the pertinent part— in late July 1981, when the *Washington Star*'s approaching demise was officially announced and the *Star*'s staff were scrambling to get off the sinking ship. It was Meg who threw me a life-vest, one which a few years earlier I would have welcomed. We had been on cordial terms during the six years that I had been in Washington, and (as I said above) during the two or three years in which, as counterpart editorial page editors of the two major capital-city newspapers, we had been rivals. It had been a friendly and collegial rivalry, with mutual regard and compliments. When the *Star*'s death notice was posted, she called and asked me to meet her for lunch at the Jockey Club. We met and talked amiably for half an hour or so. Then she sprang what she called—with a joky allusion to a bombastic radio commentator—"the rest of the story." It was to offer me a choice position on the *Post* editorial staff—the "seat" once distinguished by Alan Barth, the great civil libertarian and specialist in legal and constitutional affairs, and later by others. It was an appealing offer, for legal and constitutional matters had long been a consuming interest of mine, and there had been a time when I might have leaped at it. But I had by then supervised my own editorial departments in Greensboro and Washington for more than twenty years and I had no hankering to become anyone's subordinate. Besides, I was confident that my apprenticeship as a writer of millions of words of anonymous commentary over many years had qualified me to try to write a syndicated column—now, if ever. During the life of the *Star,* I had had inconclusive negotiations with the *New York Times* syndicate about the weekly column I was doing. That was still an option, but now I had reached a tentative agreement with the *Los Angeles Times-Mirror* syndicate. I explained all this to Meg and she immediately said, "I'll use it," *use* being the word that was to sow the seeds of such bitterness as I began to feel in time. She urged me, moreover, not to sign up with the *Times-Mirror* syndicate until I had talked with Bill Dickinson, the director of the *Post* Writers Group. We parted amiably and Meg arranged for me to see Dickinson a day or so later.

Dickinson, who was to become a good friend as well as editor, told me that his real need was for a White House column, a regular report and commentary on the doings of presidents. He had in mind something like the "White House Watch" column that John Osborne had written regularly, until his death, for *The New Republic*. It wasn't exactly what I'd planned to do; but I agreed to do it. "One more thing," Dickinson said, before we shook hands on a contract. "I need to find out whether Meg will use this column. No point doing it if she won't." Meg, always difficult for syndicate editors to pin down, signified her assent and the column was scheduled to begin, twice weekly, at the turn of the year, January 1, 1982. It turned out to be a general-interest column after all, however. Dickinson learned some time in the intervening fall months that Lou Cannon, the *Post*'s White House correspondent and a specialist on Ronald Reagan, planned to write a regular White House column for the *Post* news pages. That development suited me even better, and the initial responses to the Writers Group promotion were spectacular— nothing like it, Dickinson said, since George Will had launched his column seven or eight years earlier. Many old friends among the editorial-page editors around the country were signing on; and many would stay with the column for the whole of its fifteen-year life. It got excellent exposure in a lot of good regional newspapers and better exposure in the *International Herald Tribune,* published in Paris, and in *The Guardian* in England. In some ways, that only deepened my irritation; for if my column suited the editors of those esteemed publications, who was the editorial-page editor of the *Post* to winnow them with so casual a hand?

Of course, my mistake was to assume, amid all this good fortune, that when Meg said "use" she meant "use regularly" or "use all" on a predictable schedule—*use* in the sense in which other Writers Group regulars—Will, David Broder, Bill Raspberry—were used. But I had no staff standing at the *Post;* and I guilelessly failed to see or imagine that an outsider gaining a slot on the *Post*'s op-ed page—not only the best and most closely read in the country but now the only outlet for such exposure in the capital—might be resented and resisted. Years later, Dickinson startled me by saying that Howard Simons, then the *Post*'s managing editor, who had posed (I thought) as a friend, had tried to persuade Dickinson not to syndicate my column. Indeed, he had gone to great emotional lengths in his opposition—why, I have no idea. Perhaps others secretly joined Simons's resistance. And to complicate the matter further, the *Post* announced in August, when the *Star* closed, that it would add several *Star* regulars—Bill Buckley, Jack Kilpatrick, and Carl Rowan—to its stable of columnists, further increasing the demand upon limited op-ed page space. This produced, so I heard, squawks from *Post* writers who thought their work might be devalued or crowded by this rampant inflation. But these complications failed to register with me at the time; I simply failed to imagine that my arrival, or that of the other *Star* columnists, would stir jealousies. I was naïve, and perhaps I underestimated the degree to which Meg Greenfield was forced to ration and defer the use of aliens on the *Post* op-ed page. Certainly the *New York Times,* at least until recently, had never given op-ed columns to outsiders, except to the ex-Nixon flack William Safire. When Max Frankel took over the *Times* editorial-page editorship, he kindly offered me the job of being op-ed editor—not much of a temptation since it would have involved moving to New York. But to the present point, when I asked Max whether I might be allowed to write a weekly column in that space myself, the answer he brought back from the *Times* high command was that "aliens" weren't allowed!

Between the *Star*'s last edition in August and the turn of the year, I gave myself a leave of absence from regular writing; but Meg was quick to ask me to do special pieces. The disgraced Richard Nixon, then seeking a site for his presidential library, proposed to place it at Duke University, where he had attended law school. But the Duke faculty rose in arms to resist. Meg called and asked me to do a piece on the squabble and gave it a prominent place on her page. The same was true of other occasional contributions—any and all suggestions I might make were welcomed and my work was well displayed throughout the fall. That naturally made me even more confident—complacent would be the better word—about the "use" of my column when it began. Imagine my surprise, then, when the column officially began and the first two pieces failed to appear—a startling proclamation, it seemed, that "use" meant something materially different to Meg than it did to me. Given my expectations I hardly knew how to react. I ran into Meg on the elevator one day as I was on my way to deliver my copy to the Writers Group on the ninth floor of the *Post* building.

"You're on the page today," she said—as if to say, *I know you must have wondered where the column was until now.*

"Finally!" I said, a bit sharply. No doubt I should have fallen to my knees and kissed her hand in thanksgiving, instead of assuming an entitlement. But I was too fresh from my own authority at the *Star* to understand dependency. In any event, the January experience, as the column was just beginning, foretold a pattern that persisted for fifteen years, with tortuous variations. Well into the late 1980s and early 1990s, the column appeared regularly enough (at least once a week on the average) to maintain a presence. But no more. Moreover, it was often the offbeat pieces on literary subjects or noted deaths that Meg favored and relegated to the Saturday op-ed page. With the exception of my comments on legal or constitutional matters, often provoked by Supreme Court decisions, the columns on public matters appeared more fitfully—or not at all. It was a rare column of mine that appeared in the very political *Post* during presidential campaigns, for instance. The dearth became so stark during the 1984 presidential election that it looked for weeks as if the column might never reappear. But then a revival would begin and some sort of rough pattern would establish itself. It became maddening, prepossessing. I seemed to be listed in Meg's book as a sort of undertaker for the distinguished dead, and a celebrant of important anniversaries (the sesquicentennial of Darwin's *Origin of Species,* for instance, or the arrival of the year 1984 that Orwell's novel of that name had made ominous). Or I was allowed to rebut the absurdities of other writers, especially if they were French. Once during this period, I overtook Meg on a Georgetown sidewalk as we approached one of the rare events at which she made appearances ("all the best places," as she once said to me). It was one of Evangeline Bruce's luncheons for a distinguished visitor from England, I believe. I thanked her—I had finally learned to imitate gratitude—for using a rebuttal of mine to a particularly idiotic commentary by a French savant on the American political system.

"I always use your rebuttals," she said.

Once in the earlier years, she actually phoned one day to praise a piece, a column about Jesse Jackson's journey to Syria to persuade its rulers to release an American flier shot down over the Bekaa Valley. I had made fun of the hoopla and extravagance with which Jackson's coup was surrounded (naturally, and absurdly, it was widely compared with Saint Paul's journey to Damascus). She called in the late afternoon to say that she liked the piece. A startled silence followed; I was pleased but surprised. I knew that she rarely if ever had anything to say about any column, even the ones that passed muster. "Well, that's all I have to say," she concluded and hung up. It left me wondering what it was about that piece that in her eyes merited praise. This was the high point. The low point came some years later when a *Post* reader phoned early one Saturday morning. "I always read your column," he said, "but where is it?" I explained that it was beyond me to know when or whether it would appear. "Oh no," he said. "It's in the index this morning." Sure enough, the page-two index that listed the op-ed columns included my name; but the column was nowhere to be found. Discreet inquiries revealed that some of Meg's op-ed staff had scheduled the column, but she had pulled it later herself, without explanation as usual. I took this to be the measure of her dictatorial supervision of the page and refusal to be second-guessed. But the implications, then as ever, were mystifying and worrying.

Before I became dependent on her good will, we had frequently taken meals together. All that now came to an end, although she did invite me on one early occasion to lunch in her office. We ate sandwiches at her desk because, she said, she had to stick around to consult with Henry Kissinger, who had just begun to write his monster monthly columns. He had insisted that Meg herself edit the columns and was expected to phone. But I had the feeling, perhaps mistaken, that the editing process constituted a sort of safety barrier.

Our professional relationship had not always been so awkward or constrained. As I said by way of disclosure when I reviewed her memoir in June 2001, we had met for the first time not long after I moved to Washington in June 1975. We had sensed from the first a temperamental and political compatibility; and in some ways the difficulty I am trying to articulate may have been rooted in a surplus of identity—we looked at the world in much the same way. I liked her writing and I think she liked mine. In those early days she came frequently to dinner at our house in Alexandria, usually complaining wittily of the condition of her old car ("I think it needs to be taken out and shot"). One night I took her to a D'Oyly Carte production (*HMS Pinafore,* I believe) at the Kennedy Center. It was preceded by light snacks at her house, her "Jewish mother" caretaking, she said. It was all very easy then.

The easy and collegial camaraderie that had begun at that dinner at the Wills' house ended abruptly when the column began; and for a long time I wondered why. I had learned myself the awkwardness of dealing with old friends over whose writing one presides as gatekeeper. I had recruited my Greensboro colleague James Ross, a gifted writer of drollery, to write occasional pieces for the *Star* opinion section; but somehow his stuff, like a rare wine, did not travel well and failed to survive the impalpable cultural and tonal distances between Greensboro and Washington. For similar reasons, I would let occasional submissions from Edward P. Morgan lie about on my desk until they became embarrassing and I would have to tell white lies about them. Ed was an old friend from my pre-Washington days, a distinguished radio and television journalist, now retired, who had once offered me a job writing scripts for his radio commentary. Our inconclusive conversations about that job left us in friendly touch over the years. When I became editorial-page editor of the *Star,* he took an intense and generous interest in what we were trying to do to revive its fortunes. But his style of commentary did not, I found, lend itself to the op-ed form.

Still, what is clearly observable from one perspective is hard to digest when one is on the receiving end. No writer likes to think that his work is other than deserving of fervent attention. Kind friends, well aware of the problem I was having, suggested that some sort of rivalry, perhaps unconscious on Meg's part, was a factor. But if so, it was odd that it should have intensified when we were no longer editing rival editorial pages and when I in effect had surrendered my sword and was no threat to her. She had all the power; I had none. Besides, I am sure that she was a professional to the fingertips and I would be shocked to learn that personal feelings had ever affected her editorial judgments. (I should pause to note here, by the way, that in the six years in which the *Star* struggled for life the *Post*'s editors—Meg, Ben Bradlee, and above all Phil Geyelin—behaved with generous good will. Indeed, Phil and I became such close friends that we used to joke at our periodic lunches that we were in violation of the antitrust laws.) Perhaps there was, on the other hand, some subtle feeling—a transmuted guilt, it may have been—about Phil's unceremonious removal from the *Post*'s editorial page editorship in Meg's favor. The *Post* treated it as a long-planned leave of absence, but it was more like a deposition; and an abrupt one at that. I learned about it one afternoon in 1980 when Murray Gart, the *Star*'s contentious editor, came barreling down the hall to my office.

"Your friend Geyelin is out at the *Post*," he announced, not without a note of glee. "We're running the story tomorrow."

I was stunned, for it happened that Phil and I had lunched together only a day or two earlier and I was sure that Phil had then had no inkling of any impending change. Perhaps the changing of the guard had been tentatively bruited, without a timetable, and the *Star*'s scoop forced an unseemly acceleration. I never learned the story. What I do know is that the unceremonious transition left bitterness; and that it was intensified by the capricious treatment (as Phil saw it) of the column he subsequently wrote for a time for the Writers Group and the *Post* op-ed page. Outwardly, civility was maintained, but the wounds were so deep that when Alan Shearer, who succeeded Dickinson as director of the Writers Group, gave me a pleasant farewell luncheon in Kay Graham's private dining room, at the end of my Writers Group tenure in 1997, Phil hesitated to attend until he was assured that Meg would not be there. He indicated that he would not participate in a ritual hypocrisy; for he was, generously and loyally, among those readers of my column who thought it was mistreated. And I reminded myself at the time that when Phil himself had stopped writing his column, a similar luncheon in his honor offered by Meg had been scheduled, unscheduled, rescheduled, unscheduled, rescheduled again, and finally cancelled.

Again, much of my resentment over the fate of my column might appear in a very different light to a more detached eye. I had no doubts about the standard of craftsmanship; only George Will's seemed to me, so far as I could judge, consistently higher. The implicit judgment of dozens of other newspapers, including, as I've noted, the European edition of the *New York Herald Tribune* and a majority of the major regional papers all over the country (e.g., the *Los Angeles Times, St. Louis Post-Dispatch, Houston Chronicle, Atlanta Journal, Richmond Times-Dispatch, Raleigh News and Observer, Providence Journal, Hartford Courant, Boston Globe*, et al.), was reassuring; for most made more regular use of my pieces, to the point that friends joked that they had to go abroad and read the *Herald Trib* to follow what I was thinking.

Apart from the capriciousness, the hit-or-miss scheduling, was the impenetrability at the core of the mystery. Meg was, in that respect, an enigma whose defense was facetiousness. Any attempt I made to confer or discuss was rebuffed, beginning with that evasive luncheon in her office, with the awaited call from Henry Kissinger hanging in the air; and it soon became evident that she had no plans to offer any explanation or rationale. At one point I wrote a rash note of complaint, then on Phil's advice retracted it and apologized. Perhaps she had no explanation to offer. After all, she gave the same treatment, or worse, to others— Buckley, Kilpatrick, Rowan—though there was the vital difference that I was syndicated, as they were not, by the *Post*'s own Writers Group. It seemed at times a form of negative advertising, a vote of no-confidence, as if the *Post* editorial pages were implying that half, at least, of what I wrote was unworthy of their busy readers' notice. There can be little doubt that this did me some injury among smaller subscriber newspapers who took their cue from what was playing in the *Post*. Increasingly, the demand for columns ("syndicated columnist" has now become a job description promiscuously attached to scores of obscure writers who have no significant distribution and no audience worth measuring) is governed by one factor: television exposure.

I realize as I write this, that it is a partisan brief in which Meg Greenfield's views get no airing. My only plea is that I don't know what they were. Writers one and all have big egos, even when they pretend otherwise, and I am no exception. The implicit vanity, the assumption that one has things to say and ways of saying them that are of more than private interest, is the vital mainspring of the art. In my more modest moments, I can concede that, viewed from Meg's Olympian perspective, my grievance might have seemed petty. "After all," she might have said, and perhaps did say, though not to me, "I rescued Yoder from Washington oblivion when the *Star* closed and offered him one of the most important jobs in American editorialdom, which he refused. Without my help, such as it was, his work might have had no presence here at all, unless in the *Washington Times,* which doesn't count. And he seems not to understand that I tried to display columnists at their best, not in their mediocre moments. In the case of the *Post* regulars, who had staff connections, I was not free to select, as I was with him." And after all, Dickinson, a model editor with whom I was on the best of terms, had his own way of grading my pieces. I knew that when he called to say "this is a *neat* piece," he was awarding it an A and could almost predict that his evaluation would be verified (as in most cases it was) by an appearance in the *Post*. I also knew that when he called to suggest changes and began "I have your column about . . ." it was not A-level work in his book and it probably would sink without a trace. The difference was that I could ask Dickinson what he liked or disliked and he would tell me. With Meg, I might as well have addressed my queries to the Sphinx.

I have, I find, taken several hundred words to say what I tried to say to Kay Graham in a brief note on the day Meg's death was reported:

> . . . Meg had "no immediate survivors," but I know that you and she were very close, and that you must feel very acutely the extinguishing of such a luminous spirit. . . .
>
> As you know, my path crossed Meg's in more than one respect, and until I became a sort of dependent our relationship was easy and collegial. I can't—I won't—pretend that I liked or was not angered by the way she used (or didn't use) my column, after having directed me to the Writers Group. But she had her job to do, and her own balances to make, and in the perspective of years such personal grudges fade to a certain pettiness.
>
> The long and short of it was that I admired Meg for her wit and craftsmanship. As you, a connoisseur (and practitioner!) of fine writing, know, her touch was so special that I used to say: "You can spot Meg's pieces instantly—they might as well be printed in colored ink." I thought her columns occasionally cried out for the blue pencil, but when she editorialized it was always memorable and often definitive. In short, I am glad to have counted her as a colleague and friend in our craft. . . .

Odd as it may seem, even feeling still the scars of neglect, I meant every word of it.

As the foregoing frettings indicate, any writer is naturally preoccupied with his exposure in print and I am no exception. But these vicissitudes no doubt give a slightly distorted picture of the columnist's life as I experienced it. In truth it had many collateral benefits and satisfactions, not least a flow of speaking invitations from coast to coast and from Maine to Georgia, many of them profitable—perhaps best of all, a few fascinating journeys abroad. My friend Dick Howard, professor of constitutional law at the University of Virginia and probably the world's pre-eminent authority on comparative constitutionalism, took me along on a number of constitution-writing and consulting missions. My Chapel Hill contemporary Sam Wells, associate director of the Wood-row Wilson International Center for Scholars in Washington, engaged me to speak to German-American and Finnish-American conferences; and that carried me to cities I might not otherwise have visited: Riga, Latvia; Helsinki and the Finnish lake country; and St. Petersburg as that beautiful city was recovering from the long night of Soviet rule.

But far the most intriguing venture of those years took me for the first time in nearly thirty years back to a city I had known and loved as a student: Paris.

It must be clear by now that my life's adventures, even when unusual, have been neither dangerous nor exotic: no pursuit of ferocious beasts in far-off jungles. The adventure to which I was invited by my late friend, the vivid and lovable Timothy S. Healy, S.J., then president of Georgetown University, comes as close to the exotic as I managed; or if not exactly the exotic, the unconventional. Indeed, this little tale forms a sort of footnote to what I have written above and below about the need for perspective. The more a journalist can see of the operations of great institutions close up, the better.

One June evening in 1985 I found a surprising message from Tim Healy on my telephone answering machine.

"Ed," I heard the familiar voice say, "call me when you get in, no matter how late it is. I wonder if you'd like to go with me and a few others to Paris in early July to brief the new archbishop in preparation for his American visit. We'll pay your expenses and fly you over and back on the Concorde."

I started up the stairs from my basement study to tell Jane about this proposal when I stopped in my tracks. *A trip to Paris on the Concorde? What was I waiting for?* I called Tim and said that of course I would go. And that's how I became involved in my only Jesuit plot. I call it that lightheartedly but it was a plot of sorts, and it did involve Jesuits, several of them.

Even growing up in a Presbyterian town in very Protestant North

Carolina, I must have known a bit at an early age about the Jesuit order, founded by Saint Ignatius Loyola after the Council of Trent in the mid-sixteenth century. The Jesuits were to be the footsoldiers of the Counter-Reformation. Agnes Repplier's popular biography of Père Marquette was on our family bookshelves and I had read it; and no doubt the Jesuit role in the early history of Canada was mentioned even in the bland world history textbook I studied—occasionally—in high school. Still, I had no inkling that I would ever be part of a Jesuit conspiracy, nor that in subtlety that conspiracy would fit the Jesuits' legendary reputation for intrigue. At the height of the battle, in the sixteenth and seventeenth centuries, Jesuits were rumored to slip into Protestant countries by night and hide themselves in "priest holes" in recusant households. In England the Jesuit father Edmund Campion was burned in the cause and his martyrdom later chronicled by no less than Evelyn Waugh. In fact, I later learned from Tim Healy that the Bodleian library at Oxford houses the world's largest collection of Jesuitiana—gathered, he said, on the "know-your-enemy" principle. By the time I became involved in Tim's plot the culture of Catholicism and its image in the minds of Protestants had been sharply changed by Pope John XXIII, a hero in his time to people of ecumenical sentiments of all faiths, and the Vatican II council he had summoned to "update" the church. Thanks to him and to his successor Paul VI, Catholics and Protestants were now on better terms than at any time since the Reformation. Tim, however, was my first close Jesuit friend. He and I had arrived in Washington at the same time, he to head Georgetown, I to be editorial page editor of the *Star*. He seemed to like my work, and I his. We both were Oxonians and fellow members of a curious body, the Oxford-Cambridge Dinner Committee, whose sole function is to arrange an annual spring "boat race" dinner. Tim had taken his doctorate at Oxford in the 1960s as a John Donne scholar and was a famously witty speaker. He took a keen interest in Oxbridge academic politics and admired the finesse and urbanity with which Oxford handled student rebels in the turbulent sixties, when insurgents threatening the university were reminded that they faced men who had confounded Hitler's spies and agents in the famous "Double Cross" operation and thus bent the German intelligence apparatus in England to their own uses. This interest was surely related to his duties as president of a Catholic university, where nice balances had occasionally to be drawn between church doctrine and student whims—for instance, on such tender issues as abortion counseling and gay rights. As befitted the romantic legend, Tim was a consummate politician. As I wrote after he died suddenly of the heart attack he had courted for years, he looked as if he had been chosen to play a Jesuit college president by central casting on one of its good days.

On that June night when he called me about the Paris journey he must have sketched in some of the details, although the subtext that was to constitute my Jesuit plot wasn't mentioned. We were to fly to Paris on the Monday morning after the July Fourth weekend—Tim, four other Jesuit priests, a news producer from CBS in New York, and I. The instigator was François de Laboulaye, the former French ambassador to Washington. The new Archbishop of Paris, Cardinal Lustiger, was planning his first visit to America since he had been chaplain at the Sorbonne in the stormy sixties. François knew the American scene and feared that anyone whose impressions had been formed in 1968 would need those impressions updated. That was the service he had called on Tim and his team to perform. I was to be the "expert" on the American political scene and print journalism. Others would brief on other matters concerning the church, education, and mass media.

At just what stage Tim took me into his confidence about his special agenda I don't recall, but for him it was as important as the task of providing the new archbishop with a proper *aggioriamento*. It combined intrigue with monumental ambition, worthy of a bad novel. As president of one of the nation's premier Catholic universities, Tim was deeply disturbed by signals that the Vatican aimed to harrow heretics from the theological faculties at Catholic universities and colleges, Georgetown and elsewhere. The new Polish pope, John Paul II, was a theological conservative by any measure; and the unpublicized initiative was thought to reflect his wishes. Tim's worry, however, had only secondarily to do with the merits of theological argument. It had very much to do with federal funding of student loan subsidies, medical research, and other vital educational concerns. Georgetown University and its peers—Notre Dame, Fordham, Holy Cross, and the like—relied no less than "secular" institutions, or those affiliated with Protestant denominations, on these public subventions. And while the Supreme Court in its Establishment Clause jurisprudence had distinguished between public schools and higher education (reasoning, apparently, that students at the latter were mature enough to resist religious indoctrination), Tim saw big financial trouble ahead if the Vatican pushed.

"In Rome," he said, "they haven't a clue about First Amendment law or the courts. If the Vatican begins purging faculty at our place or others like it Washington will notice, whether or not the meddling is limited to theologians. The feds aren't interested in theological disputes but they certainly are interested in issues of entanglement." (In a case known as *Lemon v. Kurtzman,* the U.S. Supreme Court had established the awkwardly labeled "three-prong" test in Establishment Clause cases; and one of the "prongs" was whether any policy promoted "excessive entanglement" of church and state.)

I had seen no mention of the issue in the press, although in Germany and the Netherlands some dissident Catholic theologians had been silenced or dismissed. And what was the Paris mission's connection to all this? Here the Jesuit plot thickened at its core. The cardinal-archbishop, Jean-Marie Lustiger, was said to be personally close to John Paul II, the Polish pope. Lustiger's background, unusual for a prince of the church, suggested why. His Jewish parents had fled Poland before Hitler's hordes and some of his kin had died in Nazi death camps. John Paul had made it a special mission to repair the historic strain in Vatican-Jewish relations, which not only bore the burden of centuries of oppression but recently had been sharpened by the charge that before and during World War II, Pope Pius XII had done too little to resist the systematic persecution of Jews, even in Italy. It was thought that the Polish pope's sensitivity to these matters could be traced in some part to his friendship with Lustiger, and their common Polish connection. Of the inwardness of that friendship little is known; but it was assumed to be a promising link. Tim reasoned that if he could impress Archbishop Lustiger and his deputies with the dangers of Vatican meddling the warning would eventually reach the papal ear and the Roman bureaucrats might be restrained before they made a mess of things.

I tried to explain this complex project to my parents, who were as always interested in their son's distant adventures, with an amusing result later to be described. For family reasons—my father died suddenly on the eve of the journey—I reached Paris some hours later than the others. At Charles De Gaulle airport, a uniformed driver led me to a gleaming Mercedes sedan (Jesuits accept no pay, but otherwise Tim lived well) and sped me past the familiar landmarks to our quarters at the Hotel

Lutetia. From there I walked the short distance down to the Institut Catholique, where the meetings had just begun on a beautiful summer morning. Tim and the other members of our delegation sat at a conference table. Facing them sat three auxiliary bishops, plump and self-satisfied in that special way some Frenchmen have of being pleased with themselves and their world. The discussion was in French, there was no interpreter, and my limited command of the spoken language (in particular, a deficient ear) had rusted badly in three decades' disuse. As I tuned in, Tim was already discoursing on the perils of Vatican interference in Catholic higher education in the U.S. Some of the phrases of his cautionary remarks echo in the memory—not, it struck me then, that the stolid lords of the French hierarchy seemed much impressed.

"C'est un sujet très compliqué, messeigneurs, très difficile, très delicat, légal aussi bien que théologique," Tim was saying. "Si Rome continue à pousser le résultat sera malheureux. Alors, très malheureux!"

Tim obviously was moving ahead with his plan, hoping to engage the cardinal's deputies as conduits—Lustiger himself was absent. I stole glances at the placid faces of the French bishops. But they seemed impassive, even bored, as if they found it curious that Tim should be fretting himself about such obscure and distant matters.

After lunch, a break was called and we filed out into the sun-splashed courtyard and through an archway into a leafy garden, insulated by high walls from the din of traffic. One of our hosts began an account of the horrors that had occurred there during the French Revolutionary Terror, when the Institut became a place of detention for priests and seminarians. It all sounded quite grisly, and it was certain that our hosts invested more emotion in the bloody events of two centuries earlier than in the hazards of Vatican educational policy in America.

The cardinal was expecting us for dinner at his residence that evening and François led the way. François came of a distinguished liberal family whose beautiful Norman chateau, Le Quesnay, lies near Saint-Saëns. For generations, in the French manner, the Laboulayes have been hereditary mayors of their village; and after the laicizing of church properties early in the last century François's grandfather had become titular proprietor of a neighboring abbey, making the precondition that it become a conference center looking to the reconciliation of Anglicanism and Gallicanism. It had been François's great-grandfather who had originated the idea of the Statue of Liberty as a centennial gift to the American people in 1876 and raised money for it; and the original scale model was one of two striking conversation pieces in François's drawing room in the rue du Bac. The other was a magnificent ormolu clock, presented, he explained, to "an ancestor of mine" who had defended Marie Antoinette before the revolutionary tribunal. It had been the reward of his valor at the Bourbon restoration. Admiring it, I was struck, as I had been at the Institut Catholique, by the powerful proximity, the psychological simultaneity, of the Revolution in the sensibilities of late-twentieth-century Frenchmen. Until a year earlier, François had been a popular figure in Washington, like his father before him a distinguished and urbane representative of France whose luncheons and dinners were always lively affairs.

The Archbishop celebrated mass for our small party in his spartan private chapel, then we adjourned to a spacious drawing room where his butler had laid out a bar. But something was wrong.

"Non, non!" Lustiger said sharply, "Vous vous trompez. L'autre scotch! Le 'Red Label.'" The butler hastened away and quickly replaced the inferior whisky. After a quick drink we moved to the large dining table and the conversation began, again in French. His Eminence was keen to hear our views on U.S. policy in Lebanon, a place of special French interest recently marked by Israeli invasion and civil war where a terrorist had blown up the U.S. Marine barracks with great loss of life a year earlier. The Cardinal said that he did not understand American policy. Could someone explain?

"That sounds like a topic for our friend, Monsieur Yoder," Tim said with a sly grin. I waded in, at first in French. But I could see that my fractured French was merely adding to the confusion so I went on in English for perhaps five minutes. Tim, seated at the Cardinal's left, did a quiet simultaneous translation. If, I said, the French were confused they were not alone. The invasion of Lebanon and the spectacle of the shelling of Beirut had been a catastrophe, and one that could have been prevented had Ronald Reagan heeded the warning the outgoing President Carter had given him about the need to keep a tight rein on the Begin government. But there was reason to believe that Reagan's first secretary of state, Alexander Haig, had winked at the Israeli incursion, making the U.S. a silent accomplice to the disaster. Most Americans, I said, would be hard put to find Beirut on a map and our presence there was surely temporary, an accidental consequence of the mishandling of

Middle East policy and not the result of a calculated strategy. The French are sometimes given to conspiratorial views of events, being great rationalists, and would naturally have difficulty believing that our strategy in Lebanon was as much the result of blunder as calculation.

Lustiger nodded, then launched his own monologue, of some ten minutes' duration. I understood only a bit of what he was saying but his remarks had the tenor of a formal diplomatic *démarche* and once again I feared that the Cardinal and his deputies were inattentive to whatever wisdom the visiting Americans had come to impart. The dinner, in fact, was our first and only meeting with the Cardinal himself, though the conversation with his deputies continued for another half day. The following afternoon, Tim celebrated mass in one of the antechapels at Notre Dame, thoughtfully dedicating it to the memory of my father and asking me to read one of the lessons. To the tourists swarming in the dim light of the cathedral, the procession from the sacristy must have presented a mystifying spectacle—the portly and cherubic Tim Healy, vested, carrying the consecrated host; the other priests following, trailed by three laymen. The service punctuated our official agenda and following dinner with the Laboulayes that evening we dispersed. After a brief stop in England I enjoyed my first and only ride on the Concorde. As we took off from Heathrow for New York, the captain spoke: "There is no special sensation in supersonic flight, ladies and gentlemen, although when we reach the Bristol channel and pass through the sound barrier you may feel a slight bump." My two young children, Anne and Teddy, had asked me to bring them peanuts flown supersonically, but the Concorde, I was told, did not do peanuts.

I said earlier that I had explained this adventure back in North Carolina only imperfectly. A week after my father's death, while I was still abroad, Jane and my daughter Anne paid a sympathy visit to my mother. They were dining at a small restaurant favored by her and her widowed friends. As they lingered over coffee the mother of one of my boyhood companions approached.

"Of course, you remember Jane and my granddaughter, Anne," my mother said.

"Certainly. And where is Edwin?"

"Edwin," said my mother with a touch of pride, "is in Paris, *instructing the Pope.*"

"But I thought the Pope was in Rome."

"Yes, but all the same that is where Edwin is—in Paris, instructing the Pope."

My mother had epitomized the Jesuit plot precisely, if in shorthand, leaping nimbly over the intermediate doubts and obstacles. She had it essentially right. Those "instructions" were Tim's and not mine, speculatively launched like a random arrow in the air via a number of intermediaries. But Tim could be jesuitical when he needed to be and he was a wise and farsighted man. I hope his advice hasn't fallen on deaf ears in Rome.

Tim retired in 1990 as president of Georgetown and then, until his sad and sudden death, served as president of the New York Public Library. Did the Vatican pick up his signals and curb the push for a financially risky theological conformity in the Catholic universities? Tim believed that the danger had been averted, at least for a time, though just what effect, if any, his own back-channel effort had I don't know. Perhaps some historian of the twenty-third century will examine the Vatican archives and find out.

LEWIS POWELL: A WASHINGTON FRIENDSHIP

A Friend at the Court *I have recited in other chapters the origins of my long-standing fascination with the work and history of the U.S. Supreme Court. In my Washington sojourn I've been on friendly terms with a few justices and one chief justice, as well as with several solicitors general, including old friends like Charles Fried and Walter Dellinger. But none of my other Court associations matched the richness of my friendship with Lewis Powell. The relationship began, as I report, with an exchange of letters but it went well beyond the professional. As I realized when he died, it had elements of the filial as well.*

I can imagine what some journalistic colleagues, perhaps many, would say about the following account. They will say that it is ill advised, if not scandalous, for anyone in the news business to be on close personal terms with anyone so powerful as a Supreme Court justice. In the current view, friendship and journalism don't, or shouldn't mix. I obviously disagree. I greatly benefited from such personal contacts, not that they were many. I think that by taking a too-aseptic view of those it covers, American journalism is in danger of regarding, and treating, public servants as arid stereotypes, usually of the scheming sort. It hardly need be said that some are just that. But many more are complex human beings trying to serve the public good and it is beneficial to try to learn what makes them tick: not just what their programs and policies are, but what it's like for them at home, and what place their wives and husbands and children hold in their lives. The last great Washington journalist who made a point of going beyond a polite distance, and trying to write sympathetically of the after-hours lives of public officials (and I don't mean scandal) was James (Scotty) Reston of the New York Times. *He is missed, as is his example. The so-called "adversarial relationship" between press and government and the cult of "investigative journalism" have doubtless produced some benefits, but at what price?*

Recently, as I was cleaning out the basement study of our house in Alexandria, Virginia, that I've used for more than a quarter-century, I came upon a cache of correspondence from my time (1975–81) as associate editor and editorial-page editor of the late, still lamented, *Washington Star.* As I looked it over, stirring memories now dulled by two decades, I recalled how surprised I had been when I first arrived in the nation's capital by the tone of casual intimacy which allegedly important people, in journalism, politics and public life, immediately adopt with one another. The intimacy is of course illusory; for in Washington friendships, so called, are often rudely functional, ties of convenience, and soon evaporate when the opportunities for mutual back-scratching vanish. But one of those friendships did take on important personal dimensions, was to last for some two decades, and remains among the memorable benefits of my brief moment in the capital's affairs.

Not long after I took over the editorial pages of the *Star* in mid-1975, I found that we had a distinguished and attentive reader a few blocks away on Capitol Hill: Justice Lewis F. Powell Jr. of the Supreme Court. The discovery began with the interaction of two roles, that of the judge (and former military intelligence officer) and that of the journalist. It began with a lengthy "Dear Ed" letter on the justice's personal stationery. The letter carries the flavor of his exquisite courtesy and is worth quoting at some length:

> [February 24, 1977] Dear Ed: A single sentence in your interesting column entitled "Skepticism and Certainties in Arms Control" prompts this personal letter. The sentence reads:
> "And we know the story of strategic bombing both in World War II and Vietnam."
> The inference . . . is that strategic bombing in both wars was more or less a failure. Perhaps, readers, in view of bracketing the two wars together, would draw various other unattractive inferences.
>
> I write because you are a careful scholar, occupying a position of influence, and because I would like to interest you in reexamining your assumptions. Perhaps I am a "special pleader" as I served four years in the Air Force in World War II . . . as an intelligence officer with strategic bombing. . . . Myths tend to develop a life of their own and eventually are accepted as veritable truth. An example is the now fashionable view that strategic bombing was ineffective, and some critics even claim it prolonged World War II by stiffening German resistance. These views are contrary to historical facts that are well documented.
>
> In November 1944 President Roosevelt created, by directive, the U.S. Strategic Bombing Survey. . . . The Survey Commission, with a staff of more than a thousand persons, was charged with determining the efficacy of the bombing of German targets. . . . After reading your column, I obtained from the Library of Congress the enclosed Summary Report of the Survey (dated September 30, 1945) . . . backed up by a full report that is

impressively documented. I quote only selected sentences from the "Conclusion":

> "Allied air power was decisive in the war in Western Europe. . . . In the air, its victory was complete. . . . On land it helped turn the tide overwhelmingly in favor of Allied ground forces. . . . Its power and superiority made possible the success of the invasion. It brought the economy which sustained the enemy's armed forces to virtual collapse . . ."
> To be sure, the employment of air power . . . was far from flawless. As the survey indicated, a good deal of effort was wasted by poor target selection and failure to persist with attacks on critical target systems. But the conduct of war is intrinsically wasteful. Misjudgments and folly are characteristic of what men and nations then do. But the Air Force's successes far outbalanced the failures.

Powell went on to specify how Allied bombing forced the Germans to divert manufacturing resources to the production of more planes, as air superiority over Europe was established; and he noted that "the strategic air attack on the German oil industry in 1944 was, in itself, one of the most notable achievements of Allied arms." He suggested that I read Albert Speer's account of the results in his memoirs, and continued:

> But those of us involved need neither the Survey nor Speer to corroborate the result of this series of attacks. We were reading German top secret messages describing the results, and we had extensive aerial photography. . . . Moreover, when the war ended I personally visited many of our targets. The devastation was appalling. . . .
> A footnote about bombing in Vietnam: There probably never has been a greater misemployment of weapons and men than the attempt to bomb the labyrinth of Ho Chi-Ming [*sic*] trails in those jungles. But the basic decisions . . . were made by our civilian leaders; not the Air Force. . . . Quite apart from these melancholy reflections, there simply is no "linkage" whatever between what strategic bombing undertook and accomplished against industrialized Germany and what it was mistakenly assigned to do in the jungles and paddy fields of agrarian South Vietnam.

I read the justice's letter carefully, along with its enclosures, and found that he was right: I had misread my sources and parroted a common misconception, as I confessed by return mail:

> [March 11, 1977] . . . Let me first clear up a minor matter. . . . I did not mean to invite any "unattractive inference" by bracketing the two wars

together. The distinctions you draw . . . are entirely persuasive. . . . All that is really left to clear up, given the overwhelming evidence of the Survey, is the mystery of how and why I had subscribed to the conventional wisdom that strategic bombing had been a failure in the European war. Just to check, I went back to a book I had found quite good—Prof. Gordon Wright's *The Ordeal of Total War, 1939-45* . . . Not only did I find his own assessment of strategic bombing judicious, and very much in line with your own, I discovered a possible clue. He writes that Sir Henry Tizard, who as you know was the great believer in radar, was severely critical of strategic bombing after World War II, arguing that it had, all told, cost the British more than it cost the Germans. But his critique, it appears, was addressed mainly to the so-called "area" or population bombing by night which was the main concern of the British Bomber Command, and less so to the work of the American Army Air Forces. I must at some point have read the Tizard argument, without grasping its narrow focus. Beyond that, I can only conclude that I was guilty of accepting second-hand opinions and hearsay evidence. . . . Now that you have so thoughtfully corrected my misimpressions . . . I won't make that mistake again."

The full story of Powell's wartime service, to which he alludes with typical modesty, was to await the publication almost two decades later of John Jeffries's fine biography. But it was clear to me that Powell's keen interest in strategic issues rested on a foundation of rich personal experience. It was also clear that he had not checked his citizen's hat at the portals of the Court. Still, I was impressed that a busy Supreme Court justice would take time from his mule-killing schedule to write with painstaking care to a newspaper editor about a throwaway line in a negligible newspaper column about another subject: the Civil War. I did not know then, nor did many others, that during the Second World War, as Colonel Powell of the U.S. Army Air Corps, the justice had been one of fewer than thirty American intelligence officers in Europe who had been entrusted with the war's deepest Allied secret: the Ultra or "Enigma" secret. At Bletchley Park, a Victorian estate between London and Oxford, British intelligence, with the help of French and Polish refugees, had constructed replicas of the Wehrmacht's most sensitive encrypting machine. Throughout the war, that breakthrough afforded the Allies invaluable, sometimes decisive, forewarning of Hitler's military moves. But it remained so secret that it was a full thirty years before the wider world first learned of it.

At the end of his letter, Powell had extended an invitation: "I would still welcome a visit from you—either to hear an argument or (even better for me) to come to lunch sometime when we are not having arguments." That luncheon meeting, the first of many, was soon arranged. Thus our exchange on strategic bombing became the overture to a friendship. We began corresponding frequently, often about *Star* editorials or columns that touched on judicial matters, but occasionally strayed to other matters of mutual interest. We typically met three or four times a term for lunches, at the F Street Club downtown, at Duke Zeibert's or, as years wore on and Powell grew increasingly frail, at the Monocle on Capitol Hill, just down the street from the Court, where he invariably sat in the same booth, and ordered his "usual": a dry vodka martini with a twist and a club sandwich, toasted, on white bread, little of which he ate.

As an observer of Washington egos, I was struck by Lewis Powell's lack of pomp or self-importance, the endemic vices of judges. He was keenly focused on others and talked little of himself—except for an occasional fond recollection of how "crazy" his father had thought it was when the young lawyer announced in 1932 that he planned to vote for Franklin D. Roosevelt. He talked about his children and grandchildren—and about my children too, about whose fortunes he was always up to date. His genuine modesty never ceased to surprise me. Years later, I heard a story. It seems that a senior partner from the eminent Richmond firm of which he had been the leading light before his departure for the Court visited his chambers one day. Powell, his clerks noticed, addressed the visitor as "Mr." while the visitor breezily addressed him, by then the most respected of American jurists, as "Lewis." When the visitor left, one of the clerks asked why. "He has never asked me to call him by his first name," the justice explained.

As a student of the Court, I was aware that the justices, most of them anyway, cultivate (or affect) a certain monasticism—"taking the veil," Felix Frankfurter once called it. Powell honored the veil; he never discussed the merits of a pending case. But he was eager to help an outsider understand the Court, its culture and its processes. It surprised him that populist critics of the Court complained of its "secrecy." The need was elementary, as he saw it: no decision was ever final until it was formally announced in open court. Up to the very last minute, a justice if he had sudden second thoughts could ask the Chief Justice to hold the announcement up and he would.

When rumors about the Court's internal politics cropped up, as they do from time to time, I would try to wheedle the facts from him; but his discretion was monumental. There were exceptions. Bob Woodward's controversial exposé, *The Brethren,* disturbed him. As George Will commented at the time, the book implied that the justices were "brethren" in the Cain-Abel sense. Powell considered this perverse nonsense. To him, the Court was an amiable institution that functioned as a big law firm, with the justices in their separate orbits meeting occasionally in conference to vote and exchanging draft briefs and memoranda. His response to rumors of acrimony was that there was none worth remarking. No doubt his own courtesy was so disarming that colleagues were reluctant to display so much as a shade of petulance in his presence. He felt that Woodward had misled him. "He told me that he was writing a broader book about decision-making in Washington. If I'd had any idea that this was to be about the Court, and contain so much gossip, I would never have talked with him." The only colleague with whom he hinted impatience was Chief Justice Burger, and you had to have very sensitive antennae to detect even that.

When I met Lewis Powell in mid-1970s Washington, I was already a rapt amateur student of the Court. I can still recall the beginning of my romance with its lore. In the spring of my senior year in high school, I was visiting a former schoolmate, then a freshman at Chapel Hill, where I was to begin the following fall. He took me to a history class in Saunders Hall, where a young lecturer whose name I wish I knew spent fifty rich minutes on the great case of *Marbury v. Madison* (1803), the pivotal case in which Chief Justice John Marshall asserted for the first time the authority of his Court to judge the constitutionality of acts of Congress. Ultimate federal judicial checks on decisions by the state courts had been taken for granted, and the great Justice Holmes once remarked that without that authority the federal union would have collapsed. In fact, it was the absence of a federal court system, and therefore of modest legal comity and uniformity among the states, that had helped spur the formation of a new Constitution.

The details of the lecture that so engaged me that spring morning in Chapel Hill have long since commingled with all that I was later to learn about the case, as its study became a personal hobby. What I do recall was a rapt personal interest in the story of a case illustrating Tocqueville's dictum that great political controversies in America eventually become cases at law. This case had it all—two great but inimical personalities, Thomas Jefferson and his cousin the third chief justice, in angry collision; a momentous issue of checks and balances veiled as a petty controversy over the failure of the newly installed Jefferson administration to deliver a JP's appointment in the District of Columbia; and the utterance of a writ of mandamus to try to compel that delivery. It yielded a decision in which Marshall craftily denied his court a trivial legislated power the better to claim a vastly more consequential constitutional power—the first enunciation of the doctrine that under our written constitution, "it is emphatically the province and duty of the judicial department to say what the law is." This was the first but certainly not the last bold assertion of a doctrine that Justice Robert Jackson 133 years later was to call "judicial supremacy." Marshall must have been conscious of the audacity of his claim; for he was not to press it again in the three decades that remained of his tenure.

I have described how in the spring of my freshman year at Chapel Hill I wandered into J. B. McLeod's Political Science 41 course. McLeod, himself a former practicing lawyer, required the class to brief and master some two dozen major Supreme Court decisions. It was a discipline new to me but utterly absorbing. At about the same time, there began a far-reaching expansion of judicial assertiveness under Chief Justice Earl Warren, a response to the unfolding civil rights crisis. For an editorialist on public affairs, the reemergence of "judicial supremacy" for the first time since New Deal days was a compulsory (and compelling) subject. I soon became a Supreme Court junkie.

That interest guaranteed that I would be intrigued when it turned out that the *Star*'s editorials, and my columns, had an important and reactive reader at the Court. Before our exchange on the strategic-bombing matter, I had known Powell only slightly—a rail-thin and friendly jurist of great personal presence but equally great informality, in the best of Virginia traditions. Richard Nixon had dragooned him onto the Court after the death of Hugo Black in 1971. Nixon in his devious way represented Powell as a redemption of his pledge to name "southern strict constructionists" to the Court—talismanic words that did no justice to Powell's subtle view of law and lawyering. He was indeed a strict constructionist of a sort, though certainly not in the simple-minded way Nixon had in mind. Far more accurate was the description I heard one night from one of his former law clerks, Joel Klein. Powell, said Klein, was "a great common-law judge," one, that is, who insisted on digging into the particular texture of every case, examining it imaginatively and flexibly in the light of durable legal principles, not seeking to dispose of it by the facile application of some shallow doctrine or ideology.

Typically, Lewis Powell the super-lawyer and former American Bar Association president, had had doubts at first of his ability to perform well on the Court. So, at least, his biographer John Jeffries suggests. Jeffries draws a poignant picture of Powell sprawled on the floor of his Washington apartment, a lanky arm covering eyes strained by a long day of reading, being read legal briefs and memoranda by his wife Josephine. A mark of both modesty and diligence; surely, no one in Washington worked harder.

There had been earlier signals that Powell was reading *Star* editorials, the first of which was a polite note of complaint. One editorial, not especially well reasoned, had complained that the ongoing 1976 presidential campaign was being unduly constrained by the Court's leisurely review of the new Federal Elections Campaign Act, in the case of *Buckley v. Valeo*. Powell's letter was passed along to me as editorial-page editor. He protested, reasonably enough, that the FEC law was complex, with many separate features and moving parts, and that the Court could not responsibly deal with an important constitutional issue on demand. This was by no means the last time he complained to me, always courteously, when some published comment (for instance, of a confusing proliferation of opinions in a single case) made the consequences of Court custom an occasion for what he regarded as captious criticism.

Among the scores of issues a Supreme Court justice wrestles with every term, it was easy to spot those that especially engaged Lewis Powell's passion. He believed in presidential government and thought that a president's unique responsibility for keeping the nation's defenses in repair merited a measured deference from the bench. The mid- to late-1970s were, for him, a time of worry. The U.S. still faced a well-armed and aggressive Soviet Union; yet the post-Vietnam reaction and the end of the draft had brought preparedness to a feeble low. His personal letters applauded even the smallest encouragement the *Star* gave to the

Carter administration's fitful attempts to toughen the national sinews. It continued after Carter's defeat in 1980.

[April 20, 1981] . . . Your editorial on the need for military conscription was welcome. The politics of the situation—perhaps unavoidable in a democracy—is well illustrated by your point that the Reagan administration with its emphasis on restoring a seriously depleted military capability, has been unwilling so far to indicate any public interest in a draft. Yet, as you point out . . , we seem to have armed services composed for the most part at the enlisted level of marginally competent young people, under-educated, perhaps incapable of being taught to maintain and use modern weapons, and difficult to discipline or inspire. If these forces—particularly the Army—were committed to combat, you are right in saying our people simply would not tolerate heavy casualties suffered only by this comparatively small component of our society . . .

A modest history underlay the editorial Powell cited. I had heard from friends well versed in military matters that the all-volunteer forces were performing at a grossly unsatisfactory level. I suggested that the *Star*'s excellent defense reporter, John Fialka, look into the matter. He did; and his reporting startled everyone. What he wrote led, in due course, to reforms in the force structure. I thought (and still think) that for a variety of reasons the end of the tradition of citizen-soldiers was regrettable; but the revival of conscription was a quixotic cause. My Oxford classmate Bob Pirie, after a distinguished career in the nuclear navy, served in various manpower roles at the Pentagon. Pirie told me that the army would never consent to a revival of the draft because training costs would consume too large a proportion of its budget. I've seen no evidence to the contrary.

Powell was a moderate by temperament and was far from being an uncritical idolator of executive power. Not long after joining the Court (well before we became personal friends) he wrote an important decision rebuffing Nixon's claim that presidents enjoy inherent constitutional power to use electronic eavesdropping in "national security" cases without a warrant. Nixon's exotic claim was that presidents could confer legality upon such wiretapping simply by ordering it: "If the president does it, its legal," he said. Powell's changing position on the issue showed his flexibility. As president of the American Bar Association ten years earlier, he had endorsed Nixon's permissive view. But as Miles's

Law has it, an ingenious formulation of a Washington home truth, "where you stand depends on where you sit." Lewis Powell was now sitting on the nation's highest court, with different responsibilities; and after a careful look from that perspective, Powell the justice overruled Powell the citizen.

At the same time, Powell didn't want presidents hobbled by private litigation, as he made clear in the celebrated Ernest Fitzgerald case. Fitzgerald, a civilian employee at the Pentagon, was among the earliest and most notorious of the self-appointed watchdogs known as "whistle-blowers"—bureaucrats who risk their jobs reporting excesses and wrongdoing in government agencies. Fitzgerald had spotlighted a number of questionable Pentagon practices and was fired for insubordination. He then filed a civil suit against Nixon, claiming restitution of back pay. By the time Fitzgerald's case crept to the Supreme Court, Nixon had been forced to resign, and some argued that the case was moot. The basic issue was the civil immunity of presidents for official actions, and Powell supported that immunity. The wisdom of his view was amply demonstrated years later when a Powell-less Supreme Court foolishly denied even temporary civil immunity to President Clinton in the Paula Jones "sexual harassment" case. The justices saw no parallel between the two cases, since Clinton's alleged offense had occurred before he was elected president and not in his official capacity. Some of the justices, Scalia and others, noting Clinton's fondness for golf, had a great old time deriding the claim that the Jones case might "distract" him from important national business. But then the Jones affair ripened into a year-long impeachment carnival over piddling sexual misdemeanors and fibbing, greatly exacerbated by the prurient behavior of Kenneth Starr, the special prosecutor. I heard rumors that two justices now regretted their cavalier dismissal of Clinton's claim, but by then the damage had been done. I know nothing of Powell's view of the Jones matter. I suspect that he took a dim view of Clinton's private behavior. But by then he had moved permanently to his home in Richmond and our long series of pleasant lunches had ended. It is a good guess, however, that if he had been on the Court he would have seen more merit in the bid for *temporary* civil immunity than his purblind successors. Powell had the kind of long-headedness that seems often to be lacking in the post-Powell court. It is equally hard to imagine him—or the colleague he most admired, Potter Stewart—countenancing the Court's more recent headlong plunge into the raw voter politics of the 2000 presidential election.

Powell wrote to me on July 12, 1982:

> Thank you for the favorable column on the *Nixon* case. I have been surprised at the relatively few commentaries on the case. We viewed it as a constitutional decision of considerable importance, with both the majority and dissenting opinions going through a number of drafts over a good many months. . . .

I responded on July 26:

> Your opinion in the Nixon-Fitzgerald case was, I thought, both fascinating (in its rich recital of the material details of the case that the press had largely overlooked) and compelling in its argument for presidential civil immunity. Alas, the reaction in my trade was, as it too often is, distressingly superficial—"presidents above the law" was the essence of it. Justice White's dissent was, I thought, a creditable performance (his writing unusually sharp and clear) but he did not finally persuade me.

For southerners of Powell's generation, and mine, the inescapable American issue was race. John Jeffries's biography documents the intensity of Powell's opposition to "interposition," the antique legal doctrine resurrected in the mid-1950s to buttress Sen. Harry Flood Byrd's program of "massive resistance" to school desegregation in Virginia. Jeffries suggests that Powell may in hindsight have forgotten his caution on the school segregation question. But for Powell, who successively headed both the Richmond city school board and then the Virginia Board of Education, the issue was no abstraction. Massive resistance threatened tangible and irrevocable damage, including, at worst, school closings. Powell and others made it their care to keep the public schools open in the face of ferocious political pressures to sacrifice them to avoid desegregation. Schools *were* closed in Norfolk, Prince Edward County, and elsewhere, for a year or more before "massive resistance" collapsed.

We spoke of these issues only occasionally, for by the time we became friends the Court had reached the last of the line of decisions that began with *Brown v. Board of Education* in 1954. Powell viewed the "cross-busing" that began with the Charlotte-Mecklenburg decision a few years earlier with skepticism. He opposed putting the Court's imprimatur on "metropolitan" desegregation plans that would obliterate local school boundaries. Had the Court gone as far as some of the justices wished to go, it surely would have produced more short-term desegregation. But in the long run, white patrons who could afford them would flee to "private" academies, leaving the public schools overwhelmingly black and poorly funded. Powell's resistance to this ultimate extension of the *Brown* precedent—chasing schoolchildren with helicopters, as Sen. Abraham Ribicoff colorfully put it—brought a voice of experience to a dilemma with no good answers. Indeed, there was no sovereign remedy in equity for generations of racial discrimination—except perhaps for expenditures and reforms on a scale which few local governments (or the teachers' unions which increasingly had the whip hand in such matters) would have undertaken or tolerated.

The great case of Powell's mid-tenure, *Bakke v. the Regents of the University of California,* was a variant of the same dilemma; and in its resolution Powell was destined to write lasting judicial history—lasting, that is, so far as appears to date.

The University of California branch at Davis had established a new state medical school. To promote community medicine—at least that was the official rationale—it had reserved ten places in each entering class of one hundred for minority applicants, as officially defined. Bakke, an unsuccessful white applicant, sued on grounds that he was better qualified than some who had been admitted under the minority quota and therefore had been denied equal protection under the Fourteenth Amendment. His case, with its explosive implications, made its way finally to the Supreme Court in the 1978 term; and it became a *cause celebre* in Washington. The Carter administration had difficulty deciding which way to jump, with the solicitor general and Vice President Mondale urging support for the quota system and others opposing it; and within its inner councils the Bakke case became intensely politicized. The solicitor general's draft brief, which would eventually align the administration with one faction or the other, was shopped through various White House political offices. The tampering and lobbying became so blatant that Griffin Bell, Carter's level-headed attorney general, issued new rules to try to insulate the solicitor general from political interference.

No one had any idea which way the Court would go. One day that spring when the Bakke decision was pending, Clark Kerr, the president of the University of California, came to Charles Bartlett's occasional luncheon group, of which I was a regular member. None of the able journalists present—including John Osborne, Bill Raspberry, Smith Hempstone, Nancy Dickerson, Bartlett himself, and several others—could imagine how the Gordian knot would be cut. Either alternative, the endorsement of a quota system or its total abolition, seemed unwise. Yet it seemed that the Court must either endorse "affirmative action" outright, or end it cold. I was more optimistic; I observed at one point that it seemed an opportunity for Lewis Powell to write a magisterial opinion. I'm not sure what I meant, or why I thought he would; for no more than anyone else could I then imagine a creative solution. But the forecast proved accurate. Powell and I, our letters suggest, had discussed the case at lunch, indirectly to be sure. As I've said, he never talked about the merits of any case *sub judice;* but the dilemma posed by Bakke's complaint was obvious, the most widely discussed and anguishing public issue of that time—no secret to anyone who was paying attention. As it finally turned out, the Bakke case split the Court down the middle. There were four votes on one side to affirm the California arrangement, thus lodging an approved quota for government-endorsed minorities at the heart of higher education admissions policy; and there were four votes on the other side for scrapping the California policy entirely, which would have locked higher education into a rigid "color-blindness" that was subsequently to cause difficulty in Texas and California, as Reaganite judges began to drift away from Powell's solution. Powell viewed these dire alternatives, I suspect, as reminiscent of the dire, rule-or-ruin divisions he had faced in Virginia twenty years earlier. He was determined to find a third way. As his biographer neatly puts it: "Faced with two intellectually coherent, morally defensible and diametrically opposed positions, Powell chose neither." Race, he wrote in his controlling opinion, could be weighed as one of a number of material considerations by college admissions officials, along with such traditional assets as athletic or musical ability, and regional diversity. That was the essence of his "magisterial" opinion. On the day the decision came down, I was faced with the job of reading several dozen pages of opinions that obviously had cost much thought and hard work at the Court, then writing a lead editorial for the following day. I admired Powell's common-law craftsmanship, and wrote to tell him so privately:

[June 29, 1978] I hope it is no violation of protocol for a friend to write a fan letter about your fine opinion in the Bakke case. It seems to me to meet every aspect of the case with breadth of mind, a sense of history, and elegant conciseness of reasoning. I take some vain pleasure in having predicted it. At that Charles Bartlett luncheon with Clark Kerr I told you about, I ventured that "this seems to me an opportunity for Justice Powell to write a magisterial opinion." You have done so, and as time passes I believe your opinion will be viewed as a truly distinguished example of the Court at its best. I suspect that our admired mutual friend Alex Bickel [the brilliant professor of constitutional law at Yale who had died in 1974] would have agreed.

Justice Powell responded (July 10):

> . . . When I returned from our lunch, I found your heart-warming letter of June 29th that had come in the afternoon mail. It was a gracious and generous assessment of my Bakke opinion. Although I would not dare assume that the opinion merited this measure of praise, I shall be proud to show your letter to my children and keep it in my file . . .

There were, to be sure, times when I sensed, behind the veil of his courtesy, only limited accord between us on a racial issue. Powell was deeply interested in another matter with explosive implications, not then before the Court. This was the renewal of the 1965 Voting Rights Act, which was due to expire in 1981. It had been the most valuable of the civil rights measures of the 1960s, finally ending the obstruction of black voting in the Deep South and giving blacks, for the first time since Reconstruction, power over their own political destiny. Its most controversial feature, however, was a so-called "pre-clearance" provision, giving a veto over political changes in the parts of the South affected by the Act to the Justice Department's civil rights division. (Ultimately, the same provision was to produce the controversy over so-called "majority-minority" congressional seats, those tailored to produce a specific racial result by concentrating "black" precincts in a relatively few southern congressional districts.)

The original formula had been mechanical. In those districts, almost all southern, where the 1964 presidential vote fell below 50 percent of those of voting age, there was to be federally supervised voter registration. Moreover, no changes in election machinery or local government structures could be made without the approval of the Justice Department—that was the sleeper provision, little noticed at the time. In 1981, the renewal of the act was in trouble in Congress and the official view of the Reagan administration a mystery. What Ronald Reagan's personal view was, if he had one, I have no idea. His director of communications, David Gergen, assured me that the administration favored renewal. But it was often hard to discover who called the shots in race policy in the Reagan years. (Once, researching its support of tax exemption on First Amendment free-exercise-of-religion grounds for Bob Jones University and its near relations, the religiously oriented "segregation academies" in the Deep South, I tracked the major influence to the House offices of then Rep. Trent Lott of Mississippi, later the Republican Senate majority leader.) When Powell and I discussed the renewal of the VRA, he was clearly skeptical; and one exchange explains his concern. He wrote:

> [January 7, 1981] In view of our discussion of the Voting Rights Act, I thought possibly the enclosed slip opinions would be of interest. The cases are *Dougherty County, Georgia v. White* (1978) and *City of Rome, Georgia v. U.S.,* decided last April. Neither case, on its own facts, is of any great importance. Yet they illustrate the pervasiveness of the Act as construed, as well as the intrusive way this legislation is imposed only on the South and a few other narrowly defined areas. *Dougherty County* hardly could be less important, and hardly could have been within the contemplation of Congress when the Act was under consideration. The Court held . . . that a local school board—with no authority over any electoral system—must come to Washington and obtain clearance of a personnel rule with respect to employees who take leaves of absence to campaign for political office.
>
> *City of Rome* is an even more bizarre example of what seems close to vindictiveness. The case involves the question whether, by any degree of compliance . . . , a city may be relieved from its onerous burdens (i.e., "bail out"). It is conceded that for at least 17 years Rome had complied scrupulously with the Voting Rights Act. Yet it was not allowed to "bail out"— and under the decision will not be allowed—until the state of Georgia itself is out. No state has been allowed "out", including Virginia, despite a record for years of non-discriminatory voting. This is the government's view (i.e. the Civil Rights Division . . .).
>
> I dissented in both cases. . . . I misspoke when I told you that preclearance applications reached 200 per day. In 1979 the figure was about 25 per business day. Apart from a few local communities in the Deep South, I doubt that there is any need for the Act—except perhaps symbolically. For the latter reason, I would favor amending the Act . . . to embrace all 50

states, expressly limiting it to specified types of voting practices. . . . Also, I would return jurisdiction to the federal district courts in the states rather than continue to require approval by the Attorney General (actually the head of the Civil Rights Division) or by a court in the District of Columbia that has rarely (if ever) failed to take an expansive view of the Act. I share my "legislative" views with you with some hesitation, as legislating is not my role. Yet to some extent these views are reflected in my dissenting opinions. . . . The Act is so open-ended that it invites the Justice Department and virtually requires the court to legislate on an ad hoc basis.

Powell's letter reflects his suspicion of sectionally discriminatory laws, and of the tenacity with which bureaucracies cling to any power given (or merely assumed) to dictate to states and localities. It is the view of an old-fashioned federalist, and I tended to sympathize. My response shows that the justice's letter and dissents influenced my own views and thus the editorial line taken by the *Star* in favoring renewal.

[March 5, 1981] . . . . I am enclosing, in case you might miss it, a copy of our lead editorial for today—which, as you will note, cites the two cases we discussed and of which you sent me slip opinions. I must say that I found your position as expressed in the two dissents entirely persuasive. I am glad, in fact, that you opened my eyes to this aspect of the renewal issue, for I am certain it provides useful ammunition to those who want the Voting Rights Act killed altogether . . .

After some delay, the Voting Rights Act was renewed, with the excesses of the "pre-clearance" provision intact. Obviously our little collaboration, Powell's and mine, had no effect at all.

One effect of the veiled, sometimes elusive, civil rights policies of the Reagan administration became of keen concern to Lewis Powell. His young protégé J. Harvie Wilkinson was nominated by Reagan to a judgeship on the U. S. Fourth Circuit Court of Appeals. Jay Wilkinson, who eventually became the chief judge of the circuit, had served as Powell's first law clerk, recruited at the time of his midterm appointment in 1971. The son of a prominent Richmond banker who was himself one of Powell's oldest personal friends, Jay had made a fine record for himself as a writer, editor, and law-school teacher. I had heard of him many years earlier, long before he and I became friends, when I was visiting in New Haven. One Saturday morning I walked over to the Yale history department to call on one of my heroes, the historian C. Vann

Woodward. In the course of a half hour's friendly chat, Woodward mentioned that the best senior honors thesis he had directed was then being written by a senior from Richmond, who had the benefit of personal contacts with many of the Byrd Machine's premier personalities. This was Jay, though his name was then unfamiliar to me. His thesis won the Scholar of the House prize and was later published by the University Press of Virginia, the first of several significant books he would write. In the years following our move to Washington, we saw much of Jay and his wife Lossie, in Charlottesville, in Alexandria, and at Wrightsville Beach, where her parents had a cottage. They lived for a time in our neighborhood when Jay came to Washington as assistant attorney general in the Civil Rights Division. His nomination to the Fourth Circuit followed. Jay had written one of the better books on race (*From Brown to Bakke*) and was no enemy of racial change. But some Senate liberals presumed him guilty by association with some of the conservative—to them, foot-dragging—civil rights policies of the Reagan Justice Department. Some Virginia lawyers were irked (and perhaps a bit envious as well) that he had never practiced law. Believing as I did that he would make a fine judge, and that intellect of his caliber was too rare on the federal bench, I wrote several columns supporting the nomination, all of which appeared opportunely in the *Washington Post*. One that I wrote with special zest came when Sen. Ted Kennedy cited, as weighing against confirmation, the middling rating Jay got from the American Bar Association ("qualified" but not "highly" qualified). I remembered that some years earlier Kennedy himself had pushed for the appointment of a manifestly unqualified Kennedy family friend to the federal district bench, whom the ABA had inconveniently pronounced "unqualified." It was fun to catch the amiable but occasionally shrill Ted Kennedy in this blatant inconsistency, and I like to think that my advocacy helped a bit. Certainly the rough ride Jay got from some partisan Senate Democrats was a source of worry and vexation to Powell, who kept me informed about rumors he heard in Virginia legal circles:

[March 2, 1984] I read your column in the *Post* of March 1 with special interest. Acknowledgment by you of your friendship with Jay was admirable, though unnecessary. Your piece reflected the intellectual detachment that . . . judges should strive to attain . . . The only real negative in Jay's qualifications is the absence of experience in the practice of law. I agree—as most lawyers would—that this is not an insignificant negative. Yet, as you also observed, at the appellate level, this will be a negative only with lawyers who prefer not to argue cases before "professors." In my view, Jay will make an exceptionally able judge, and lawyers will recognize this.

It is a reflection on journalism, as well as on the level of discourse at the Judiciary Committee hearings, that Jay's overall qualifications are rarely mentioned. His academic records at Lawrenceville, Yale and Virginia were distinguished (in addition to his tennis playing); he had published three books, each of which had real quality in substance and form; because of his brilliance as a professor of constitutional law, he was tenured unusually early; he was chosen one year by the entire UVA faculty as the most distinguished faculty member under forty years of age; he remains, I believe, the youngest person ever to have served on the UVA Board of Visitors; and his three years of experience as the editor of an editorial page (as you know better than most!) gave him a range of experience and insight that few lawyers ever obtain. Not many persons in the federal judiciary can match these qualifications.

The recent [Washington] *Post* article, with the exception of his Yale education and a quote from Dean Merrill at the law school, mentioned none of the foregoing. On the contrary, by quoting unidentified sources, the article suggests that Jay will be confirmed only because he is "rich (which he is not) bright, Republican, white and male." Has America come to this?

[May 30, 1984] . . . In view of your interest, I enclose the exchange of letters between the three senators and me about Jay Wilkinson. So far as I know, no mention has been made in any press story of the final paragraph in my letter in which I express the view of Jay's qualifications that you and I share. No doubt you saw the story in Sunday's Post about the black student calling an ABA member on Jay's behalf. When politicians and the press go after a person, there is no relenting. I would hesitate to advise any one to accept an office in the federal government. The financial rewards are much less than in the private sector, and one rarely escapes criticism that may be fair or unfair and few persons leave a federal office with an enhanced reputation. . . . So it goes in the late Twentieth Century, and happily there are some competent people still willing to serve—often courageously and well.

To Powell's relief, Jay Wilkinson's nomination was eventually confirmed by the Senate, though not without turbulence, and he has won recognition as a judicial craftsman of originality and distinction. But it was a close call and in some respects foreshadowed the brutal donnybrook over the Robert Bork nomination to the Supreme Court that followed Powell's own retirement.

Powell retired from the Court, to widespread lament, in 1987, the year of the constitutional bicentennial. He had turned eighty and thought it was time to go. But he continued, after retirement, to sit on Fourth Circuit panels, often joining forces with Jay Wilkinson. Meanwhile, he took on one of the more thankless public duties of a long career. He agreed to head a study group appointed by Chief Justice Rehnquist to examine the way the federal courts were administering the death penalty, with a special focus on the bewildering tangle of parallel federal and state appeals that often dragged out capital cases for years: seven years was average, a decade not unusual. At issue was the use, and abuse, of habeas corpus proceedings to launch multiple federal appeals when some, often obscure, procedural ruling raised a new "technical" issue of due process. The Great Writ could be invoked to contest almost any finding, whether or not there was new evidence of innocence.

Some journalistic characterizations of Powell's ensuing report made it sound as if this gentle and thoughtful man were marching at the head of a screaming lynch mob, greasing the skids to rush condemned men to the gallows. Nothing his commission proposed would have disallowed any number of appeals grounded in new evidence of innocence. It would have been scandalous if the case were otherwise, as the increasing use of DNA analysis in death-row cases, in Illinois and elsewhere, has shown. In dozens of instances, genetic analysis has proved that the convicted, whatever their flaws or faults, could not have committed the crimes for which they had received the death sentence. Lewis Powell was nothing if not a kind and humane jurist. He knew, and was appalled by, the risks that an innocent person would be executed and he was careful even of the rights of the egregiously and obviously guilty. He had taken a lot of heat while still on the Court for voting to throw out, as coerced, a confession by a child-murderer who'd been pressured emotionally during a long, lawyerless ride with the police. But the treatment of his recommendations in the press was almost uniformly hostile. Also, the Chief Justice unwisely tried to rush Powell's proposals into effect without fully consulting the U.S. Judicial Conference; and the effort was wasted, at least for the moment.

> [October 2, 1989] A brief note to say that I read with appreciation your article in Saturday's Post. I think some of the reporters and editorialists who have commented on the report and recommendation of the committee I chaired, simply have not read the report carefully or with understanding. It is clear that you have.

I believe it was his experience with the report, coupled with later-life reflection on the finality of the death penalty, that persuaded Powell that capital punishment should be abolished. Unlike some other justices, who had trumpeted personal opposition from the bench and in public speeches, Powell did not say so publicly as long as he was still occasionally sitting as an auxiliary judge on the Fourth Circuit. He was mindful that the Court had made one failing attempt, in the early 1970s, to rid the country of capital punishment, and he was respectful of the contrary views of the public and the state legislatures. He would have seen it as self-indulgent posturing to announce a unilateral view of a constitutional question which had been repeatedly rejected by most of the state legislatures. I had learned of his view earlier. One day as we were lunching at the Monocle, discussing the delays that tended to distance this ultimate punishment from the crime, he said simply: "It isn't working and it ought to be abolished." I reported as much in my column, but could offer no attribution, since the information was privileged. I knew from many discussions, and some of his votes on the Court, that while his record was pragmatic, and he was certainly no hanging judge, Powell had his doubts about the Warren Court's refinements of criminal procedure. He often said he thought it would be better if American courts permitted trial judges more discretion (judges' rule, as it is called in England) to admit questionable evidence. The exclusionary rule, that no evidence obtained illegally could be used, had been enunciated in an opinion written by his favorite colleague on the Court, Potter Stewart. But it was too rigid for his taste.

In April 1992, Washington and Lee University, where I was then teaching, opened its Powell Archive on a gala weekend, with speeches by Chief Justice Rehnquist, Jay Wilkinson, and others. Powell's former clerks had raised money to add a magnificent wing to the law school to house his papers. At a formal banquet, guests received autographed "Lewis Powell" baseballs and baseball cards—a gesture rectifying W&L's failure to make him a varsity baseball player as an undergraduate.

In a special issue in his honor of the *Washington and Lee Law Review*, my colleague Alan Ides, a former Byron White clerk, wrote a perceptive piece about the case Powell had come to regard as his single great blunder: *Bowers v. Hardwick*. Police searching Hardwick's Atlanta house for illegal drugs found him in bed with another man. He was arrested on a "sodomy" charge but shortly released and not prosecuted. Hardwick himself brought a civil complaint in the federal courts seeking a declaratory judgment that the law was unconstitutional. Close students of constitutional cases know that no decision can be understood without taking account of the sometimes arcane jurisdictional and procedural issues. The *Bowers* decision pivoted on just such an arcane custom and thus was made to order for public misunderstanding. At a glance, it seemed that the Court, with Powell's agreement (the vote was five to four) had endorsed a primitive law in the age of dawning gay activism; and the disappointment was especially keen when somebody at the Court leaked word that Powell had first voted in conference to overturn the law, then changed his vote. I had been filled in on the fine points soon after the decision by my old friend Jim Exum, chief justice of North Carolina, who explained that it would have been highly unusual for the Court to strike down a statute in a *civil* suit for declaratory judgment, when there had been no criminal case. That nice point of judicial custom was obscured, however, and the case was widely viewed as a primitive affirmation by a narrow Court majority of state "sodomy" laws and of police invasions of private bedrooms. Powell made it clear in his concurrence that he would routinely vote to overturn any criminal conviction under such a law. But the damage was done. It became an embarrassment, and Powell said candidly that if he had it to do over again he would probably have stuck to his original vote:

> [July 3, 1991] I am happy to enclose a copy of the Madison Lecture I gave at NYU last October . . . A student did ask me about my vote in *Bowers v. Hardwick*. If the issue had come up in a different way and had been fully argued I may well have voted the other way. Actually, the Georgia statute had not been enforced since the 1930s. There was no actual case or controversy before us. The petition was for a declaratory judgment, something the Court rarely gives. . . .

A few days earlier—this must have been the occasion of our exchange on the subject of the *Bowers* case—he had written to me about
a longer piece I had published in the Sunday opinion section of the
Washington Post, assessing the Supreme Court term:

> [July 1, 1991] I will keep among my papers your article in the "Out-
> look" section. . . . You are more than generous in what you say about me.
> I agree that the "conservative majority" promised by Republican presi-
> dents has "finally arrived." On the last day of the 1990 Term the Court
> overruled two of my decisions. The first was my decision in *Booth v. Mary-
> land* in which the Court invalidated Maryland's "victim impact" statute.
> The second was *Solem v. Helm* in which the Court relied on the doctrine
> of proportionality in reviewing a state statute that authorized life impris-
> onment without parole where the offense consisted of minor crimes (three
> misdemeanors).

The cases he mentions show how the Court without his balancing
wisdom has tended to allow hyper-emotional testimony in the sentencing phase of criminal trials that is sure to poison the minds of a jury in
ways often irrelevant to the gravity of the crime. And of course the grim
rigidity of "three strikes" sentencing is sure to lead to harshly disproportionate sentencing. Such was part of the cost of Powell's departure from
the Court, and I am sure there were others as well. But by the mid-1990s
his health was failing; our correspondence and lunches had ceased, and
I heard of him only indirectly, through friends. He died in August 1998
and the turnout for his funeral filled the large Covenant Presbyterian
Church on Monument Avenue in Richmond.

"Turn left at Stonewall's statue and begin looking for the church on
your right," Jay Wilkinson said when I called to compliment him on a
graceful op-ed piece about Powell and to ask for directions to the last
rites. Jay's directions took me quickly, that hot morning, to the church.
I was an hour early but I was not surprised to find the church filling
up. There were familiar faces from Washington and Richmond, and an
unusually high turnout of black people, including Douglas Wilder, who
was sitting with other former governors of Virginia a few rows in front
of me. A decade earlier, Wilder had become the first black governor of
any American state, and he had asked Powell to administer the oath of
office. I could still see Lewis Powell, frail but erect, his robe and hair
tossed by a stiff midwinter breeze, leaning down to intone into the open

microphone: "A great day for Virginia": a cry of satisfaction that it was his state, the Old Dominion of all places, that had been the first to elect a descendant of slaves to its highest office. Powell knew well that Virginia's example had not always been so exalted.

It happened that George C. Wallace, the former governor of Alabama, died in the same late-summer season, as if the fates wished to flaunt an odd but revealing sense of occasion. Wallace was the noisiest of the dozens of southern politicians of the 1940s, '50s, and '60s who had worked to prolong the death agony of Jim Crow. It was he who proclaimed "segregation, now and forever" at the old Confederate capitol in Montgomery, and he who went through the charade of obstructing the admission of the first black student to the University of Alabama, he who had sought with disturbing success to export the white supremacist faith (only thinly disguised) to other regions in three presidential campaigns.

An American Plutarch with a sense of irony might have paired the two, Lewis Powell and George Wallace, as representative opposites in the South's long quarrel with itself over race and justice. Powell was all that Wallace wasn't—gentle, responsible, reasonable, with a patrician's sense of the duty the fortunate owe to the unfortunate. Wallace was a pert and gifted demagogue from crossroads Alabama with a stripe of vulgar cleverness that went over well in the 1960s in the courthouse squares (and, alas, some drawing rooms as well). With his flat face, pug nose, and slicked-down hair, he looked every inch the amateur boxer he once had been: a banty fighting cock with a sharp tongue. But they were as unlike as two men could be, parallel lives that met at no point, except that both were southerners of an age. Virginius Dabney, the distinguished Richmond editor and a friend and contemporary of Powell's, had once remarked that when the arch-secessionists from the Deep South moved to the newly transplanted Confederate capital in Richmond in 1861, they were as coolly received by old Richmond as the Visigoths had been by the old Romans. The feeling lingered, I suspect. By the time Lewis Powell and I had become friends and occasional luncheon partners after that exchange about strategic bombing, Wallace was all but forgotten, a shell of himself, paralyzed by a would-be assassin's bullet and remorseful over his misguided crusade against racial justice. Wallace's view had been as crudely simplistic as Powell's had been nuanced and responsible. Powell's stand for public schools, like his exclamation at Wilder's inauguration, like his pride in the Bakke opinion, pointed to where his heart lay. It helped explain why an unusual number of his black friends and associates would turn out for his funeral and burial at old Hollywood Cemetery. And it seemed significant to me that just down Monument Avenue from Lewis Powell's place of worship there now stands a statue of the late, great Arthur Ashe, in an honored place in a once uninterrupted gray line of Confederate heroes. The day after the funeral I wrote to Lewis Powell's son to express my sense of personal loss.

[September 1, 1998] So many thoughts have crowded to mind since your father's death that I hardly know where to begin, though all are pleasant. Among the senior figures I came to know in Washington . . . he stands preeminent in every way. He had all the virtues of the great public man—conviction, integrity of purpose, breadth of mind and spirit; but beyond that, he had all those qualities that one values in a friend: gentleness, courtesy, and genuine interest in one's personal well-being. Of course, I don't need to tell you all this, for your eloquent and moving tribute to him at the funeral yesterday recapitulated much of what I say, and more besides. . . . In short, I not only esteemed your father but loved him as a son might; and I shall miss his friendly counsel. . . . The long letter he took the trouble to write to me [about the strategic bombing survey] was typical in its genuine concern for the integrity of history but also in its entire freedom from irritation, condescension or rancor, so often, alas, the marks of controversy now. How I wish his spirit might somehow redeem the casual and mindless savagery of our public life, especially here in Washington, where the civility and consideration he represented and personified have become so rare. . . .

WILLIE MORRIS

"The New College Morris" *In the long years of our post-Oxford friendship, Willie Morris and I developed a familiar routine. The phone would ring. "Is this the Jesus Yoder or the Merton Yoder?" a pseudo-English voice would inquire. "Is this the New College Morris or the Magdalen Morris?" I would respond; and the conversation would resume, wherever it had left off. It has been true for me as perhaps for many others that the oldest and earliest friendships, when maintained, are the deepest. As different as we were in so many ways, by temperament and habit, Willie and I had affinities that ran deeper than any differences; and we were destined to be the closest of friends for as long as we both lived. Willie was, I believe, the largest figure it has been my fortune to know, large in every dimension, one of those people of whom we say, "larger than life."*

But it would be a mistake to turn this account into a caricature and to scant Willie's significance as an editor and writer, especially during his too-brief tenure as editor-in-chief of Harper's Magazine *in the early 1970s. Some traditionalists didn't like it that he transacted a good deal of the magazine's important business in a Chinese restaurant on Park Avenue South, although his critics seemed to forget the connection between the* New Yorker *in its early heyday and the Algonquin Hotel. Willie transformed the magazine almost overnight into the hottest book in Manhattan. Under his direction it became a monument to his powers of imagination and attracted brilliant writing from such figures as Bill Styron, Norman Mailer, and David Halberstam. Their work graced its pages, not for dollars, because its budget was never grand, but because they could see that Willie was writing a memorable chapter in the history of American magazine journalism and offered them a starring role in it. After he died, I was asked how he edited. Strangely, he did not edit, certainly not in the fussy sense, nor did other great editors I worked under: Bill Snider in Greensboro, Eve Auchincloss at* Book World, *Jim Bellows at the* Washington Star. *All had the imagination and perception to detect a writer's strengths and what could be done with them. They did not edit; they encouraged.*

Willie Morris, my most gifted friend, and one of the dearest too, died unexpectedly in his native Jackson, Mississippi, one August day in 1999. He was only sixty-four and his literary powers were undiminished. I say that his death was unexpected, but that isn't quite true. It was sudden and shocking. But for years Willie had lived close to the edge, burning his candle at both ends. Often in his later years his gathering embonpoint and a once handsome face now red, puffy, and splotched, reminded one on his bad days of the more sybaritic Roman emperors, and prompted friends to fear for his life. He had enjoyed an Indian summer decade of survival—and physical revival—under the loving care of his second wife, JoAnne Prichard ("she saved my life," he once told my wife Jane). But the damage done by years of hard drinking and smoking, bohemian hours and habits, could hardly be undone. And while he seemed at times almost to court death, it nonetheless came as a terrible blow to us all when it did come. Some of his friends, including my wife Jane, had a reaction not unmixed with anger, knowing as they did how recklessly Willie had lived for so long. "Willie has cheated us of his company far too soon," she said and meant it literally, for he was the most entertaining of companions. Her sentiments were echoed at Willie's lying-in-state in the old Mississippi state capitol building by another close friend, Dean Faulkner Wells. "The son of a bitch went and died on us," she said in the soft voice that sounded so much like that of her immortal uncle, tears welling in her eyes. I understood their view; for Willie was ever the most diverting of companions, among all his many other contributions to our lives and dreams. Few writers and editors (or friends) will ever bequeath so rich a legacy as Willie did. And his last bequest, appropriately, was his fine posthumous novel *Taps,* a book that he had viewed for a very long time as his masterwork.

But before I get to that, a few words of reminiscence.

Risking cliché, which had no foothold in Willie's richly original world, one could say that nothing defined his life so well as the leaving of it. Two days after his death he became only the third Mississippian in this century to lie in state under the dome of the old capitol building in Jackson, an edifice that figures richly in William Faulkner's *Requiem for a Nun.* Hundreds paid their respects. Then some three dozen of Willie's close friends adjourned to a nearby beanery whose cheerfully seedy décor and crepuscular lighting recalled those many hangouts Willie had graced over the years, from the front parlor of the King's Arms pub in Oxford to that nondescript Chinese place on Park Avenue South where he transacted business and held court during his editorship of *Harper's* magazine, to Bobby Van's bar in Bridgehampton, New York. Later that afternoon, the cortege proceeded to the First Methodist Church in Yazoo City, where he had grown up on the very edge of the great Mississippi Delta. William Styron, the novelist, with whom he had enjoyed doing road gigs labeled the "Bill and Willie Show," paid eloquent tribute and so did others. Will Campbell, a hero of the civil rights movement in its stormy days, brought the house down when he called for a standing ovation. Finally, thirteen steps from the witch's grave in the old Yazoo cemetery, Willie was laid to rest to the sound of taps as he had played it so many years earlier for the Korean War dead.

We had been the best of friends for more than forty years, even before destiny put us on the same boat to Oxford in October 1956. As fellow college editors in the preceding academic year, we had both landed in hot water—his far hotter than mine. For in *Daily Texan* editorials, Willie had questioned the sanctity of the oil-depletion allowance, heresy of heresies in Texas. We had formed by correspondence a sort of mutual-support association.

As a writer, Willie was a rare combination of artistry and intellect. Behind the sometimes drowsy or passive-seeming exterior he was a polymath who knew a great deal about a great many important things, especially American and southern history and letters. He had that most invaluable of the writer's devices, famously described by Ernest Hemingway as a reliable "shit detector." In my view Willie was the finest reporter of his age on the texture of the turbulent southern experience in this century.

As a man, Willie was without detectable vanity or egotism. He was a wonderful listener, missing nothing, recalling everything, with an exquisitely sensitive emotional register. Once when he and Jane and I were sitting late at Elaine's, the New York literary café where he was a fixture, he and Jane began talking about Scott Fitzgerald's novel *Tender Is the Night*. That led to a discussion of the tragedy of Scott and Zelda, a recollection that so upset Willie that he left Elaine's to walk around the block for half an hour.

When we traveled all over Europe together, he carried his clothes and books in a worn old suitcase without a handle which he would hoist and carry on his shoulder. It was heavy, too, for we all lugged heavy tomes with us on these hegiras, in the usually vain hope of intervals of study between the cathedrals and the bullfights. When we traveled together I always took extra money along, because Willie had no idea how much he would need and usually ran short. He always repaid these debts promptly; he was a man with a most acute sense of honor. His reading glasses were missing a rim for God knows how long, a year or more, after which the newfound rim would be attached with adhesive tape. In later life, he came to hate ringing telephones and often shut his in the refrigerator to mute the sound. You had to use an elaborate dialing code to get through to him, and even that was chancy. Willie never cared about clothes, so far as I knew, or shoes either. Even on formal occasions, I never saw him in a pair of pants that were not a bit baggy. He preferred ratty old pullover sweaters to jackets and ties; he was no fashion plate. Jane said when he died: "Among superbly creative people, who usually have big and sometimes unmanageable egos, he was the freest from petty neurosis and self-absorption of anyone I have known. He had no defenses and needed none."

Not the least of my reasons for beginning Willie's story with its ending is that he had followed Dr. Freud's advice and made friends with death. The friendship took the form of a passionate interest in cemeteries. He had prowled every notable burying ground from Oxford to Hollywood, from Boston to New Orleans—not in a spirit of morbidity but because their quiet precincts, the resting place of "the great silent majority," as he called the dead, offered an aperture into the human comedy. There, past merged with present in that incremental narrative of people and events, past and present, that constituted Willie's slant on the world. There was, of course, a hint of the wise old counsel, memento mori, in this. He wrote of this early affection in a poignant passage in *North Toward Home:* "The cemetery [where he now rests] held no horror for me. It was set on a beautiful wooded hill overlooking the whole town. I loved to walk among the graves and look at the dates and words on the tombstones. I learned more about the town's past here, the migrations, the epidemics, the old forgotten tragedies, than I could ever have learned in the library."

Yet no one was ever less defined, or preoccupied, by death itself. Willie was an antic spirit, centrally animated at his core by the soul of the mischievous ten-year-old boy he once had been. He loved to play jokes and pranks on his friends, most of them amusing and benevolent. It could have surprised no one who knew him that his last known dream involved the amusing sabotage of a fancy dinner party at the Martha's Vineyard summer house of his friend Styron. (He dreamed of putting Ex-Lax in the red wine.) There was, as I have good reason to know, a beguiling charm in Willie's practical jokes and tricks that almost made one want to be fooled. That is why his friends so often were. Once as we were being driven through the kudzu-shrouded woodlands of north Mississippi, Willie persuaded me that the man who had imported the now uncontrolled anti-erosion ground-cover plant to the U.S. was still alive, in Oxford, Mississippi. When I asked if I might be able to interview him, Willie was sadly silent for a moment (perfect acting, as usual) and then said that the man was so mortified by the vine's fecund rampancy that he had become a hermit and withdrawn from all human society. When I naïvely reported the tale in my newspaper column, a southern editor I knew was on the phone within minutes.

"What's this shit about kudzu?" Claude Sitton demanded.

"Shit?" I asked, surprised. "What do you mean, Claude?"

"If the man who imported kudzu is still living, he's at least 158 years old." Claude knew. He had once written about the menace of kudzu for the *New York Times*.

Willie once convinced my daughter Anne, then twelve, during an after-dinner walk on Long Island, that if she listened carefully at dusk she could hear the ghost of John Philip Sousa playing his horn on the front porch of his summer cottage—a dark house up a long tree-lined lane. "Listen, Annie," he said, cupping his hand to his ear. Her eyes grew big. "I can't hear it, Uncle Willie." Willie then elaborated, spinning out a story with that uncanny circumstantial improvisation that his friends knew so well, but not well enough to beware of. Willie told us as we stood there in the gathering darkness that the composer of "The Stars and Stripes Forever" and other great marches had come to America as an Italian immigrant boy, John Phillipe. He was so proud of being a new citizen, Willie continued, that he would sign his semiliterate postcards back to the old country, "John Phillipe, USA," soon elided to John Philip Sousa. It was only later, after a credulous recitation of this romance to someone more knowledgeable about the history of American band music, that we learned that John Philip Sousa, native born, had followed his father as director of the marine band!

If life for Willie was a narrative, growing with experience like the rings of a great oak, and compounded not only of his deep learning in history and letters but of his fabulous memory for old scenes and talk, one striking ingredient was a skein of fables whose quota of truthfulness (as in the Sousa romance) was often hard to fix. Memories of these fables flowed all but nonstop during those sad early-August days in Jackson, after his death, as friends sought to measure the vacancy he had left behind. David Halberstam, whose gifts as a chronicler of American life Willie was among the first to recognize and display in the pages of *Harper's* magazine, recalled a typical tale. When Halberstam's best-selling book *The Best and the Brightest* was bumped by a diet book from the top of the *New York Times* bestseller list, he had a call from Willie, affecting a donnish voice and speaking as the supposed author of the diet book. The "diet doctor" begged Halberstam's pardon for replacing him, but then proposed a collaboration that would make them both rich. "I even have a title," he said. "We shall call it *The Best and the Fattest.*"

From a thick album of similar antics, I recall the night in the fall of 1957 when Willie telephoned the Royal Humane Society offices in London from our digs at 22 St. Margaret's Road. Speaking in faux broken English for the fictitious "Oxford East European Society," Willie lodged a protest against the propulsion of the dog Laika into space by a Russian *Sputnik*. "Do ze Roshian parparians haf any vey of gettink this poor creature back to ze earth?" he asked the puzzled but sympathetic lady at the other end of the line. When the same whimsical mood came over him, Willie would suddenly lean forward in those boxy London taxicabs and loudly address the bewildered driver. "Rooshian people do not vant var," he would bellow through the glass partition. "Only crazy Americanskis vant var. Do Ainglish people vant var? Do not hang out vit varmonger Americanskis!"

With all of this, Willie was a gregarious creature with a gift for mimicry and entertainment. It accounted in part for the acolytes who gathered around any table or event, wherever he perched. That gift rested on a verbal edge whose subtlety sometimes emerged only with the years, like the bouquet of a great wine. Thus the grandsons of John Hancock, improbably buried in Yazoo City, had died of "some colorful disease." The impersonal funerals Willie occasionally witnessed in New York City told a bleak tale, for him, of the loneliness of "natural death." Perhaps one needn't be a writer, or a connoisseur of verbal invention, to sense the ingenuity of those exact adjectives, "colorful" or "natural." But the fact is that Willie's sense of words was pristine. He had the artist's capacity for seeing and making it new. It was Willie, contemplating a gray day in Oxford not long after we arrived there, who said, echoing Browning, "O, to be in April, now that England's here." Having coined this enviable bon mot, he gave it away, generously attributing it to Jess

Woods, a classmate who had died just after returning from England. When he answered my call to speak to this or that group in North Carolina, he would say: "Yoder, I'm going to attack the Red Chinese." After he had digested the tangled royal genealogies of Anglo-Saxon England, he described any fatuous reactionary as being "to the right of Ethelred the Unready," a great improvement on the hackneyed Genghis Khan. He loved to point out that his son David, born on the National Health Scheme in Oxford, "cost eighty-seven cents." Of the Confederacy and the event of our Civil War, he said—in fun, but still with a southerner's nostalgic edge—"We had the greatest armies ever put in the field, but our machines failed us."

Willie's unwearied flow of nonsense was a big part of him, obviously, for he did view life as fundamentally comic. But it was only a part, and perhaps the lesser part, after all. He was otherwise a very serious man, chastened and deepened by the experience of a sensitive childhood in race-obsessed Mississippi. His distinctions, literary and civic, to say nothing of his good works, would require many pages to list. But three paramount accomplishments may be representative.

I believe that he did more than any Mississippian of his generation to recall his troubled state from the brink of political terrorism, to hearten its better angels, and to coax it toward the vibrant racial good will that prevails there today. His return to Mississippi from two decades of exile in 1980, to be writer-in-residence at Ole Miss, was an effort of will and reintegration. As he wrote in *New York Days:* "Here I was back again in the sweet and deep dark womb of home. The eternal juxtaposition of . . . hate and love, the apposition of its severity and tenderness, would forever baffle and enrage me . . . But these forever drive me to words. Meanness is everywhere, but here the meanness and the desperation and the nobility have for me their own dramatic edge, for the fools are my fools and the heroes are mine too." The theme of redemption and reconciliation in a troubled but beloved society figure in two fine books, *Yazoo,* about the belated integration of schools in his hometown; and *The Courting of Marcus Dupree,* in which he explored the ironies of interracial amity in Philadelphia, Mississippi, a bare generation after even the law-enforcement officials of "bloody Neshoba" had colluded in the unspeakable assassination of three young civil rights workers.

During his tenure as associate editor and then editor-in-chief of *Har-*

per's (1963–71) he transformed a sedate magazine into the most vital and admired forum in the country for fine writing on great matters at a time of national troubles. His recruitment of writers was spectacular. Norman Mailer's memorable history-as-novel *On the Steps of the Pentagon* was a Willie Morris production, delivered at one hundred thousand words, all of which would run in a single issue of the magazine. As were Styron's "This Quiet Dust," a prose overture to his great novel about the Nat Turner slave rebellion, and David Halberstam's searing profiles of "the best and the brightest" who had blundered into the Vietnam calamity. Willie was an editor and impresario of boldness and imagination, from the same rare mold as Harold Ross of the original *New Yorker* and the unsung Briton Hadden, the creative spirit behind the early *Time* magazine. But his administrative methods were unorthodox and sometimes disorderly from the point of view of his owners; and his more or less forced resignation as editor in 1971 brought down a brilliant regime. When Jane and I and our two children spent a week with him shortly afterward, he was living in Muriel O. Murphy's huge house on Georgica Pond in the Hamptons and saturating himself nightly in Mahalia Jackson gospel songs and a recorded recitation of General Lee's farewell to his troops. I saw several huge boxes of unopened correspondence, all probably tributes to his fallen editorship. I offered to help open and sort them. Willie was content to ignore them and I wonder if he ever read them at all. (Jack Bales, Willie's dedicated bibliographer, tells me that the collection of Willie's papers at the Ole Miss library numbers some seventeen thousand items.)

Finally, but not least, Willie's precocious autobiography *North Toward Home* will surely live after him as one of the immortal American self-portraits, with those of Mark Twain, Henry Adams, and John A. Rice. (Rice, a South Carolina Rhodes Scholar of an earlier vintage, wrote a delightful memoir called *I Came Out of the Eighteenth Century,* which I had the pleasure of recommending to Willie. He read and liked it. Then out of the ether one night came a distressed call from New York. Willie had loved the book and, as was his custom, had tried to call Rice to tell him so. "But Yoder," he said, despairingly, "he's dead.")

Those who were not only friends but fellow writers knew, as I did, that Willie watched over them and their work from a distance, like a friendly guardian angel. He poured great energy into matching writers with their proper subjects and destinies, destinies which he often saw more quickly and clearly than they. In Jackson on the day of his burial my old Chapel Hill friend Eli Evans said, "Willie changed my life." It was Willie, then editor of *Harper's*, who suggested to Eli one day at lunch that he could and should write a fine book about the peculiar shaping experiences of southern Jewry. The suggestion led to a distinguished book called *The Provincials: A Personal History of Jews in the South*, recently reissued with a Willie Morris introduction by Free Press as part of its own fiftieth-anniversary celebration. A few years later there followed Eli's widely admired biography of Judah P. Benjamin, the Confederate secretary of state. Two of my own books were published in Mississippi, largely through Willie's patronage. Eli's experience and mine are merely representative cases among scores or hundreds. A significant part of the significant journalism of the 1960s and 1970s bore Willie's imprimatur in some form. He had planted the seed, or edited a manuscript, or conceptualized an unarticulated book, or encouraged timid writers to spread their wings and tap their hidden strengths.

Willie's perceptive obituarist in the *New York Times* of August 3, 1999, Peter Applebome, wrote with unusual candor of Willie's notorious indifference to the rules of good health: "Mr. Morris drank too much bourbon and red wine, smoked too many Viceroys, stayed up too late and caroused too much." It was true. When his Oxford classmates of 1956 first met him when the *Flandre* sailed from New York, Willie was a lithe, athletic, and fresh-faced boy, an accomplished athlete who had played varsity baseball at Texas. But some time in his late twenties, or thereabouts, Willie, a born night-owl in any case, had turned his back on the life of fitness for wine, women, and song and never looked back. It was not a bad swap, perhaps, for an artist. But it was as if Willie wished to be numbered among the great American writers, Wolfe, Fitzgerald, and many others, who had lived at the edge and paid a price. "They say I have a bourbon problem," Willie remarked to Jane and me one night, in one of his more reckless moods. "Hell, I don't have a problem at all. I can get all the bourbon I want." Some of his friends doubt that Willie would have survived even to sixty-four without the great stroke of fortune of his later life: that he met and married JoAnne Prichard, a fellow editor of great sensitivity, who valued him as he was, for his unmatched kindness and originality. There followed a final decade's renaissance, of fine writing and new accomplishment, including a deepening interest in movies and their making. His friends, however, had long since been forced to see that there was in Willie's incandescent temperament some hidden strain of the incurable wound that strengthens and aims the magic bow of art, even as in Edmund Wilson's memorable essay. The wound and the bow were intricately fused, as they often are in those of comic genius.

When we first met in New York on the eve of that sailing of the 1956 Rhodes Scholars to England, I soon heard the tale of his playing of "Taps" at funerals for the Korean War dead. The novel he wove from that memory became the fictional counterpart of his memoir *North Toward Home.* It went through many versions and vicissitudes on its way to ultimate publication—so many, in fact, as to delay its appearance until after his death. On occasion he became so discouraged that he set it aside. But now, lovingly edited by JoAnne, it is at last in print. And to know Willie is to know *Taps;* to know *Taps* is to know Willie. As I read it, Dilsey's words in the last section of *The Sound and the Fury* kept coming to mind—"Ise seed de first en de last."

The situation in *Taps*—that of a small-town southern boy, having barely survived adolescence and its vague paranoias and a hovering mama as well, playing "Taps" at Korean War funerals—was among Willie's strongest memories when we first became friends. Willie often said back then that he hoped someday to write a novel about the experience. In view of Willie's lifelong romance with cemeteries, that is hardly surprising; but, of course, *Taps* is about much more than war deaths or ritual burial.

I was nonetheless in the early years intrigued, and a bit puzzled, by Willie's almost obsessive desire to leave his mark in the field of fiction. We were still college journalists, learning a craft; but Willie already showed promise of the mastery of reminiscence and reportage that would yield *North Toward Home* and *Yazoo,* and other fine works of nonfiction—all in my view fit to be mentioned in the same breath with the best of Joseph Mitchell, A. J. Liebling, James Thurber, and the other great *New Yorker* writers. Moreover, his first published novel, *The Last of the Southern Girls,* though full of grace notes, was transparently the instant product of a torrid summer romance with Barbara Howar. It had not undergone the necessary transmutations of real storytelling.

What more could fiction add?

I am older, and perhaps wiser, than when this question began to puzzle me. I think I understand better Willie's itch to fictionalize. It is, after all, the highest ambition of any writer to tell a true story so well that it will survive the erosions of time. I believe that *North Toward Home* will survive; I am sure that *Taps* will. The long steeping of this book in the pools of memory has been rewarded by that magical metamorphosis from mere anecdote to story that is the essence of fine fiction.

Taps addresses, with thematic depth and resonance, the ageless theme of mutability, the longing for permanence amid decay and flux. In *Taps*, Willie has challenged mutability with powerful recall. His memory, one in a million, was, as I have already said, powerful and comprehensive. It embraced verbatim, with uncanny completeness and accuracy, bygone conversations; hundreds of people personally known or observed; books read and recalled to the letter; landscapes rural and urban explored down to the last blade of grass or flowering shrub; seasons cold and hot and in-between; scents and smells and sounds, of autumn leaves burning or the freshness of a girl on a spring night; crises of the heart, whether of pain or fear, loneliness or joy, love or friendship. Willie's memory, in short, had that vivid particularity that is always the key ingredient of enduring narration. In Willie's novel, it assumes the etched clarity of that unforgettable scene in Homer's *Odyssey* where the old nurse washing the vagabond Odysseus's feet when he returns to Ithaca in the beggar's disguise discovers the scar left in boyhood by a boar's tusk, is impelled to cry out in recognition, but is sternly silenced on pain of death.

Browsing in a bookstore in Madison, Connecticut, not long after *Taps* was published, my daughter Anne saw the novel prominently displayed among the current favorites of the store's staff. "This is Faulkner you can read," one of them had said, perpetuating of course the silly view that Faulkner is unreadable, but also making a point about the permanence of Willie's novel. There are no Mozarts of writing; even the best writers serve apprenticeships to the masters, as Willie did not only to Faulkner but also to Thomas Wolfe, whom in so many ways he resembled—not only in his verbal exuberance but in his living. He had absorbed Wolfe's trademark thematic search for the missing father and for "lost and wind-grieved ghosts." He was forever fascinated that I myself hailed from "Old Catawba," that I had walked the sandy walks of Pulpit Hill in the footsteps of Eugene Gant of *Look Homeward, Angel*.

One dull reviewer—where else but in the *New York Times Book Re-*

view?—noted the rich vocabulary of *Taps* and had the effrontery to mistake verbal fearlessness for "lushness." The poor reviewer must have been frightened in his youth by an English teacher, and I assume that he is similarly disturbed when he reads Faulkner and Shakespeare, who never hesitated to reach for new words or adventurous juxtapositions of old words.

Of course, *Taps* falls into the familiar realm of the *bildungsroman*—the tale of a young man's growth through experience. It is about the discovery of love and friendship in all their varieties; and certain passages are of such obvious durability that they remind me of the story told by the youthful figures Keats discovered on his immortal Grecian urn: lovers forever fixed in art who need never fear the decline of beauty or passion. Willie has many passages in *Taps* that sound that note:

> We remember what we wish to remember. It is all there to be summoned, but we pick and choose. . . . We are sixteen. She and I are standing in the side lawn of her house, under an ancient water chestnut. . . . We stand in an amiable embrace. . . . I gaze down from the summit of the years, all the losses and guilts and rages and shames, the loves come and gone, and ravenous death, and I conjure now that instant when I was standing in the shade of the chestnut with Georgia, and I am caught ever so briefly in a *frieze of old time,* the high school years stretching before me as in a Lewis Carroll dream: "Come, lad." *Artifice, all of it.*

Whoever fails to see the fineness of that, and many passages like it, is a clod with no nose for poetry. And "artifice" *is* at the heart of it. Experience is mere raw, random recollection before it undergoes the refinement of memory and artistry. *Taps* shows me that Willie, from the days of our youth together, understood something fundamental about life and letters. Having seen the first, I have been privileged to see the last; and it is very fine.

Two years after Willie died, his hometown of Yazoo City staged a celebration of his life, rich testimony to his legacy. Old friends, including many who had been inspired one way or another by his editing or his encouragement, gathered in an old schoolhouse Willie had once attended, now a city museum and arts center. And it was a touch of genius on the part of his widow JoAnne, and her fellow planners, to link "place and friendship" and invite some of us who had known him to reflect on that indelible connection. Anyone who entered Willie's orbit quickly learned that the sense of physical place was central to his view of life and character—therefore of friendship as well. I don't believe I've ever known anyone else who had so intense a feeling for places and for the tactile and visual values they represent.

The opening words of *Taps* are typical: "We were flatland people. . . . The hills came sweeping down from their hardwood forests and challenged the flatness, mingling with it in querulous juxtaposition." As I shall note in a moment, that mode of identity is echoed by the narrator of his unfinished Oxford novel, *Chimes at Midnight*.

Willie's intense solicitude for unspoiled land inspired his antic campaign against a New York real-estate developer who was building suburban houses—houses shot from guns, as another old friend of mine used to call them—just down the road from his country place near Pawling. Until this apostle of exurban "progress" went to work, the neighborhood consisted almost entirely of gentle, rolling pastureland, marked here and there by mellow old farmhouses, and Willie hated to see it blighted by mundane bricks and mortar.

One night when the bulldozers and hammers had fallen silent, Willie slipped down the road and taped a cryptic handwritten message to the seat of one of the bulldozers. It was that passage from Faulkner's story "Delta Autumn"—in *Go Down, Moses*—about how the Delta had been "deswamped and denuded and derivered in two generations," and continuing: "No wonder the ruined woods I used to know don't cry for retribution! . . . . The people who have destroyed it will accomplish its revenge."

It would have been a treat to see the puzzled faces when this ominous prediction was discovered the following morning—not that I imagine for a moment that it arrested the ravaging march of urban progress across the New York countryside. But like so many of his gestures it gave Willie amusement and satisfaction. And there was no doubt of the passionate feeling that inspired it.

The other day, going through some of the many letters that he and I exchanged over more than four decades, I was reminded of yet another project that had a great deal to do with place. At a point in the 1970s—I believe it must have been when he was working on the Oxford novel—he asked me to help him find a place in Chapel Hill where he could live incognito for a few weeks, steeping himself firsthand in an ambience he already knew from his reading of *Look Homeward, Angel* and from his interrogations of me about what it had been like to follow Wolfe's hero Eugene Gant to Pulpit Hill. Those who know from of old of Willie's gregariousness, and the ease with which he could draw a crowd, will find it amusing that he planned to be incognito. Still, he was determined to absorb the texture of the place and I wasn't surprised to discover in the unfinished Oxford novel that the narrator is a Chapel Hill man bearing minor similarity to yours truly. But his narrator's imaginary family, unlike mine, are rooted in the desolate, swampy northeast of North Carolina:

> The broad river estuaries and coastal sounds of east Carolina are in the blood of me and my people. They were farmers, lawyers, teachers and politicians—Chapel Hill men; one of our forebears was an early president there, back when the campus was little more than a clearing in the woods. The most natural act of my life was being a Chapel Hill man, because of everything it ever was to us, the aristocracy of its intelligence, its integrity, its beauty in the forested hills. I was shaped by it—trained to excel in all it offered.

I found this passage remarkable and moving because I knew the energies and imagination that underlay it—the more so because it was I, one bright late September day in 1958, who introduced Willie to Chapel Hill. This eloquent passage from the fragmentary *Chimes at Midnight* bears witness to Willie's uncommon capacity to imagine himself into a place, a landscape, to know it vicariously more deeply than many for whom it is an accustomed habitat. Willie certainly loved Wolfe's evocative description of the place, transmogrified into Pulpit Hill—"like an outpost of great Rome . . . The wilderness crept up to it like a beast."

Willie, of course, quite literally put Yazoo City on the map. I don't mean the banal maps of the geologic survey or the Exxon stations; rather that livelier map of the American literary imagination, where it joins Mark Twain's Hannibal, Willa Cather's Nebraska, Scott Fitzgerald's East and West Egg, and of course Wolfe's Old Catawba among immortal places.

It was at Oxford, as I've said, that Willie and I first got to be friends, brothers really. When Larry L. King was writing his fine recent profile of Willie for *Texas Monthly,* I was glad to share some "informed speculations" about Willie's response to that most powerful and haunting of physical places: the Oxford invoked by Matthew Arnold, by Chaucer, by Gerard Manley Hopkins, and so many others. Since Willie wrote relatively little about his Oxford years, and since he was a practiced converter of every experience into rich prose, his partial silence had led some to assume that Oxford had disappointed him, or he it. The notion astonished me, knowing as I did that Willie was easily the most celebrated and charismatic American Oxonian of his years and—with the possible exceptions of Pete Dawkins and Bill Bradley—of his era. For one thing, he managed to spend four years there, a record for Rhodes Scholars, so far as I know. I suggested to Larry that the clue to Willie's reticence about Oxford is to be found in his essay, *My Two Oxfords,* elegantly edited by JoAnne and printed at the Yellow Barn Press. Willie calls a long and daunting roll of eminent Oxonians and observes that following in their footsteps could be intimidating for a boy from the New World. (Willie never quite got over the realization that his college, New College, was "new" before Columbus set sail.)

I believe that Willie and others among the Americans of our time there—those with a grain of sensibility at least—held Oxford in awe, and that he was haunted in that special way of his by the ghosts of the great figures who had preceded us. No doubt, as his unfinished novel suggests, he yearned to try his hand at subduing to words that powerful place. But he feared, because he knew it would be a deadly sin, to be glib or superficial. Willie, I am confident, shared the view that when you're moving in the shadows of Shelley, Arnold, Gibbon, Dr. Johnson, Cardinal Newman, and others, modesty is in order. It risks impudence to contest their like in casual reminiscence. But that is a measure of the depth of Willie's feeling, not of disappointment or failure. And in fact, Willie was in his way a jaunty bard of Oxford and England, in a manner appropriate to his genius. In that magnetic memory of his, small phrases of place and association lingered in mythic resonance. "How do you like our muddy little island, Yoder?" he would sometimes ask. We remembered it as the timid query put to him by a meek little man who had sat long in silence beside him at a Christmas dinner in London and then suddenly popped that vivid question. *Our muddy little island!* Willie liked that, far though it might be from John of Gaunt's gem of an island set in a silver sea.

I have already mentioned Willie's fascination with cemeteries. They were places of instruction in the human comedy and tragedy, laconic and lapidary and leaving much to the imagination. I was led on several such expeditions and pilgrimages, not only to the grave of William Faulkner in Oxford but to the country graveyards in the hills around the university town where fading photographs of the departed in little glass and plastic frames struggled against wind and rain to keep memory green. One day he drove us all the way to Holly Springs to stand among the tombstones of Confederate generals. A few years ago, when Jane and I visited Yazoo City for the first time, Willie arranged a special communication as we wandered through the place where as a boy he had played "Taps" at military funerals. "Yoder, why don't you and Jane look at that marker over there?" he urged, pointing to a large gravestone some twenty yards away. We knew what was going on, and obliged. When we returned to the witch's grave, lo and behold the witch herself had left Jane a letter—and Jane's correspondence with the witch, always in care of Willie, continued for months.

And Willie, being so distinctly a man of places, tended to identify friends in that way also—and indeed, what superior index is there?

You see Willie's conviction in the passage I quoted in which the narrator of his unfinished Oxford novel speaks of his ancestral connections with Chapel Hill. It is a matter of *rootedness*. As I wrote in my introduction to the Yoknapatawpha Press edition of *North Toward Home,* our southern small-town America, his and mine, has been much homogenized since Willie and I were boys in the 1940s. We were lucky to have grown up in a world whose regional flavors and colors had not faded to pastels, and whose distinctive regional accents—those liquid, patrician voices of our mothers and grandmothers, aunts and sweethearts—had not been puréed into an indistinguishable Valley Girl patois. There was plenty of nourishment for memory and storytelling. The vividness of particular memories made it easier to become friends then—"We grew up," I wrote, "on the same books, the same Protestant hymns, the same popular tunes and radio programs [and] . . . heard the same ceaseless family talk."

Throughout our long friendship, Willie took pleasure in identifying me as a son of "Old Catawba," and also with my college in Oxford which (to the unending stimulation of Willie's imagination) happened to be Jesus. "What a friend we have in Jesus," he would say. Not one of our telephone conversations over forty years failed to begin with the pseudo-English voice, easily identifiable as Willie's asking: "Is this the *Jesus* Yoder, or the *Merton* Yoder?"

If you were so fortunate as to be a friend of Willie's, it was as if you were filed by place in the capacious spaces of his memory; and this filing system, in turn, implied a traditional view of human character—that it springs, at its best, from rootedness and from piety for one's ancestral places, a sense of that spiritus loci known to antiquity. Beyond doubt, that was true of Willie himself. He knew where his roots were, and in the end they were the key to all he was and wrote.

FOSSIL'S FAREWELL

Admitted Fiction *The title of this farewell chapter is, of course, a small joke, echoing the title of the book. Any journalist who isn't self-deluded is aware that fiction is often committed, even unintentionally, in the name of reporting. I wouldn't go as far as Janet Malcolm of the* New Yorker, *who in her little book called* The Journalist and the Murderer *expressed the same idea in much stronger language. Of late, however, part of the news in journalism is about journalism: the scandal of brazen and quite intentional fictionalizing. Prestigious newspapers, including both the* Washington Post *and the* New York Times, *have been victims of it. A young man writing for the* New Republic *(whose notoriety has now been enhanced by a novel and a movie about him) wrote such lifelike and entertaining reports as to fool his editors for months, like a canny art forger whose canvases are more convincing than the Old Masters they imitate. Then came Jayson Blair of the* Times, *whose fictionalizing brought about the fall of an editorial regime.*

Dare we admit the obvious—that journalism is liable to such impostures in part because fact and fiction are separated at all times by a porous membrane, rather than an impermeable barrier? And is it possible that the increasing intrusion of entertainment values into journalism, even at high levels, is augmenting that vulnerability? In any case, the dimensions of the foggy borderland between the true and the invented is a part of my new interest in writing historical fiction, "admitted fiction" as I call it below.

In my final column for the *Washington Post* Writers Group in early 1997, I noted that my colleague Jonathan Yardley had labeled me a "journalistic fossil." He undoubtedly meant that the conditions that beckoned me—and him, and many others of our vintage—into the newspaper trade forty years ago no longer prevail. We made our debuts when print was paramount, television news in its infancy (and still almost exclusively written and broadcast by great figures like Walter Cronkite, Howard K. Smith, Eric Sevareid, and others who cut their teeth as newspaper reporters); the cable spectrum undreamed of and "talking heads" a dismissive TV term for a situation in which nothing happens but talk. How different it is now! Pulchritude would seem to be more important than literacy in local television news, if only there, and a strident voice and instant opinions more salable than beauty or good sense. No one would accuse the renegade Jesuit John McLaughlin of beauty, but as the founder of a noted "shouting heads" program in which lightning judgments are meted out, yes or no, "on a scale of one to ten," he has the distinction of being a journalistic revolutionary.

His isn't a revolution I care for, and to tell the truth "journalistic fossil" is a sobriquet in which I take satisfaction—insofar as it implies that the standards my generation sought to honor are threatened if not antiquated. Journalism today is permeated with entertainment values and by attitudes which the French call *bien-pensant,* right-thinking. When the "virtuecrats" of right or left aren't in cry, the private lives of public figures, whether or not they involve any public interest, are being poked into. Whatever zone of privacy once existed in public life vanished when the U.S. Supreme Court in a famous 1964 decision abolished (for good reason in the immediate instance) the common law of libel. At least as it might protect "public figures."

Entertainment and prurience are ageless and endemic flaws of journalism, to be sure. A century ago, Henry James took his cracks at the minions of publicity in such works as *The Reverberator* and *The Papers.* President Cleveland, James's contemporary, never recovered from the shock of news hounds spying on his honeymoon. These vices vary in viciousness over time, however; and up-to-date terms like "infotainment" and "tabloidization" suggest, just now, an unseemly scramble by print to lure back the young audience siphoned off by the more sordid aspects of television or the Internet. Even as I write (July 2003), the media critic of the *Washington Post* describes a berserk competition touched off by a sensational rape charge against a young National Basketball Association superstar. No holds are barred; no restraints honored. The anonymity traditionally (and questionably) accorded victims in rape cases is gone; and indeed the medical history and confidentiality of the complainant, along with her identity, are an open book. And so it goes. The *New York Times* and other traditionally reserved newspapers adhere to the old restraints; but even they sometimes follow the journalistic herd over the top into a territory that was rarely if ever visited when I entered journalism. Human nature and the follies that go with it are timeless; but the disposition to thrust them to center stage, often at the expense of more important public matters, is something new. A sort of journalist Gresham's Law seems to be at work, whereby the bad coin of sensationalism drives out the good of legitimate news.

And that is why I pause here, briefly, to pay homage to the writers and editors who inspired me to go into journalism when that trade was the only practical professional avenue open to someone who wanted to write; and who, more to the present point, set standards and goals that guaranteed my own rapid fossilization.

I grew up in a news- and history-conscious household. My father (see chapter 1) was one of the few people I've known who invariably turned first to the editorial pages of newspapers (even before sports or the stock quotations) to gauge their character and quality. Interpretation, he deeply believed, was essential to the understanding of events—not merely what the "news" was or seemed to be, but what the news *meant,* how it might affect the moving stream of history or shape the future. He consequently viewed commentary as an essential aperitif to reporting. He read the pundits avidly, whether or not he liked what they said. He listened to others on the radio, some of whom he very much disliked. He often came to the dinner table grumbling about H. V. Kaltenborn of NBC, the most eminent of the radio commentators of my boyhood. The stuffy, Republican-leaning Kaltenborn was sponsored by the Pure Oil Company, and my father entertained little doubt that he was oil's paid-up front man. It was Kaltenborn and his clipped, idiosyncratic way of speaking, that Harry Truman hilariously mocked at a victory dinner after his upset victory over Thomas E. Dewey in 1948. The parody delighted my father for the same reason that he greatly preferred Truman and his views to Kaltenborn and his. Still, he listened and took commentary seriously, even when he violently disliked it. He came by the taste honestly, for according to one story he told me, my grandfather, a militant supporter of progressive political causes at the turn of the century, so heartily disliked the stuffy views of the *Charlotte Observer* that he sometimes ripped out the editorial pages before reading the rest of the paper. There were of course not a few commentators my father found more compatible, foremost among them, perhaps, the Olympian Walter Lippmann and the earthier Bernard De Voto whose "Easy Chair" essays in *Harper's* magazine were a special favorite of his, often commended to my reading.

A boy nurtured in such an atmosphere naturally attached a premium to commentary journalism. And North Carolina in my youth was a rich climate for such an interest. I don't know why North Carolina sustained so strong and serious an editorializing tradition. Perhaps it can be traced to Walter Hines Page, a Tar Heel newspaper editor after the Civil War who later flourished in New York magazine and book publishing and, still later, as Woodrow Wilson's anglophile ambassador to the Court of St. James. Other figures—Jonathan Daniels of Raleigh, William T. Polk and Gerald Johnson of Greensboro, Wilbur J. Cash of Charlotte—were exemplary. All were accomplished stylists and Cash's *Mind of the South* remains an acknowledged classic. Polk and Johnson had written for the *Greensboro Daily News,* where I was to spend fifteen happy and productive years. When I came along, there were younger mentors worthy of that tradition—W. E. Dowd, Brodie Griffith, Cecil Prince, and Perry Morgan at the *Charlotte News* and H. W. "Slim" Kendall and William D. Snider in Greensboro. All were exacting craftsmen and generous mentors for whom the act of writing itself approached the hieratic—as nearly, anyway, as was compatible with the rush and tumble of daily deadlines.

I sense that the tradition I knew, and others like it elsewhere, are fading; and that is one reason why my own preoccupation with craftsmanship may mark me as a fossil. We are told these days that we now live in the "digital age," although just what that proclamation implies is uncertain. The video-display terminal and word-processing programs are merely the latest successors to the quill, the fountain pen, and the typewriter—and for that matter the stylus on wet clay or the cave wall-painting. All, early and late, are tools with the neutrality of tools, for uses good and bad, elegant and stupid, graceful and ugly. Whether on flickering screens or on paper, grace and elegance, precision, accuracy, and richness of expression continue to be supreme writerly virtues. Thomas Mann has said that "a writer is someone who finds it hard to do what others do easily." Capacious garbage bins may await us all; but those too casual of the values and disciplines that inspired Mann's remark will surely—and deservedly—be the earliest to disappear. Hard words, perhaps; but loyalty to my earlier models and mentors shortens my patience with the glibness and inaccuracy that seem the earmarks of the "digital age."

Such, then, are the centrifugal forces at play in journalism as it was when my fossilization commenced. But I can hardly blame them altogether for my transition to another line of writing. That story is more complicated.

One November day in 1989, when I was lecturing at Washington and Lee University as a Class of 1963 visiting fellow, my friend John Wilson, president of the college, summoned me to his office in Washington Hall. John and I had become friends as fellow members of the Virginia Rhodes Scholarship selection committee and I assumed the visit would be social. But it wasn't—or wasn't entirely.

"What would it take to get you to come down here and do some teaching for us?" Wilson asked. The question was seconded by the dean of the college, John Elrod, who was also there. I was surprised and hardly knew what to say.

"What about a chauffeured helicopter?" I asked.

"I don't think we can manage that," John Wilson said, chuckling, "but we might be able to make it worth your while."

It has been my odd destiny—and good fortune—to have such attractive propositions fall my way, unbidden. I agreed to think it over. Like the sudden invasion of my life by Joe Allbritton, Jim Bellows, and the faltering *Washington Star,* this proposition too was destined to change my interests—and, as I shall relate, in unexpected ways. I had long thought, rather vaguely, that at about this stage of life—I was then in my mid-fifties—I might like to teach. I had tried it briefly before; the academic life was in my genes; and in a sense I had always been something of a misfit in daily journalism, much as I liked it. I had assumed that I might some day get such a call from Chapel Hill, but it didn't come and John Wilson's idea seemed far less disruptive. I had no special ties with Washington and Lee, although my mother's elder sister, my Aunt Florine, had been so ardent an admirer of Robert E. Lee that she had sent her sons, my Warthen cousins of Warthen, Georgia, there many decades earlier. We had been visiting our close friends John and Martha Evans there every fall for decades; but there my Lexington ties ended. Or perhaps began. After some weeks of reflection I said yes to John Wilson's offer and became Professor of Journalism and Humanities; and a gradual sea-change began to transform me from working journalist into a very different kind of writer.

Washington and Lee is distinctive among private liberal-arts colleges in having a journalism department; and that department is distinctive, in the special Lexington way, in being a legacy of Lee's presidency of the college just after the Civil War. Marse Robert had appointed the first known professor of journalism in the world, for reasons which are not entirely clear. The consensus of speculation is that he had in mind what we would today call a form of "extension" education, beneficial to journalists and editors who often emerged from the printer's trade with less formal schooling than might be expected. That was the authoritative view. I liked to fancy that perhaps Lee also had a warm spot for newspaper reporters because the Confederacy, like any insurgency, had had every interest in getting its story out. And with Lee consistently whipping Yankee generals before his fateful blunder on the third day at Gettysburg in early July 1863, it was a famously appealing story. It is certain that Lee and his officers got along better with reporters than their great adversaries Grant and Sherman, who loathed them.

Under whatever auspices, I found myself teaching journalism courses, but not those alone. Part of my title was "professor of . . . humanities," and at Washington and Lee, a collegial place whose faculty was not obsessed with departmental boundaries, I was allowed, indeed encouraged, to teach fall and winter courses in European fiction and spring seminars in the English and American novel: Henry James, Faulkner, Conrad, and Joyce.

Although my syndicated column had enjoyed good circulation and display in major regional papers (and abroad in the *Paris Herald Tribune, The Guardian* in England) circulation lingered in the range of sixty to seventy-five and it never won the mass audience that provides a comfortable income. It had perhaps been my fate to launch a career as a syndicated columnist a generation late, when dozens of would-be pundits described themselves that way, even when they were neither. That, along with the increasing popularity of the TV talking-head shows, tended to inflate and devalue all commentary. I still enjoyed writing the column on certain days, but teaching draws upon identical psychological and intellectual energies, and my column, I sensed, was steadily losing altitude, foot by foot. By working six and a half days a week, I strove for five years to teach seven courses an academic year and write two columns a week for fifty weeks. My academic duties also required a grinding weekly round trip between Alexandria and Lexington of some 380 miles. It was too much.

But these were the mere exteriorities. Although I neither planned nor expected it, the new routine would gradually wean me from journalism and stir in me the yearning to create, to write what I jocularly call "*admitted* fiction." It wasn't that newsprint had ceased to charm; only that a subtler chemistry was at work and leading in new directions. I didn't foresee that I might develop an itch to be a teller of tales. But I did. Melo-dramatically, and with a certain contraction of the time sequence, you could say that I went to bed one night half a decade ago as a contented journalist and woke up the next morning wishing to be a "real" writer. The transformation was less grim than the one that befell poor Gregor Samsa of Kafka's unforgettable parable "The Metamorphosis"; it was nonetheless very real.

No one had warned me that this might be the special vulnerability of an overaged pundit, although looking back I can detect one or two instances of good-natured foreshadowing. Charles Lloyd, who at the end of his career as a scholar and teacher was professor of English at Davidson College, was one of the most dazzlingly literate men I have known. He was also a family friend—in the early 1950s, my father had hired him to teach high school Latin and French as he left U.S. Army occupation duties in Germany. One day as I was just starting out in full-time newspapering, Charlie, by then at Davidson, read a piece of mine in the *Charlotte News*. He wrote a remarkable letter of friendly exasperation and reproof, culminating in a magnificent burst of Lloyd-speak:

> What, in short, is the prime concern of newspapers? And what, oh what is Edwin Yoder doing among those space-merchants? Of course, I know the answer; you have written some powerful and fine editorials that swayed people's minds and actually made some events transpire. You would have done that, perhaps not with such scope, if you had been getting out a house organ for Warner & Swasey. Because I am impudent and meddlesome, I shall now tell you what to do. Write those powerful editorials with your left hand five days of the week. With your right hand make pictures in paint and verse and prose of *people*. Shakespeare and Chaucer located the mother lode . . . but their time was too short for them to do more than pack away a few panniers. Individual human beings are the true frontier; most people, even most artists, have not the heart and mind to penetrate to them. You have, and you will do it. Eighteen months from today I expect to review your first verse drama in the *Zeitschrift für German-ische Philo-logie*. You can have a little longer for the epic.

My first verse drama! A good natured burst of blarney, obviously. In fact I had last committed epic verse at the age of fifteen or sixteen on an old upright Underwood typewriter my father had taken home hoping, I believe, that it might cure my academic indolence. It didn't; but it was for a time a powerful stimulus to adolescent literary creation. The other occasion when I missed the bell involved Peter Taylor, a merry Tennessean and a great storyteller whom we were lucky enough to befriend in Greensboro. One Sunday after church, he complimented a reminiscence I had written about my comic misadventures in air force basic training and asked if I had ever thought of trying my hand at fiction. Of course I had!—don't we all at some stage? Flattered as I was, however, those early efforts were long forgotten, and Peter's suggestion went right over my head. I was too busy then trying to improve the world, which as usual was in dire need of improvement.

I should mention yet another impediment. At that point, in my late twenties and early thirties, I had read a good deal of classic fiction—I was, after all, a Chapel Hill English major—and I had read, and sometimes reviewed, a good many journalists' novels. They almost always missed the point of storytelling that Charles Lloyd understood and articulated: *pictures of people are the mother lode.* News oriented, the authors of these brittle tales assumed that intrinsic interest inheres in, say, the machinations of Big Tobacco or Big Oil, whether or not the story flows from human character or illuminates the human comedy. Sometimes, the portrayal of character seemed almost incidental, as if people were reluctantly dragged into the thrilling world of industry or politics as puppets or props, for convention's sake. The born storyteller, which I wasn't, though I believe I knew one when I saw or read him, knows in his bones that the power struggle in which the wicked Richard III loses his crown is secondary to the thematic inner struggle, the study in brazen personal evil and ambition. *Macbeth* isn't a discourse on Scottish dynastic politics and would be long forgotten if it were.

Could a journalist, then, become a real writer?

That does beg the question. There are hosts of fine writers whose forte is not fiction, not storytelling as it was practiced by Tolstoy, Chekhov, and Peter Taylor, though certain journalists (the immortal Joseph Mitchell of the *New Yorker,* for instance) are exceptions who test the rule. They, too, are storytellers, inventors, and fabricators. Mitchell's sketches of New York City fantastics like Joe Gould fuzz every usual distinction between fact and fiction, so called. H. L. Mencken's hilarious and scathing reportage from the 1925 "monkey trial" in Dayton, Tennessee, descends to us in most anthologies not as he wrote it on the scene but as he dolled it up creatively after the fact in Baltimore. In fact, the mere assumption that fiction is superior to the best reportage had long intrigued me. Willie Morris was, as I have written in an earlier chapter, among the most accomplished and compelling nonfiction writers of his age. His books of reportage were luminous with imagination while, oddly, his maiden venture into fiction, a novel called *The Last of the Southern Girls,* was the byproduct of a mood, a fling, a personal episode, and never quite took wing. The needed transmutation from personal experience into story never quite emerged. Yet for all his brilliance as a writer of nonfiction, Willie had it fixed in his mind that "real" writers write fiction, *imagine* stories, not report them. For a long time I had viewed this prejudice as a kind of folly, akin to Conan Doyle's chagrin at the popularity of his Sherlock Holmes stories, which he regarded as inferior to his "serious" novels, all of which are now forgotten. I dismissed Willie's superstition, little imagining that I would wake up one day bitten by this virulent bug myself. Live and learn!

But enough. The foregoing is only to say that the itch to write fiction—historical fiction, in particular—is my current bid for that "second act" in our lives that Scott Fitzgerald warned never happens. We shall see. Whatever comes of it, it is great fun. I have, so far, placed the young Hamlet as a student at Wittenberg University, where he has become a disciple of Martin Luther, professor of scripture there and, as we know, religious revolutionary. I have carried forward the unpromising life of Faulkner's Caddy Compson of *The Sound and the Fury,* imagining that she and her German officer friend (last seen, and despaired of, in the lengthy appendix of the Compson family that Faulkner wrote for *The Portable Faulkner)* are actively involved in the July 1944 plot to assassinate Hitler. More recently I have brought Sigmund Freud and Henry James together in Rye, Sussex, in 1908, when in fact Freud did pay a visit to relatives in England. In the course of a visit to James at Lamb House, Freud does a "short-term" psychoanalysis of James, a fragmentary case-history version of which turns up in Freud's papers after his death decades later. James's letters to his pen pal Edith Wharton give the other side of the story. One feels even about these homely literary children a natural parental fondness, and I have hopes for these late offspring. The market conditions for what is called "literary fiction" (should the adjective actually be "literate"?) are notably inhospitable just now, especially for those who have no record of successful fiction. But knowing as I do how many fine works have found truly weird destinies, I think of them—of, for instance, Giuseppe di Lampedusa's *The Leopard,* for which he sought a publisher in vain during his lifetime; and of course of Proust, rebuffed by none other than André Gide, publishing the first volume of *A la récherche du temps perdu* at his own expense. And not least of Joyce and his volunteer publisher Sylvia Beach, and their loyal printer down in Dijon, braving the censors. And these are three examples of many. Even if nothing comes of my autumnal children beyond electronic publication, there is at least that. As usual, my wife Jane has put the matter into perspective. We both work at home, she seeing her psychotherapy clients in her consulting room upstairs, I contentedly toiling at my fiction in my book- and paper-crowded basement study.

"I don't think you believe I am really working down there in my study all day long," I observed one day.

"Well," she said, "if anyone publishes this stuff, it's your work. Otherwise it's your hobby."

Just so. Stay tuned.

Appendix: A Portfolio of Columns

The pieces that follow this brief introduction are chosen to illustrate a few of the journeyman's tricks gathered in my own half-century as an editorialist and columnist. Many of them spring from personal experience or memory, and that might remind us of a basic rule of all effective writing: *Write what you know about or, at least, what you care about.* A mere glance at most opinion pages most days in most newspapers, large and small, suggests that their creators are haunted by a spirit of deadly earnestness. Of course, no one would wish to squander space on the frivolous and inconsequential. But the examples of such masters as E. B. White and H. L. Mencken, to name only two, show that the serious and effective need not be ponderous or solemn. The typical vice of commentary journalism, especially on newspapers with an inflated sense of their own importance, is a plodding dutifulness, a deadly resolve to write about every event that comes bearing the label, "this is important," whether or not it truly is and whether or not the writer has anything fresh to say about it. The impulse should be resisted; for when duty calls silence is not often improved upon. Some duty pieces are inevitable—a good word for the Red Cross blood drive or the Christmas Empty Stocking Fund. But duty pieces are usually dead on arrival, as is routine political commentary that is written without heart or passion. American politics is increasingly the playground of spinmeisters and PR agents, and it is useful to bear in mind the historian Daniel Boorstin's ingenious term, the "pseudo-event." Pseudo-events abound nowadays, especially in campaign seasons. So a dull official day should be seen as an excuse to ignore what is allegedly important and write what I used to call the "invented" piece, the piece created as the universe was said to be, *ex nihilo:* something personal with a dash of intimacy about it.

The newspaper column has a long history and many cousins, including the sermon. So far as I can discover, the remotest recognizable ancestor of the modern opinion piece is the sermon of late antiquity in colloquial Latin, filled with pointed personal anecdotes and homely personal testimony. You can trace its ensuing history into and through the eighteenth-century coffee houses and the editorial wars of the early American republic, when Hamiltonians and Jeffersonians were slanging each other in their respective party presses. But that era also produced something permanent and even glorious, the Federalist Papers. Anyone aspiring to commentary can still learn a lot from two master opinion writers, James Madison and Alexander Hamilton.

There is an abiding superstition that opinion pieces consist primarily of opinion, a view that isn't discouraged these days by all the ideology-driven barking and howling that imitates commentary on television and talk radio. But the sober truth is that no thoughtful reader is impressed by anyone's mere opinion, unless the writer happens to be the pope, the president, the chief justice, or the archbishop of Canterbury—and even in those cases only fitfully and because the speaker or writer has undoubted power to make things happen, good and bad. The name of the game is *persuasion,* and persuasion demands a balance between assertion and information. Of the two, information is almost always the more important. A telling fact, artfully cited, will carry more weight than any view, however colorfully phrased. Please note: *a telling fact, artfully cited.* Amateurs at persuasion often labor under the illusion that a weighty argument consists of turgid parades of fact that glut the writing without amplifying the point.

Opinion writing is a craft; and like other crafts it can be learned. But it differs from some others in the nature and extent of the resources a good practitioner must bring to it. By resources, I mean, apart from a feeling for words, knowledge and perception. A good commentator cannot have read too many books in too many fields, especially of history, or seen (or read) too many Shakespeare plays, or perused too many passages of the King James Bible, or looked too closely at too many pictures by Leonardo or Giotto, or heard too much of Mozart, the Beatles, and Louis Armstrong. Or listened to too many country storytellers weave their tales, as the great William Faulkner used to do, incognito, at local Mississippi courthouses on Saturday afternoons. Which is to say that everything embraced by the term literacy must be the pundit's food and drink and fuel.

When I was an active columnist, I was occasionally asked who did my "research." The question is hard to answer without sounding cocky. If you don't have the stuff at your fingertips, or know where to find it quickly, an army of researchers won't make up for the lack. And in fact, nothing is more artificial than a flourish of pseudo-learning drawn from Bartlett's or the encyclopedia and smeared on like garish grease paint. Students of good writing know the touches of the tart when they see them. Obviously, a columnist must often write about matters of which he or she knows far less than all; it goes with the territory. But like the legendary British civil servants who believed that a good Oxford degree in the ancient classics primed them for any administrative challenge, however formidable or far-flung, the bold pundit needs a good education in the arts and sciences, the more thorough the better. There is no substitute for it and no shortcut to it. It is a lifelong undertaking that really begins when you leave the last classroom, when in all likelihood you will have tasted only a few samples.

How then, given these formidable barriers, to proceed? Notwithstanding what I said above, it does help to be opinionated. Fortunately, not everyone is; it is a special affliction. As may be clear from the portrait of my father in chapter one, I came by it naturally and perhaps genetically. It is even more useful to be blessed with a pristine slant on the world, a capacity to view its follies from a fresh and uncommon angle, whether of irony or wit or chronic impatience. To "make it new," as Ezra Pound said; or see it new. Reading the master writers of opinion is crucial. Any reader of the writings of George Will, Jonathan Yardley, Mary McGrory, or the late Meg Greenfield of the *Washington Post;* or of Rick Hertzberg of the *New Yorker;* or of such past masters as Vermont Royster of the *Wall Street Journal,* James Reston and Walter Lippmann and Murray Kempton; any such reader will realize that fine writers of commentary have a unique angle of their very own on the world. H. L. Mencken certainly had it, along with a gift for flashy diction. (No one "*guilty* of golf," he once wrote, should be eligible to be president.)

Are great commentators born, not made? Possibly. But again, for the would-be journeyman the craft can be learned, at least to a degree, by constant practice. It used to be said that a good French chef could make a tasty dish of a shoe tongue. That seems unlikely, but I mention the jest because the journalism of opinion—of "telling others what to think" in the puckish title of this memoir—often poses the shoe-tongue challenge. There are days when the news is barren of inspiration—no catastrophes or distinguished deaths or great follies; yet space must be filled by day's end. The pundit's task is often to concoct a convincing sauce for the otherwise unappetizing shoe tongues.

In his essay "Politics and the English Language," and others, George Orwell left us memorable rules for writing. My own are few, but one is paramount: *revise, revise, and then revise again*—meaning, don't just reshuffle stale words and phrases on the VDT but re-imagine, re-envision, what you want to say and how you want to say it. Thomas Mann said it best, and it is worth repeating: "A writer is someone who finds it hard to do what others do easily." We do well to imitate the novelist in Philip Roth's novel *The Ghost Writer,* who tells his young admirer, the ubiquitous Nathan Zuckerman, that he spends the day writing a single sentence and then turning it around again and again. Within limits, since writers of opinion, unlike the novelist, face deadlines. But however narrow the window for work, revision is essential. Certainly it always has been so for me, if only because the theme, also known as the point, often refuses to declare itself on the first or even the second or third try. It must be harried from concealment by revision, for without it the piece will lie lifeless on the page and waste the reader's time. We all recall that Sir Winston Churchill, one of the most inventive of wordsmiths, once said: "Waiter, pray remove this pudding. It has no theme." The themeless puddings of commentary should be removed uneaten and boiled again.

LESSONS IN LITERATURE FOR A TEN-YEAR-OLD

This piece can easily be dated, for if Teddy is ten this must be 1973. But the theme is perennial, one of my hobby-horses, sharpened by amusing combat in print with a prominent modern linguist, a professor in Greensboro named Norman Jarrard, whose gospel it was that language, as it evolves, has little or nothing to do with "right" or "wrong." I admit to being a reactionary on this matter. I had the good fortune to be taught by people who cared about language, including my parents, who thought good reading had a lot to do with it. I was eager to return the favor with my own children. My mother had edited a college lit magazine (at the age of eighteen) and seven decades later knew more poetry and Scripture by heart than almost anyone else. Poor Teddy may seem to a neutral reader the hapless victim of an overbearing father. That case can be made. But I like to think that one reason he writes well today is that he still hears the echo of those distant readings. I am sure that this piece was widely read, but the congregation had heard me preach on this text too many times to find it unusual.

A rhetorical note: Under the subhead "Danger of loss," I write: "Those of us who came along a generation or more ago, through no great virtue of our own . . ." etc. A piece that can be read as a puffed-up celebration of one's own literacy needs a self-deprecating grace note or two. In this case, it happens to be accurate. I was far from being an especially deserving case, for as I write elsewhere in this memoir I was a pretty indolent student at Teddy's age.

My son Teddy, who is ten years old, belongs heart and soul to the brave new world of science and technology. He never misses an Apollo launch or a rerun, however familiar, of "Star Trek." He has inherited his grandfather's instinctive understanding of electrical and mechanical gadgetry—a trait as clearly genetic as eye color, so far as I can tell, and wholly recessive in my case. For these endowments, I am thankful.

But like so many children of his time and place. Teddy has not acquired what I believe—if memory isn't tricking me—I had begun to acquire at his age: a love of words, a sense that their magical properties can be quite as enthralling and entertaining as the rockets, machines and chemical reactions that delight small boys.

Of late, accordingly, he and I have been having regular evening sessions which, it is my hope, may stir this love of words. The device is simple: We sit down together with the King James Bible and read, each in turn the familiar old stories. We speculate on their meaning; we discuss the unfamiliar but arresting way in which words are used. Here, for example, it says that someone is "compassed about" with enemies.

Teddy knows what a compass is; and it isn't difficult to move from an instrument of direction to the sense of being surrounded. Other passages, the genealogies once called "the begats," offer another sort of challenge.

The tables turned

We are now several weeks into the regimen, having covered the Creation, the story of Adam and Eve, Jacob and Esau, Abraham and Isaac, and of course the magnificent story of Joseph the interpreter of dreams—his betrayal by wicked half-brothers, his rise to power in Egypt, the just turning of the tables.

Although we plug away undaunted, Teddy to my dismay claims to be "bored" by these readings. Almost every night he argues that we should be reading Greek mythology, always a favorite of his. I think I understand why. For a small boy on whom the superior power and insight of the Bible has not yet fully dawned, the horrendous events of mythology—the magical metamorphoses and heroic exertions—are indeed more compelling fare. By comparison with Hercules, or the quest for the Golden Fleece, or the bizarre history of the House of Atreus, even Samson seems a rather commonplace brawler, whose deeds might well belong among the squalid records of an ancient police blotter.

Still, we press on, arguing down the protestations of boredom, because of his father's quaint conviction that where the English language is concerned we seem to be headed for an age of dreary flatness in which, before we know it, the whole mode of understanding represented in classics of language may be lost. I have visions of a time when the old words in their old orders will strike the ears of our children, or their children, as the strange tones of some unfamiliar oriental music.

Danger of loss

Those of us who came along a generation or more ago, through no great virtue of our own, were not in the same danger of losing our ears. By comparison with Teddy's world, with its rocket kits and chemistry sets and the dreary passiveness of television, it was a world of astonishing stability. Words still occupied an essential place in it. Even those of us who had no uncommon endowment of memory were constantly presented with opportunities to absorb words in fixed and expressive order.

The King James Bible (there were no others at hand) was a staple of public reading and recitation. One had a whole succession of grade-school teachers who believed unshakeably in memorization—not only of certain psalms and stories from the Bible, but of poems, songs, hymns, and patriotic documents. We stored these things not out of striking aptitude, but the way flannel accumulates lint.

Everyone of a certain age who spent a reasonably attentive childhood in the South knows what they are—dozens of familiar hymns, songs, and psalms; the Gettysburg Address and the Declaration of Independence; Robert Louis Stevenson, Rupert Brooke, and Wordsworth; "I wandered lonely as a cloud", "In Flanders Field"; dozens of lines, soliloquies, and epigrams from Shakespeare ("the taste of sweetness, of which a little more than a little is by much too much"); Milton's description of Satan's plunge, "hurled headlong flaming from th' ethereal sky / With hideous ruin and combustion down to bottomless perdition"; unforgotten responses from old childhood catechisms ("Sin is any want of conformity to, or transgression of, the law of God") whose words had a splendid force and clangor to them even if you didn't fully grasp what they meant. And of course countless stories went along with all this.

Vacuums and reservoirs

For all I know the teaching that goes on in the schools today is vastly superior to the mnemonic concerns of the gentle school marms of my youth. But who can be sure? Certainly if my children have been required to memorize anything I don't know what it is, and I have trouble accepting the vacuum that will exist for them in later years where this reservoir exists for me. I can't help feeling they will have missed something of value and that is why Teddy and I have been reading about Samson, Moses, and Joseph.

A PARANOID TAR HEEL LEAVES POLITICS BEHIND

In the fourth chapter, "Greenhorn Days," I have described my involvement in the great Red conspiracy battles of the 1950s and 1960s. The objects of conspiracy theory vary over time, but the weird angle of vision remains. It baffles me that a man of Robert Welch's reputed intelligence could have believed what he said he believed. But then, according to the polls, a majority of Americans even after forty years and ample proof to the contrary believe that John F. Kennedy was shot by a second gunman from the so-called grassy knoll in Dealey Plaza in Dallas, and that Lee Harvey Oswald's second bullet had a weirdly devious trajectory, including one right angle turn—this by way of disbelieving the Warren Commission's (erroneous) analysis of that bullet's pathway, since corrected by better observation. But let us not start that hare, for it is only incidental to the point. I don't know why so many people subscribe to conspiracy theories about all sorts of things. In some cases they are uninformed; in others, they are masters of the most intricate detail and logic but argue from a flawed premise. But the determination to believe in a rational universe is, I think, at the root of it. They are reluctant to accept the demonstrable freakishness and irrationality of human affairs, even in the face of St. Paul's ancient warning: "The good that I would do, that I do not; the evil that I would not do, that I do." Freakish events, in which a large effect seems grotesquely disproportionate to a trivial cause ("a punk with a mail-order rifle," as David Brinkley said on November 22, 1963) demand complex explanation. Perhaps conspiracy theorists are the ultimate rationalists.

Soon after I moved as a fledgling newspaper editorialist from Charlotte to Greensboro, North Carolina, in May 1961, my new editors began to hear a strange rumor: I had been "fired" from my old job.

It was, as they well knew, nonsense and we ignored it until, a few weeks later, a friend took me to a meeting of a local college history club. The speaker of the evening was the "area coordinator" of the John Birch Society. We expected to be amused but, like Queen Victoria, were not.

As that gentleman, a stranger, was expounding the Birchite view of the world—how, for instance, the communists might at will "take over" Western Europe with a single telephone call—he suddenly blurted something still more astonishing. The real obstacle to sensible anti-communism in his area, he said, was an editorial writer for the local paper who had recently been fired in Charlotte. . . .

A powerful rush of adrenalin as I heard myself identified sent me bolting to my feet. "That's a lie," I shouted from the rear seats, as the audience gaped, "I know, because you're talking about me."

Macbeth, at the unwelcome apparition of Banquo's accusing ghost, could not have been more rattled than the "area coordinator" of the Birch Society, who soon fled into the night. My newspaper's lawyers sent him a gentle note, and the rumors ceased.

This old scene came freshly back to mind when I read of the death, at 85, of Robert Welch, founder of the Birch Society. Where I now feel sympathy and amusement, I felt, those long years ago, the outrage of injured innocence.

Not that I was wholly innocent. I had prodded the hornet's nest with a long review of Welch's notorious *Blue Book*. Welch had delivered this diatribe a few years earlier; and around its apocalyptic view the Birch Society believers had swarmed. I had haughtily called it "a tract in political neurosis," which it was. But I had rubbed in the insult by also calling it, in a letter to my fellow Tar Heel Welch, "seditious trash."

This reaction now seems at least a bit overwrought, lacking the urbanity that always builds better cases than raw epithet. But then, I was 25; an excitable kid.

Robert Welch, who grew up on an eastern North Carolina tobacco farm and was known as something of a child prodigy, had made a fortune in the candy business. Then, like other wealthy men of eccentric turn of mind (H. L. Hunt was a parallel case), Welch set out to press his political insights upon his imperiled countrymen.

Among those insights, unfortunately, one found not only such amiably kooky notions as that Norway was secretly communist, or that Bolshevism had been cooked up by the Bavarian Illuminati. One also found that such trusted public heroes as Dwight Eisenhower were "dedicated, conscious agents" of communism.

My word "seditious" was not, therefore, misplaced. An alleged conspiracy so monstrous left no place for Marquis of Queensbury rules. The roughhouse tactics which Welch openly urged on the Birch Society cells (evidently including disinformation campaigns against critics) tended to sap public trust, confidence and civility.

As to Eisenhower, Welch's suppositions seemed both puzzling and scandalous. In those days, of course, we were still disputing who in the last days of World War II had left Berlin prey to Stalin's hordes. And indeed Ike had made a battlefield decision not to send Anglo-American salients into eastern Germany. Ike's own explanation—that American generals do not make "political" decisions—made far more sense, however, than the hypothesis of furtive Muscovite sympathies.

Precisely when or why Robert Welch, Tar Heel farm boy made good, was smitten with his conspiratorial vision I do not know. In *The Paranoid Style in American Politics*, Richard Hofstadter expertly laid out the usual pattern of such visions. But he did not, perhaps could not, persuasively explain why one of us is prone to them, while another is immune.

Surely most of us discover in history some reflection of our own temperaments. Welch clearly relished plots and secrecy (witness the initial structure and tactics of the Birch Society). He seems to have projected the same pattern on history, not only in the Kremlin but in the White House as well.

The great Armageddon that Welch envisioned has taken some surprising twists since Blue Book days. China has wandered out of the strict Marxist orbit, and Western Europe never wandered into it. This must have struck Robert Welch as odd, though no doubt he found a way to fit the odd facts into the all-enveloping theory.

At any rate, now that he has left us for another shore I hope he finds rest from his monumental worries.

WHO WAS TRULY AMBUSHED?

In an earlier passage of this memoir, I recall the historian Daniel Boorstin's useful term, "the pseudo-event." We sometimes soften the phenomenon by calling it a "media event," when some scene (for instance, George W. Bush's landing on the USS Abraham Lincoln in a flight suit) is patently arranged for the cameras with the aim of getting it on the television news. Dan Rather's famous interview with the pseudo flyboy's father, George H. W. Bush, that provoked this piece was a pseudo-event in essence. It happened in the midst of the 1988 presidential election season when much was at stake and at issue for the country, including Mr. Bush's role as vice president in the so-called Iran-Contra scandal in which the Reagan administration tried to trade arms for hostages held in the Middle East. Yet the face-off contributed nothing save a brief, visceral passion to the discussion. Marshall McLuhan, the great analyst of "media," observed in one of his books that television is "iconic," meaning—as millions of Mac computer users will now know—that it is a medium using graphic symbols that usually say or "mean" more than the words that accompany them. The Rather-Bush interview, which had the gracelessness of two dogs circling one another snarling, was a classic McLuhanesque encounter—iconic, exciting, provocative—and vacuous.

Since there was little middle ground here, the mail this piece generated was sharply polarized but ran to misplaced sympathy for the vice president and his violated dignity. I can't recall whether or not "the women-folk in my home" were persuaded. Probably not.

The great Bush-Rather shoot-out on the CBS Evening News sent the women-folk at my house (my only available test market) into orbits of outrage.

My wife, a practicing psychotherapist, is a subtle student of the human comedy. But if she'd been a cartoon character, little puffs of smoke would have hissed from her ears. Imagine! An anchorman treating the vice president of the United States so rudely!

An hour or so later, my daughter, who is a doctoral candidate in arcane sciences, was on the telephone long distance. She too was steaming over the antics of dangerous Dan.

If these two astute and subtle women, neither preternaturally sympathetic to George Bush, were irate, Bush had surely scored a bull's-eye out there in television land. And that, I insist, is exactly what he planned to do from the outset. Dan Rather was had.

High officials should be treated with respect, even when their behavior undermines it; for they embody the dignity of their offices. But Bush was plainly acting (and not badly, at that). His anger over the alleged ambush—his complaint that he had expected to be questioned about his educational ideas—was a polished replay of his calculated anger in the recent debate in Des Moines.

There, Bush borrowed a leaf from the Gary Hart press-bashing manual. He assailed the stolid and proper Jim Gan-

non, editor of the *Des Moines Register,* for allowing his newspaper to rehash Iran-Contra questions he, Bush, claimed he had already answered. He resented this deeply. Wild applause.

Both performances seemed to me about as spontaneous as dancing the lead role in *Swan Lake,* or playing Hamlet (no, make that Henry V). They were as spontaneous as the arrangement of things on the vice president's vast, polished, unlittered desk—as spontaneous as the angle at which the framed photo of Ronald Reagan had been turned. Perhaps George Bush keeps the president facing that way, just in case someone drops in unexpectedly with a TV camera.

Look. If George Bush were truly ambushed or double-crossed, as he claimed, if he really thought CBS was wheeling all those monitors, lights, and cameras into his office to ask him about the decline of scholastic-aptitude test scores and such, he should be sent back to remedial poly sci in New Haven, not to the Oval Office.

You simply aren't invited for big, live, much-publicized interviews on the world's most-watched news network, in the midst of a campaign, to bandy puffballs about education. Such naïveté, if real, would disqualify the vice president for dogcatcher, to say nothing of leader of the free world.

And another thing. The switchboards

reportedly lit up at CBS affiliates everywhere, and some stations even disgraced themselves by apologizing for Rather's behavior.

Come on, couch potatoes of the nation, grow up. The press—as, to the considerable disgruntlement of us pencil-pushers, you insist on calling television—is a new game altogether. And your confusion about what was going on in the Bush-Rather clash argues a dangerous innocence. Television isn't print, and it ain't beanbag. It is an explosive mass medium in which entertainment values constantly color news and debate and—when political power is at stake—annihilate all sorts of old Gutenberg rules of civility and rationality.

This is true in spades of presidential campaigns. Night after night, candidates scramble for a microsecond of exposure on the network news shows. They pant after the electronic Mephistopheles (in Godfrey Hodgson's fine phrase), offering that table-turning sound bite that can make or break them in the boondocks of Iowa or New Hampshire.

A bit of Gannon-bashing or Rather-bashing isn't a spontaneous response to unexpected aggression by the wicked media. It's a vote-winning device, long ago perfected by Richard Nixon and other great nice guys of politics.

Bush, and all those whose hearts bled for him when Dan Rather was so beastly, should save it for the Red Cross. This raucous and amusing wrangle was great political television, just what the symbiotic media war dance between politicians and television accomplishes on your luckiest day when absolutely everything clicks.

Of course, it also shows how the demands of media politics can degrade two professions which, in quieter moments, are capable of dignity and even reflection. But never mind that; these are unquiet moments. Rather used Bush, and Bush used Rather to appear ill used. It was the usual stuff, raised to the max. Come on, ladies, give me a break.

DNA AND A DEEPER INQUIRY

When it was suddenly announced a few years back that DNA analysis in a lab in Oxford, England, had "proved" that Thomas Jefferson was the father of at least one of Sally Hemings's slave children, my friend Steve Rosenfeld, then editorial-page editor of the Washington Post, *asked me to write this piece. He knew of my interest in Jefferson. Notwithstanding the "disclosure" in the first paragraph, I remain skeptical of this widely believed chapter in the personal history of our most intriguing national sage. Fortunately, my daughter, a molecular biologist by profession, weighed the evidence for me and saved me from swallowing the "proof" whole. Her cautionary words have been borne out. It has emerged, for instance, that at least eight of Jefferson's contemporary male relatives could have contributed the telltale Y chromosomes to the Hemings family line. But while it is of paramount concern to a genuine biologist, little attention has been paid by lay people to the crucial probative differences between male and female chromosomal evidence.*

"Why not let Jefferson be Jefferson?" I ask. That's the key question, after all. Human and political complexity are, alas, frequent casualties of our headlong age, which is gorged with information and credulous (up to a point and depending on the subject) about anything sporting scientific credentials, but often too busy for discrimination and reflection.

There was the usual reaction. My critics remarked that I seemed not to take sides clearly on what seemed at first blush a yes-or-no matter. That was true. The fact is that no one who really wants to believe some "fact" about the past, or an historical personage, is likely to be stopped. How many times have we now read that Mr. Jefferson is guilty as charged by the lab technicians? As if emphatic repetition made a debatable thing true.

First, a disclosure: When the late Fawn Brodie's "intimate history" of Thomas Jefferson revived the then dormant Sally Hemings story twenty-five years ago, I was among its vociferous detractors, damning her book as a travesty of historical method and an insult to Mr. J's memory. Its one redeeming virtue, I thought, was that she thought this imaginary liaison with a slave woman humanized the somewhat chilly third president.

Now the latest in this long-running dispute has transformed an argument over remote historical possibilities into an argument over real scientific probabilities.

Or so I am assured by my daughter, Anne, a molecular biologist at Northwestern Medical Center who sequences DNA for a living. When I queried her, she wrote:

"The important scientific considerations are that the Y chromosome is the flip side of the mitochondrial story. Because Jefferson has no legitimate paternal descendants, the researchers have used the lineage of his paternal uncle as a surrogate. Various assumptions must be made, such as that Jefferson's father was really his father, and that no other paternal relative could have fathered the Sally Hemings son in question.

"It's possible that the Y chromosome resemblance is accidental, but the chances of that, according to the study, are only one in one hundred. As scientists, we usually like better numbers. Certainly, the one in one hundred would never stand in isolation as enough evidence to convict a murderer. But in this case, we have strong circumstantial evidence within which to assess the statistics, making a much stronger case."

If the scientific case is so solid, what have we gained for history? Perhaps less than we imagine, given the peculiarly moralistic cast of our political and academic dialogue these days. The new discussion may be as sterile and self-serving as the old.

A friend of mine remarked in a recent letter that we Americans have become "gnostics," quick to divide the world between light and darkness, good and evil; quick to force people who give every sign of being the usual mixture of good and bad traits into rigid moral niches: paragon or villain, hero or cad, sheep or goat. He was commenting on a little piece I had written about Captain Vere, the ship commander in Melville's tale "Billy Budd" who is forced by what he sees as military necessity to hang the angelic Budd for impulsively killing the repulsive Claggert. It is now fashionable to typecast Vere as the very model of a heartless martinet, never mind the grim imperatives of command at a time of war and mutiny.

I detect a similar impulse on all sides to iron the wrinkles and ambiguities out of Thomas Jefferson. Either he remains the giant philosopher who broods on Higher Things in his marble temple by the Tidal Basin, or he's rudely unveiled as just another exploitative hypocrite slaveocrat, stealing around to the servants' beds by night.

Question: Why can't we let Jefferson be Jefferson, all enigmatic six feet three inches of him? Why not ask why and how he might have done what the chromosomal evidence suggests he did? Which is to say that the (still disputable) "solution" of one puzzle merely invites a deeper human inquiry.

Sally Hemings was—reportedly—the half sister of Mrs. Jefferson, who died in childbirth in 1782 after begging her grieving husband never to remarry. Very possibly, Jefferson saw in this lovely young woman an entrancing image of his lost love and as a man of normal passions felt himself secretly, scandalously, irresistibly drawn to her across the barriers and taboos of the age.

He whose "Notes on Virginia" are the most scalding of all condemnations of the master-slave relationship ("a perpetual exercise of the most boisterous passions, the most unremitting despotism on the one part and degrading submissions on the other") can hardly have failed to be tormented by this betrayal of that other, loftier self who wrote the soaring words on human equality—and, incidentally, savagely denounced "miscegenation." In the eyes of his deist God, Mr. Jefferson must have felt deeply compromised; and perhaps that consciousness pushed him into ever higher clouds of abstraction. Who knows?

In any event the man who once, in his Parisian infatuation with the artist Maria Cosway, wrote a dialogue between heart and head cannot have been alone in letting one get the better of the other. But I am beginning to sound like Fawn Brodie.

DISNEY'S AMERICA DOESN'T CUT IT

More here on the dilemmas of history, also with a personal touch. The daffy plan for a Civil War theme park near the Manassas battlefield west of Washington was ultimately cancelled, thanks to articulate opposition from landowners and historic preservationists. Yet the urge to devise easy ways of beguiling lazy youngsters into an effortless understanding of the past lives on, in the ersatz history of dozens of theme parks and other pablum-like devices. No wonder so many Americans have little more than a comic-book notion of what happened in the yesteryears. It was coincidence that our cousinly visit to the site of our ancestor's death in battle at Deep Bottom came along just as the battle over Eisner's theme park was hot. But personal testimony can add an element of persuasiveness to an argument.

Kind friends told me that this piece, which appeared in the Washington Post *during the fight, may have helped turn the tide. The pen mightier than the corporate pocketbook? I hope they were right, but, after all, historical causation is a tricky thing.*

DEEP BOTTOM, VA.—A visit to this tree-shaded landing on the James River south of Richmond, now a Sunday-afternoon launching place for recreational boaters, is poor preparation for yet another defense of Disney's America by Michael Eisner.

But there he goes again, the cheery chairman of the Walt Disney Co., explaining in a recent *Washington Post* that his controversial theme park project in Prince William County, a few miles from the Bull Run battlefield, is to "reconnect Americans with their heritage."

Eisner is disturbed that his college-age son and his friends "have never been to a Civil War battlefield." But his solution is not to collar this historyless youth and drag him off to Gettysburg—or even Deep Bottom. It is to substitute for the past a sort of virtual reality—serious, he says, but also humorous, entertaining, and even celebratory.

Only in Hollywood!

Some cousins and I came to Deep Bottom for a special reason, at once historical and personal. During the siege of Richmond in 1864, two battles began at this crossing of the river and draw their names from the place. In the second of

these engagements, on August 16, my Georgia great-grandfather was killed.

How the grueling struggle of several thousand boys in gray and blue on that infernally hot summer day could be made entertaining or celebratory it is hard to imagine. What could easily be imagined, as we walked the sites, was what an ordeal it must have been. Survivors reported, in letters home, that dust and drought had withered the foliage and turned everything a dull brown, filling the air with a choking haze that intensified the one-hundred-degree heat and made sunstroke as great a hazard as flying lead.

Our guide to the second battle of Deep Bottom was a Washington-based Civil War historian, Bryce Suderow, whose dedication to this largely forgotten battle may yet place it on the historic registers. He and a National Park ranger, Mike Andrus, are slowly mapping the terrain around Curl's Neck and White's Farm and Fussell's Mill for a book.

The grim end game of the Civil War, of which this battle was a part, lacks the dash and glamour of earlier set-piece battles. But with the help of Suderow's writings and Andrus's maps, we stood on the crest of the stubbled pasture where the Confederate defenses stretched from a ravine on the right across the Darbytown Road. Here, Alabama, Georgia and North Carolina boys contested an attempt to breach the Confederate capital's outer defenses. That was the strategic stake. It mattered enough to draw the battlefield to the personal attention of Lee himself, who later in the afternoon of this close-quarters engagement with bayonets and rifle butts suddenly appeared on Traveler.

As I stand here imagining my great-grandfather's last earthly hours, I am intrigued by the thought that his last glimpse was of the charismatic warrior he had followed for three long years, surviving Chancellorsville and Gettysburg.

In the last spring of 1861, he left a good life as a Georgia planter, judge, and legislator because, I suppose, he found satisfaction in the military life (for which neither he nor other officers of his outfit were professionally trained). Or maybe because he believed, as my uncle speculated years ago at the unveiling of a handsome monument to him in his hometown; that he and others "were fighting to repel unconstitutional invasion of their homeland." Such exertion must be explained by an ideal or personal bond of some sort, for it is inconceivable that men would endure all this for a mere system of chattel property.

Today the legatees of such self-sacrifice have the luxury of choices. We can abandon the sites of struggle—brambled fields, overgrown rifle trenches, old sun-splotched millponds hidden in the trees—to bland suburbanization and garish strip cities. And we can compensate ourselves for the loss with a plasticized air-conditioned, sanitized, flyless, and lifeless theme-park past, deluding ourselves that this is history.

Eisner seems not to know the difference. He is right in thinking we are disconnected from our heritage. What he seems not to understand is that the kind of reconnection he recommends is no improvement at all.

THE POPE ACCEPTS NATURAL SELECTION

I include this piece because it ends with an honest confession that the ancient evolution argument is good fun. A few years ago, I wrote another column pegged to a PBS television program that examined children's views of the evolution controversy. Why, they were asked, did it happen that dinosaur bones are found so deep in the earth if there were, as biblical literalists insist, only some six thousand years since the mass extinction? With wonderful children's logic they offered an obvious answer: in the first place, these huge creatures with their pin-sized heads were too notoriously stupid to run when the meteorites began to fall; and being so big and heavy they sank rapidly to a deeper level than the smaller animals. No nonsense about specific gravity, as I put it.

One morning after I had some naughty fun with the subject, I had a polite call from a "Christian" radio station in Florida. The talk-show host on the line told me, to my surprise, that my piece was the talk of the letters columns in all my client papers down there. He was polite and deferential and seemed surprised that I saw no conflict between the acceptance of Darwinian theory (as modified) and the Bible. We sparred for a bit but it was a case of ships passing in the night. The anti-evolutionists are right about one thing: the apparent randomness of natural selection is a disturbing thing in a world in which we human beings fancy that we detect something called Purpose.

The bemused observation of the perennial culture wars in the South (and elsewhere in the sun belt) over Darwinism happens to be an old hobby of mine. And a recent papal statement on evolution seems likely to touch off yet another round of fireworks.

Evolution versus antievolutionism is a Victorian controversy with more lives than a cat. Polls show that millions of Americans reject the well-established Darwinian mechanism of natural selection as an explanation of the development of life forms. The state of Tennessee, at last notice, was still attempting to resuscitate the "monkey law" under which it put a high school biology teacher named John Scopes on trial almost seventy-five years ago.

Yet the business is full of paradox. Even fierce anti-Darwinists peacefully coexist with the benefits of modern biological inquiry. They don't, for instance, shun medical treatments that arise from the intricacies of modern cell biology.

Now along comes Pope John Paul II to declare, after a mid-October scientific consultation at the Vatican, that evolutionary theories are "more" than mere hypotheses and now may safely be affirmed by the devout. The Catholic hospitality to ideas that most biologists affirm but millions of religious fundamentalists deny isn't exactly a novelty; but it is a curiosity and is likely to be taken as a provocation in the well-defended redoubts of "creationism."

My own fascination with the evolution controversy would seem to have something to do with a stray gene or two in the family tree. My mother's family has produced physicians, and good ones, for several generations. My father was trained in biology, as was a paternal uncle, an entomologist who was fondly known to his college students as "Bugs." The gene skipped me but both of my children majored in biology, and my daughter, having a doctorate in the field, is at the cutting edge of evolutionary investigation. She still encounters taxi drivers who, discovering her line of business, ask: "Are you one of those people who think we're cousins of monkeys?" She has a show-stopping reply: "Why? Is that a problem for you?"

My own underschooled interest in biology does not at all impair respect, even reverence, for the majestic biblical account of creation, nor my sense of the mystery at the heart of life. Those who detect a conflict between biology and belief suffer, in my observation, from philosophical naïveté, whether it takes the form of fundamentalist religion or its mirror image, scientism. Scientism is the dogmatic naturalism that springs from ill-understood science and it stands to science as fundamentalism does to well-instructed theology. There is in both a psychological yearning for certainty and unity in a world of doubt and multiplicity.

The imagined contradiction between the account of creation in the Book of Genesis, mythic and poetic in form, and the evolutionary account of the development of life forms, is misplaced. It arises from what the British philosopher Gilbert Ryle called a "category mistake"— the confusion of different orders of truth. Even in the age of Einstein and Darwin, poetry and myth remain our only avenues to human self-understanding. For however profound or interesting biological or physical inquiry may be, it isn't about first causes. Science abandoned metaphysical claims centu-

ries ago. Any scientist who finds "design" or "intelligence" in natural phenomena may well be right; but he is expressing a poetic claim, not a cognitive one, and it is neither more nor less authoritative by virtue of his scientific training.

None of these observations, of course, is original with me; indeed they're all old hat. But such is the deficiency of philosophical training that what was once the "queen of sciences" rarely guides or disciplines the disputation that has been going on between evolutionists and fundamentalists since Wilberforce and Huxley tangled over apes versus angels in Oxford a century and a quarter ago. You can be sure that the recent words had no sooner passed Pope John Paul's reverend lips than the old antagonists began sharpening their dull and rusty old swords. And to tell the gospel truth, I love it.

DARK WITH LIGHT

Notwithstanding what I said in the introduction to this appendix about the dreariness of duty pieces, I am a firm believer in seasons and anniversaries. Newspapers could, if they would, help rescue these occasions from the frivolous and blatant commercialism that now envelops every American holiday. I still mourn the transformation of Armistice Day (as it used to be known, when everyone stood in silent remembrance at the eleventh hour of the eleventh day of the eleventh month, the end of World War I) into the bland "Veterans Day." It is now no more than an excuse for blowout department-store sales and self-interested lobbying.

The American Christmas, likewise a super-orgy of commercialism, now begins at Hallowe'en (whose connection with All Saints' Day is long forgotten) and ends on Christmas Day, when it ought properly to begin on Christmas and last for twelve days. All that remains of the twelve days of Christmas is a song. In the face of all this, I tried to mark each Christmas with a piece that I hope

was of ecumenical interest. The 1993 film about C. S. Lewis, based on his book
A Grief Observed, *offered a peg. Of course, the practice of theology without
a license is hazardous. But mainstream journalism makes a mistake by largely
ignoring the palpable importance of religious belief in the modern world (for
both good and evil, and indeed plenty of the latter) or relegating it to the Saturday "religion page," or worse, treating it as something weird and freakish.*

Even in the happy Christmas time we sense undercurrents of sadness—a confirmation of the widely reported prevalence of mild depression. We deny it because it seems inappropriately uncheerful.

I thought of that the other day, when we went with friends to see Richard Attenborough's new film *Shadowlands* with Anthony Hopkins as the famous Oxford scholar and Christian apologist C. S. Lewis, and Debra Winger as the stricken American poet Lewis married. The movie takes a few poetic liberties but they hardly matter. This is a story of the heart, a Christmas story.

It is set in the Oxford of the 1950s, rich in architectural and musical echoes of the Middle Ages—the age of Oxford's origins and the age of faith. But it is a story of suffering as well as beauty, a study in how human and divine love are linked; and it is told without a false note.

Millions of readers of books like *Mere Christianity* and *The Screwtape Letters* knew C. S. Lewis not as a distinguished scholar of English Renaissance literature, though he was that, but as a genial and provocative guide to religious faith—or, at least, a guide around and beyond shallow doubt. That is how his friendship with Joy Gresham began. She was an American reader of his books,

some twenty years his junior, a recent convert to Christianity, estranged from a violent and alcoholic husband. They corresponded; she visited him in Oxford.

Lewis at first appears as the embodiment of the cloistered monasticism of the Oxford of that day, when women almost needed a passport to enter the men's colleges. He is fascinated by this intelligent, sassy, outspoken woman, and soon has come to love her. As "lapsed atheists"—wonderful term—they share a faith that deepens, though it brings no easy consolation, when she suffers and dies. Not far into the marriage, now stricken with terminal cancer, she teases him by suggesting that he finds it safe to love her because she will soon be off his hands.

There is some truth in this. Lewis's emotional constriction has deep roots. His mother died when he was nine. He has managed, before meeting Joy Gresham, to seal himself from the risk of emotional involvement and disappointment.

Why is this a Christmas story? It concerns at least three of the "four loves" Lewis explored in one of his books—human friendship and physical love, and their connection to divine love. Astringently, without glibness or cheapness, the movie addresses one of the knottiest of theological questions. If God is good—if, as men have ventured to write, God is love—why does he countenance suffering? Aren't the cruel tricks that befall his creatures better evidence that God is some sort of cosmic sadist?

The question is posed in the most shattering fashion imaginable in *Shadowlands*. The happiness of married love and friendship is overshadowed by disease, pain, and death. In the opening scenes, before he meets Joy Gresham, we see Lewis wowing audiences of bookish ladies, in his best professorial style, with brilliant lines about the pain God inflicts with his chisel as he sculpts children into mature adults through suffering. We soon see that these metaphors are leftovers from his childhood, only mildly foreshadowing how cruelly he will be "chiseled" by the suffering and death of his beloved. When his wife dies, Lewis can only conclude that while as a

boy he chose the "safety" of protecting himself emotionally, as a man he must engage suffering and that somehow, as she has taught him, the pain will be part of the happiness. "That's the deal," says Joy Gresham in her breezy way.

There is, I think, a clear connection between this powerful story and the Christmas story of the next twelve nights. We are enthralled by the modern superstition that religion is a proposition rather than a poem, that it is about certainty rather than wonder. But the Christmas story can only be true in the way that all faiths are true, and all require fullness, dark with light. Maybe that is why the Christmas story connects the wickedness of King Herod and the inhospitality of a rude world to the divine with the wisdom of the magi and the singing of angels.

As Joy Gresham might have put it, that's the deal.

WE CANNOT CONQUER TIME

Wrightsville Beach on the south coast of North Carolina has been a late-summer retreat for us, and for many old friends, for more than forty years. The consistently warm reaction to my annual "what I did on my vacation" column (why should schoolchildren enjoy a monopoly on that subject?) shows that readers of op-ed matter react with happy relief to any break from the stale diet of politics. Like the seasonal Christmas piece, the beach piece, flavored with an ecological issue or two and seasoned with a mild dash of the tempus fugit *theme, offers a chance to go beyond the temporary. Here, it also offered me a chance to pay brief tribute to a brilliant and influential friend, Jimmy Wallace, who almost single-handedly founded the coastal-environmentalist movement in North Carolina.*

A rhetorical note: Antithesis is a familiar device in the writer's toolbox, immortalized by John F. Kennedy's "ask not what your country can do for

WRIGHTSVILLE BEACH, NORTH CAROLINA—Our yearly retreat to the seaside restores the soul, but it also calls mocking attention to the obsolescence of the body. Last year's photographs tell the story. It is a story of thinning hair and thickening waistlines.

That obsolescence is inevitable. But this is also the year when used hypodermic needles and other squalid medical debris washed ashore and forced the closing of several mid-Atlantic beaches. Somehow, as the years turned, it had never registered that we might be dragging the seas with us on our journey.

"And the earth was without form and void; and darkness was upon the face of the deep. And the spirit of God moved upon the face of the waters." So we read as children. The deep was there, even before there was light or breath or land. It was here before us and we had always assumed it would abide. Now that is in question.

Wrightsville, thanks to some wise choices and a few happy accidents, has been spared the worst of the great beach boom of recent years, as well as the needles and other litter. This year, a sort of red seaweed drifted in with the tide, and its filaments could be seen dancing in the otherwise clear water. But that was all.

Wrightsville is an old beach, neither fashionable nor elegant nor well known to the great megalopolises of the eastern seaboard. Even the northernmost mile of this four-mile-long island (the part we used to call the Empty Quarter) was for obscure legal reasons spared "development" until about four years ago. Even that development is restrained by the settled doctrine that all North Carolina tidelands up to the mean high watermark are common property.

That fortunate vestige of common law, now reinforced by statute, means that developers are not free to so much as set a covetous eye on the vital wetlands that protect the barrier islands on the landward side. Moreover, a kind of folk wisdom among the fishing and beach-going native tribes made it understood long ago that without healthy dunes no strand will be with us very long.

Yet not even Wrightsville is immune to our more thoughtless modern habits, including the possibility that some stealthy hauler may someday dump tons of inorganic junk offshore. Multiplying humanity is already crowding the Outer Banks, a desert in my youth, and turning the Cape Hatteras area into a bustling chain of pleasure beaches. Or so one hears. Friends of mine from Northern Virginia vacation at places like Duck, which thirty years ago would have drawn only determined hermits.

There is no cure for what the yearly photographs reveal about aging bodies, though of course we aren't taking creeping mortality lying down. One of us—names will not be revealed—was into pill-augmented tanning, and another was swimming laps every afternoon. There was heavy teasing about these stopgap measures. We know they are small fingers in the dike, that on its other side waits the great relentless tide of time that, as the hymn tells us, bears all its sons away.

But what we are doing, or about to do, to the great life-giving mother sea is curable. Unlike youth, seas are salvageable. Not long before we left to come here, I read in the papers a letter from a New York surgeon. He had conducted a recent postsurgical inventory that showed how much of the refuse of surgery is new: "disposable" things replacing equipment that used to be sterilized and reused. The summer's beach refuse tells us that "disposability" is a delusion. We knew that, of course, though we didn't want to admit it, when that Flying Dutchman of a garbage barge roamed the hemisphere a year or so ago in search of a dumping place.

The surgeon's letter recalled the wisdom of my old friend Jimmy Wallace, scholar and sometime mayor of Chapel Hill, who did so much to raise the consciousness of North Carolinians about ecological principles. Wallace, who has a pithy way with the language, had it exactly right twenty years ago. Enough, he said, of the "anal" approach to waste management. It was a loser. For by the time undegradable waste becomes waste, it is too late. The real ecological art, Wallace suggested, is the "oral" approach: being careful about what you throw away and what it is made of.

This summer's insult to the beaches has vindicated his wisdom—in spades.

REFLECTIONS ON A DAUGHTER'S MARRIAGE

Like the two columns that precede it, this one is offered as an example of the occasional piece. It is literally factual, nothing invented: The bridal regalia was locked accidentally in a shop on Franklin Street in Chapel Hill; the wedding was accordingly delayed for half an hour; and the bride did call it a "silly" wedding, which on the whole it was not. But what is life without its small contretemps? They are the seasonings that turn routine and ritual into the exceptional and connect them to the great human comedy. As important, they offer the columnist a way to write about formal occasions and to convey their importance without resort to drippy sentimentality.

This column, by the way, ranged widely. Scientific colleagues of my daughter read it in the jungles of Madagascar—where she had done her doctoral field work—thanks to the International Herald Tribune. *And a young friend, clerking at the World Court at The Hague, read it in the same newspaper with fascination and curiosity before he wondered, "whose wedding is this?" and looked at the byline.*

CHAPEL HILL—She looked up at me laughing, this young woman whom I first saw, red and wrinkled, through a maternity ward window in August 1959. "Daddy," she said, "this is the silliest wedding I've ever been to."

She squeezed my arm, which was beginning to tremble a bit. The organist played on . . . and on, omitting nary a note of Bach before sounding the first notes of the processional march. She looked radiant in the wedding dress her mother had worn, years before, in this very church. To a father's fond eye, she rivaled the Botticelli Venus.

Her own eye sparkled, as usual, with merriment at the comedy of things. The processional was twenty-five minutes late, and the throng of friends at the old church was now quite steeped in Bach.

What she meant by "silly" was that, earlier that afternoon, much of her essential wedding regalia had been locked up in the dressmaker's shop, and the dressmaker had herself disappeared. Her shoes, her lovingly handmade hairpieces, the blue garter and the lucky sixpence borrowed from our old friend Judy Exum, and her grandmother's engagement ring—all had been accidentally locked behind doors the Chapel Hill police said they could not force.

Now, however, the crisis was over, the dressmaker was found, her door unlocked, the precious items retrieved and relayed to the church and hastily fitted, while the guests, now going down for the third time in a sea of Bach, had been assured that "a wedding will indeed begin in a few minutes."

Maybe silly was the word. But the great ceremonies of life have a way of developing such mixups, just to remind us of life's own larger uncertainties. A ring is lost, a door locked, an item misplaced, a plane fogged in, or the best man wakes up with a nervous stomach.

The affair of the items left at the dressmaker's shop was no sillier, in any case, than the toast offered by the father of the bride the evening before. The father's memory was very dim. He had the happy impression that he had been eloquent, that a rather bibulous evening had set wings to his words. Actually, he is alleged to have called this accomplished and beautiful daughter, a new-minted doctor of esoteric sciences, "a good egg" who, with her young man, was entering "a complex relationship." He had gone on to philosophize extensively and fatuously. Or so he was informed, to his surprise, the next day.

The father of the bride was admittedly a bit spacey. It was, after all, his second most important wedding—and, exponentially, shockingly expensive. Yet somehow the champagne was drunk, the toasts offered, silly and sober, the photos taken, the feast consumed, the dance band tuned up, the dear friends gathered in a warm glow, and the two youngsters hitched.

Later, as they drove home, the parents compared notes. Both felt pleasure, but also a touch of sadness and perhaps a touch of anxiety—that old visceral tightness that parents feel when they must let go—as if paying out yet another untested length of that tether of love and concern that binds generations, which must be both infinitely strong and infinitely flexible.

But what was a locked dressmaker's shop, or the challenges of the marriage estate, to this resourceful girl, who had already explored more of the wide world than either of her parents? What terrors could life hold for one who had trekked the jungles on the trail of mouse lemurs, who had galloped her horse through the fields of Tennessee (with a cracked noggin to show for it), who had even walked a dog in Central Park? What failures of invention could be feared of someone who could sequence DNA? A cherished family photo shows her, all one hundred and ten diminutive pounds, surrounded by "natives," peering in boots and jodhpurs and pith helmet from amid what look like carnivorous plants, somewhere in the wilds of Madagascar lemur country. What is marriage, after challenges so splendidly weathered?

Well, it may not be terrifying, but it is something. If you listen closely to the old and awesome words of the ceremony—two people joined, till death, by a power mightier than man or science—it will take your breath away.

Marriage is an act of grace, faith and hope, in part beyond mortal capacities. But there is a human side. Our old friend David Williams, the officiating clergyman, said it best. A wedding is no solo act for two, of which the others are mere spectators. It is an act of community affirmation as well. For without the friends and family, gathered to testify to their love and regard for these two, and to reinforce the solemn vows they were making, where would they be? David Williams was so right. Without community, where is marriage? Or the world itself?

THE BATTLE OVER THE BATTLE FLAG

Even as I write this note, a presidential candidate's offhand characterization of a certain cadre of southern voters whose votes he seeks shows, for the hundredth time lately, that the Confederate flag remains an electric issue. For me, as I tried to argue in this piece, the controversy too often involves misplaced emphases. Flags are in themselves symbols to be honored, when the causes they represent—or represented—are honorable, as I believe the Confederacy's was, and when the display is dignified. Certainly those who fought and died in the Civil War, on both sides, believed so. By the same token, I intensely dislike the use of the flag as a symbol of bigotry, or, for that matter, of ostentatious nationalism. Both are perversions, in my book. Indeed, there is a disquieting parallel between the use of the Stars and Bars as a racist declaration, and the casual wearing of tiny U.S. flags on the lapels of politicians, as if to say, "I am more patriotic than thou." If pins, why not those vulgar star-spangled neckties? Why not coats and trousers that look like Uncle Sam's? Why not go the whole hog? But I am turning a serious point into a jeer. Abuses of a flag, whether by racists or superpatriots, do not affect its intrinsic value. But they make it harder to pay due homage and invite its burning by outraged dissenters. Incidentally, the pro–Stars and Bars advocate on the television discussion mentioned above was the great Shelby Foote, who made a more outspoken case for its display as the South's ancestral banner than is offered here.

A few days ago, a small incident reminded me how neatly we like our issues packaged these days.

After South Carolina's overdue decision to lower the Confederate battle flag, a television producer phoned to "preinterview" me on the issue just resolved—that is, to test me for suitably categorical views.

Her program is far less given to mindless bombast than most, but when I began to explain the complexity of my views, I sensed disappointment. I probably should have exclaimed, "Damn those South Carolinians! High Time!" Or, "Damn the NAACP for meddling in South Carolina's business!"—or something equally stark. If you happen to think the earth bulges a bit, you fare ill in television arguments between flat-earthers and those who think our planet is as impeccably spherical as a billiard ball.

So far as it goes, which isn't terribly far, the South Carolina matter was elementary. A flag that lacks official standing and that a solid minority of South Carolinians view (alas) as a symbol of racism has no business flying from the main capitol flagstaff.

That said, however, there remain appropriate uses for the Confederate battle flag, discredited or even hated as it may be by those who have no reverence for symbols. At Washington and Lee University, where I teach, Edward Valentine's recumbent statue of Robert E. Lee, in the apse of the chapel named for him, is surrounded by Confederate battle flags, perfectly appropriate in a memorial to Lee. Julian Bond recently spoke there—so far as I know, without complaint.

But my personal feelings about the flag are not entirely abstract and can't be, since two of my great-grandfathers were Confederate officers and fought under it. I feel a lingering loyalty to their memory and character, if not necessarily to their cause. And anyway, what was their cause, exactly? It certainly wasn't identical in the two cases.

One great-grandfather, a North Carolina Lutheran schoolmaster and farmer, owned no slaves and opposed slavery and secession. He survived the war to become a historian of some local note, and he directed that his tombstone in the old Grace Church cemetery near Hickory bear the inscription: "Colonel, CSA."

The other great-grandfather, a Georgian, had been a planter, judge, and legislator before the war and helped to frame the state's secession ordinances. He owned slaves and presumably favored slavery. He fought many campaigns with Lee's army before being killed in battle on the James River in August 1864, and is buried in the Confederate Officers Cemetery in Richmond. When the village of Gibson, Georgia, for which he had donated the land, raised a handsome monument to him many years later, my uncle, a U.S. Navy captain, said in his dedication speech that our ancestor fought to repel what he regarded as "an unconstitutional invasion of his homeland." Perhaps he did; many southerners believed that was what they were fighting for.

Would I have made the same choice in 1861? I have no idea. But I can imagine having done so, with malice toward none. Lee himself, after all, deplored secession and agreed with Lincoln that it was "revolution." Yet he made the same painful choice.

It is such considerations that make me shy from the clashing categorical certainties that mark the battle over the battle flag. Those certainties strike me as yet another depressing sign that Americans too often dispense with history (which teaches respect, at least, for lost contexts and causes) and substitute for it a brittle, present-minded moralism.

This perennial tension between historical contextualism, as we might call it, and moralism is not new and in fact has respectable antecedents. A century ago, the great English historian Lord Acton admonished his students at Cam-

bridge to visit upon the wrongdoers of the past "the undying penalty which history has the power to inflict on wrong."

But who are the wrongdoers? For Lord Acton, who believed that "great men are almost always bad men," the targets were perhaps obvious. But for the rest of us, wrongdoing in history isn't always easy to identify—there are virtuous men in bad causes and vicious men in good ones. Indeed, the same Lord Acton was as articulate an apologist for the Confederate cause as could be found in the Europe of his time. In his essay "Political Causes of the American Revolution," he wrote its most impressive defense.

In his own person, then, even Acton embodied the sublime ambivalence of true historical judgment. The past is a strange and complex place, and it often resists our self-righteous certainties.

MENTOR

In chapter one of this memoir I have said far more on the subject of this column than could ever be said in seven hundred words. But I include the column here because there are times when a writer—and his readers—sense that a bull's-eye has been scored. I am glad to recall that this was such an occasion. Columnists learn that there are certain subjects that inflame readers and yield tons of angry mail (abortion, for one). But the obituary piece is a special art, appropriate for the ancient adage, de mortuis nihil nisi bonum (speak only good of the dead). It offers a chance to write with the perspective that journalism only rarely provides. I wrote this column a month after my father's death on July 7, 1985; and in the interval the unconscious had—as it dependably does—winnowed many memories down to the essentials. It was pleasing to hear of it not only from many friends and readers, but from three colleagues in the trade whose craftsmanship I greatly admire—Vermont Royster, Tom Wicker, and George Will.

A rhetorical note: "My most influential mentor died suddenly," I write in the opening sentence. And at the end, "a fresh sense of the great honor . . . of having had such a man as my teacher and friend." "Mentor." "Teacher and friend." Why? It would have been easy enough to begin, instead, "My father died suddenly" and to have ended similarly. But my ear told me that a less intimate term would set a more appropriate tone for what I wanted to do in the piece—that is, to avoid intimate personalization and to pay tribute to my father's virtues as I had experienced them. Tone is to prose what hue is to painting. A good writer must try to get it right. And the more personal a piece is, the more essential it is to do so.

My most influential mentor died suddenly at eighty-five one Sunday a month ago, as he sat reading his newspaper at the nursing home.

None of us chooses the hour or setting of this unwelcome summons, yet his had an uncanny fitness about it.

There was, in the first place, the mastery of a stubborn, often willful spirit over physical frailty. Merely to read the morning paper, as he always did, cost great effort. He would be wheeled to a dining-room table, where the journal would be spread before him. A nurse would return periodically to turn the pages his once powerful farm boy's hands had become too arthritic to handle.

This careful, observant scrutiny of a world he could no longer affect, even barely, suggested, too, his unquenchable curiosity.

Early on the day of his funeral, I watched a long freight train crawl through the small North Carolina town whose schools he had run for forty years. I thought: he was the only man I knew who could have told you (for instance) what those odd-shaped cars were built to carry, whether they still did, and, if so, where the cargoes were mined and made. For good measure he could have named the founders of the rail lines (rascals, most probably) and told by what imposture against the public interest they had prospered.

His information was, in short, vast and seemed especially so to a boy. It pained him that I could never identify the cover crops that whizzed past the car windows as we pursued vacation routes through the southern countryside. "What is that, sonny?" I would look up blankly from my book. "Oats?" "No, clover."

A few summers ago he sat patiently listening as a babbling mob of newsless children and grandchildren on vacation idly guessed where the United States had shot down two Libyan planes. The Gulf of . . . of . . . ? Persian Gulf?

"Sidra," he finally said. Others guessed; he knew.

That he was stricken over his newspaper suggests, also, another great fact about him: that as to public matters he was never neutral. Perhaps it is not impious to wonder, in fact, what public folly in the papers of July 7 stirred the fatal agitation.

Until I was no longer a young man, his views weighed with me because they were his, rarely unemphatic, and usually wise.

In mid-1964, as the mess in Southeast Asia worsened, he followed my editorial errors in pained silence, as was his custom, until one day he brought himself to say in the kindliest way that I surely must realize that Vietnam would be our ruin, as it had been of the French. Even Douglas MacArthur, of all people, could see that.

No, I assured him; his worries were misplaced. We would gently bomb these people for a while, and they would come to terms. The Bundy brothers had it all worked out. No small peasant society could long endure the benevolent displeasure of the world's strongest power. Wait and see, he said; and read your Walter Lippmann.

There seems to have been something genetic in his lavish investment of feeling in public issues. His father before him had been a militant populist leader until, as he put it, "the Democrats caught up" by nominating William Jennings Bryan.

One day during the crazy presidential campaign of 1972, I tried calmly to tell him that, while *of course* there could be no question of my voting—ever—for Nixon, McGovern seemed to me to be saying such silly things that I might just not vote.

"If I ever become so indifferent," he all but roared, "just bury me." (I voted.)

Oddly, these gusty political passions were a sort of hobby, incidental to his consuming interest in the nurturing and education of the young. Incredibly, his farmer/schoolmaster/politician father had sent ten children through college. Education was so central to his family's vision of the world that to be without it, or to treat it lightly, was unimaginable. And by the way, to know was to know exactly. He conceded little to the twilight.

His funeral services were, as he had wished, unadorned and ecumenical, with a few psalms and prayers and the last lines from Bryant's "Thanatopsis," expressing the rational faith and hope of a public man. Quite without his leave, we ventured to add Luther's great hymn, "A Mighty Fortress," as seemed appropriate for a seven-generation Carolina Lutheran.

The death of fathers is an old theme and, regrettably, some weeks of fond reflection yield no striking variations for me. But rising above the pain and indignity of his long decline, there is a fresh sense of the great honor—and luck—of having had such a man as my teacher and friend.